Driven to Distraction

Driven to Distraction

JEREMY CLARKSON

MICHAEL JOSEPH
an imprint of
PENGUIN BOOKS

MICHAEL JOSEPH

Published by the Penguin Group
Penguin Books Ltd, 80 Strand, London WC2R 0RL, England
Penguin Group (USA) Inc., 375 Hudson Street, New York, New York 10014, USA
Penguin Group (Canada), 90 Eglinton Avenue East, Suite 700, Toronto, Ontario, Canada M4P 2Y3
(a division of Pearson Penguin Canada Inc.)
Penguin Ireland, 25 St Stephen's Green, Dublin 2, Ireland (a division of Penguin Books Ltd)
Penguin Group (Australia), 250 Camberwell Road, Camberwell, Victoria 3124, Australia
(a division of Pearson Australia Group Pty Ltd)
Penguin Books India Pvt Ltd, 11 Community Centre, Panchsheel Park, New Delhi – 110 017, India
Penguin Group (NZ), 67 Apollo Drive, Rosedale, North Shore 0632, New Zealand
(a division of Pearson New Zealand Ltd)
Penguin Books (South Africa) (Pty) Ltd, 24 Sturdee Avenue,
Rosebank, Johannesburg 2196, South Africa

Penguin Books Ltd, Registered Offices: 80 Strand, London WC2R 0RL, England

www.penguin.com

First published 2009
1

Set in 12/14.75 pt Monotype Bembo
Typeset by Rowland Phototypesetting Ltd, Bury St Edmunds, Suffolk
Printed in Great Britain by Clays Ltd, St Ives plc

A CIP catalogue record for this book is available from the British Library

HARDBACK
ISBN: 978–0–718–15554–4

TRADE PAPERBACK
ISBN: 978–0–718–15573–5

www.greenpenguin.co.uk

To everyone who made my Range Rover.
Well done, chaps. It's brilliant.

The contents of this book first appeared in the *Sunday Times*. Read more about the world according to Clarkson every week in the *Sunday Times*.

Contents

Part 1

Part 2

Part I

Okay tubby, you could get a nation out of a jam

Renault Clio

Once again the mysterious Highways Agency has claimed that the slower you drive the faster you will reach your destination. It sounds preposterous, but if you're a subscriber to the teachings of Lenin and Marx it's true.

If everyone trundles to work at the People's Tractor Factory No 37 in their Ladas at a state controlled 40 mph, the motorway will run smoothly and efficiently. Especially if the government radio is playing calming songs and the People's Roadwork Johnnies have not closed a selection of lanes so they can sit in a hut all day drinking vodka and playing cards.

Unfortunately socialism like this doesn't work because in reality roadwork people do tend to close lanes and then retire to their huts for a game of whist. And what's more, you will always have people, usually in BMWs, who think their journey will be completed a little more quickly if they duck and weave. And why not? It's by ducking and weaving in life that they ended up with such expensive cars.

Similarly there are those, usually in N-registered Peugeots, who drive as though they've been plugged into the mains. They cannot maintain a constant speed, which means they creep up to the car in front and then brake. And then repeat the process. Endlessly. These people, like those in the Beemers, cause the big metal traffic snake to judder and stall. These are the ones who bring the socialist ideology crashing to the ground.

Of course, to try to prevent people in Peugeots and BMWs messing up the Leninist theory of how traffic should flow in an ideal world, the sinister Highways Agency has developed a whole new state control system to quash individualism on the motorway.

Nowadays men in bunkers armed with sensors and predictive programming are able to change the speed limit at will and automatically activate overhead cameras to catch and prosecute those who flout the law. Sadly, this doesn't work either. I drove round the M25 recently and in a twenty-mile section the speed limit changed eleven times. For no palpable reason.

To make matters worse newly installed gantries designed to flash socialist messages from Downing Street to the masses keep us up to speed with problems ahead. Problems that usually don't exist. 'Warning. The Conservatives are not to be trusted.' 'Think before you drink.' 'A worker is more productive if he takes a break.' And of course, 'Congestion after next junction.'

There never is. What's happened is that a sensor somewhere has detected a man in an N-registered Peugeot braking and decided quite wrongly that there must be a reason for this. Down goes the speed limit and up go more messages about how the firemen are on strike and that it might be a good idea to drive carefully until the KGB's got them back to the station again.

This was one of my favourite gantry messages. Because I sort of assumed that when they did go back to work we'd get a new message saying that it was okay to drive recklessly.

You might assume that the sheer complication of it all is specifically designed to confuse the motorist into going past a speed camera too quickly and therefore having to pay a £60 fine to the state. But you'd be wrong. Recent figures show that Britain's 6,000 Gatso cameras earned £110 million last year but made a profit of just £12 million. That's rather less than the government gets in tax from someone like Sir Anthony Bamford.

The facts are these. There is no proof that speed cameras have saved a single life and plenty of evidence to suggest they haven't. They have simply raised a fortune that is then wasted on massive state inefficiency. The sort of inefficiency that we see every day on the motorway. Ludicrously low speed limits, especially when the People's Navvies are out and about digging holes, idiotic safety messages and warnings of hazards ahead that could have come from the hand of a fiction writer like Alistair MacLean.

Or Piers Morgan.

What's to be done? Well, in recent weeks the great white Tory hope, David Cameron, has made some unusual appointments. There's Zac Goldsmith, who's been taken on to help shape the party's green credentials, and – more bizarrely – Bob Geldof, who's been asked to help out with Third World debt. So why has he not yet approached me to sort out the transport mess? Because it's simple. You replace the overhead gantries with police marksmen who are allowed to shoot anyone who changes lane for no reason or who brakes when there's no need.

I'd also like to have special powers to deal with the man who allowed the Oxford ring road to be cordoned off recently so that someone could dig a hole in the grass verge . . . and then go home, for ever. I'd like to think these special powers could involve battery terminals and some pliers.

Then there's the PR issue. We need to get the message across that 3,200 deaths a year is tragic but not excessive. With 30 million vehicles on the roads it's nothing short of a bloody miracle. And then we should set to work on the big problem. You don't cure congestion by slowing traffic down. You cure congestion by speeding it up.

And that brings me on to the new Renault Clio. Apart from the fast versions, I never used to like the old model much. Oh, it had transparent windows and some wheels but it felt like it was going to fall apart at any moment. And it looked fat, somehow, which meant it was a bit like driving around in Rory McGrath.

The new version is much more handsome on the outside and feels a lot more substantial on the inside. There's so much soft touch leather-look plastic you could almost be fooled into thinking you were in a German car.

Unfortunately, by being loaded up with lots of luxury trimmings the Clio has become a real fatso. It doesn't feel like Rory McGrath any more. But it weighs the same. A whopping 130 kg more than the old one.

And that's a problem, because Renault couldn't very well launch this car onto the market saying: 'Hey, everyone. It's heavier than the last version and that means it uses more fuel.' So to make sure it uses less they've had to cut the power. And then, to make sure it didn't actually go like a nunnery, they seem to have shortened the gear ratios.

The price, then, of having a car that feels like German granite is that on the motorway it sounds like a German prison guard. GRRRRRRRRRRRR.

Off the motorway it feels French again. There's a looseness to the controls that you just won't find in, say, a VW Polo or even a Ford Fiesta. The gearbox feels more baggy than a sack of bubble wrap and the steering's all wobbly. It's weird, gazing out over a Teutonic view and then finding the undersides are not hard at all. It's like one of those liqueur chocolates. You gird your jaw to tackle the outer shell and then find the soft centre has dribbled all down your shirt.

Some semblance of order is restored if you're a teenager, because while the Clio may appear to be a cheap, practical and jolly safe little thing – the sort of car your parents might buy for you to go to university with – it's actually very good fun to drive.

Once you put your foot down the whole package seems to come to life: I liked driving it fast about as much as I didn't like driving it slowly.

This makes it the perfect car for Britain's transport problems. Because if you dawdle along, braking every now and again, you'll find it a rather ill-conceived mishmash. But if you drive to work like you really want to get there, you'll have fun and perform a social service all at the same time.

Sunday 15 January 2006

Whee, it's a tax-dodging style guru's dream ride

Nissan Navara

I don't think I'd like to be a trawlerman, truffling around in a stomach-churning ocean for fish that the Spanish have caught, cooked and eaten already. I also wouldn't like to be a removals man, smearing my fingers down dado rails while trying to get a bossy woman's sofa into a corridor that just isn't wide enough.

But most of all I wouldn't want to be a public relations executive. Yes, PR works for celebrities and PR put a buffoon into No 10, but mostly there is no tangible measure of success. Did the iPod become a global phenomenon because of great PR? Did the Sinclair C5 fail because the PR wasn't good enough? Maybe. Maybe not. PR people sit in that murky grey area between the vagaries of chance and the certainty of advertising.

In theory what you try to do in PR is raise awareness and shape public perception. But in reality what you do is take journalists and radio disc jockeys out for lunch and try not to look too embarrassed when they don't turn up.

You spend weeks trying to get a mention of the foot spa you're promoting in any publication, no matter how small or insignificant. And you'll find yourself punching the air in a dopamine-drenched moment of ecstasy when you find that two dozen phone calls, the promise of some light sex and six redrafted press releases have got the product on to page fourteen of *Lincolnshire Life*. In the middle of an article about financial services.

Things, however, are rather different if you work in public relations for the car industry. Because here you're not cajoling the journalists. It's the other way round.

Here's the problem. Most young car journalists are paid less than £15,000 a year, which means they have barely enough money left at the end of the week to buy food. And yet, each week, a brand new car is delivered to their house, full of fuel and insured.

What's more, twice a week they will be flown, first class or on a private jet, to Florence or Tokyo or wherever. Here they will stay in a thirty-eight-star hotel where they will be showered with tasty morsels and refreshing wines.

The next day, after driving the new car through some lovely scenery, they will have a £150-a-head lunch and then board the jet for home clutching a nice freebie. A laptop computer, perhaps, or some expensive luggage.

So, are they going to give up being Elton John by saying something awkward about the car they've been driving? Would you? Or would you bend over backwards, or forwards even, to ensure you were on the guest list for the next big global freebie? The car industry PR people know this. They know they have the power. They also know they have the budget to make sure that every single new car, no matter how dull, is guaranteed to get full-page coverage in all the magazines and all the newspapers.

This, then, is one of the best jobs in the world. You farm out the tiresome business of writing press releases to some poor hack who's down on his luck and then you spend all day eating grapes while telling journalists that if they want some new car for a photo-shoot ahead of the launch there'd better be a lot of sucking up.

You don't believe me? Well ring Porsche or BMW in the morning, ask to speak to the press office, and I can pretty much guarantee you'll spend the rest of the day bouncing from voice-mail to answerphone.

My favourite motor industry PR person is a girl who works for Nissan. The first time we encountered one another she lunged out of the audience in the *Top Gear* studio to berate me for a less than favourable review of the 350Z. It wasn't the time or the place so I told her to go away, and now all motor industry personnel are banned from the hangar and the track when we're recording. If I had my way I'd ban them from all of Surrey.

Then, the other night, she suggested at the *Top Gear* awards ceremony that I don't write my own newspaper columns. Well sorry, love, but as you've probably just realised, I do.

And to make matters worse, this morning I'm doing the new Nissan pick-up truck. Getting it wasn't easy. Normally when I want to review a car I simply ring up and ask to borrow a demonstrator. But Nissan was reluctant to oblige, saying it was too expensive to deliver a car over Christmas. Quite why this should be so I have no idea. Perhaps it's because the PR staff wanted all the demonstrators for themselves over the two-week break.

Though quite why anyone might want a pick-up truck I have no idea. They are, to the world of cars, what Mexican food is to the world of cuisine. They exist, they are popular in Texas, and, er, that's it.

There are some tax advantages I suppose. If you have a Vat-registered company and you use a pick-up truck to do your business then you can get the Vat back. What's more, you pay only an annual flat tax rate of £500 a year, whereas with a car it's all worked out on how much global warming you do. And employees with pick-up trucks don't have any tax liability even if they use company fuel at weekends.

Doubtless if you're an accountant you're probably nursing a semi at this point but if you're a normal person, well I'm sorry, but going this far to save money on tax is daft.

No really. It would be like moving to Andorra or Belgium to cut your tax bill. Why? I mean would you rob a bank, knowing you'd do time in jail, just so when you came out you had a lump sum to play with? No? Well that's what you're doing if you move to a bleak and friendless place like Andorra. And it's what you're doing if you drive a pick-up truck.

These things are classified as commercial vehicles because that's what they are. Oh, they may have leather seats and CD players but that's like putting a painting in a cowshed. It's still a cowshed.

The Nissan Navara Aventura I drove had rain-sensing wipers, cruise control, Bluetooth connectivity, a voice-activated mobile phone and satellite navigation. It also had five leather seats and deep-pile carpets. But underneath it had leaf springs, such as you would find on an ox cart on a Chinese farm.

So it rode with all the comfort of the Middle Ages and handled with all the poise and panache of a boulder tumbling down a hillside. It wasn't what you'd call quiet, either. Unless you test shotguns for a living. In a blast furnace.

Nor was it wieldy. I found myself attempting to park in spaces that would have swallowed a Hummer and, much to the amuse-ment of bargain hunters who were in town for the sales, giving up after half an hour. You really do have to think of the Navara as you would a skip lorry.

But if you're prepared to live with these drawbacks, if you really want a pick-up truck for work or to make some kind of weird neocon style statement, then it's not bad. Even though it's built in Spain it will almost certainly be mechanically bullet-proof and the four-wheel-drive system means it'll keep going in muddy bits.

What's more, the Navara has a torquier diesel engine than any of its chief rivals and a bigger load bay, which comes with all sorts of clever mounting points to ensure stuff doesn't roll about. This, then, is probably the best of the bunch.

And don't you find that interesting? No free suitcases. No first-class travel. No PR input whatsoever. And still a favourable conclusion.

Sort of.

Sunday 22 January 2006

Wiggle your hips and drive like a Norwegian

Mercedes ML 320

Norway completely ruined my bladder. Normally I can drink a pint or so without needing to visit the lavatory, but up there among the elk and the permafrost it was so damn cold that an above-average dew point was enough to keep me at the urinal for up to six hours at a time.

And I don't want to lower the tone over your breakfast table, but it wasn't only my bladder that shrank in the chill. This makes life difficult when you're wearing long johns, jeans and heavily padded waterproof overstrides.

This is the weird thing about Norway. On the surface it appears to be a monochrome and rather chilly version of Britain. There's the same northern European efficiency, the same things make us laugh, and the town centres are full of vandals who like to key your car. I was there ten days and liked it a lot.

But behind the veneer of normality it's as mad as a box of hovercraft. First of all there's the bothersome business of reading the signs. There are no reference points. Norwegian doesn't seem to be a language that's evolved, or migrated. It isn't an amalgam of dialects, a European potpourri of sounds and expression. If you ask me I'd say it was derived from the noises made by mooses.

I learnt after a few days that the Norwegian for 'parking' is 'parkering', but this doesn't work with other verbs. The Norwegian for 'talking', for instance, is not 'talkering'. And if you say you want to go drinkering, they won't have a clue what you're on about.

Though that's because in the frozen north you need to drive for 500 miles to find a beer and when you get there you'll be charged about £500. To make your evening out even less pleasant, you aren't allowed to drink outside and you're not allowed to smoke inside. I spent most of my time in doorways, freezing to death.

You might think everyone can talk English and of course most do – even A-ha – but there are exceptions. Last Tuesday I asked the proprietor of a remote highland cafe for the rest room and he recoiled in such horror I began to think 'rest room' might be Norwegian for 'Hey, troll, I've got a gun and if you don't hand over all your money I'm going to shoot your husky'.

Perhaps difficulty with communication is why the hotel room in which I stayed had a fold-out whiteboard nailed above the bed: so guests can use diagrams and cave drawings to explain to their girlfriends what they have in mind next.

I can't imagine the whiteboard is for any sort of management meeting because in the whole of human history Norway's only contributions have been the paperclip and the cheese slicer. Only Australia has achieved less, with the rotary washing line.

So sex, speaking, drinking and smoking are all laced with complications. And you try walkering. Yes, eco people, 2006 is alarmingly warm up there, but even so you still need your collar up. In Lillehammer it was a nippy minus nine.

This meant the pavements were encased in a sheet of ice. So to move around you have to develop an unusual gait. Some time back the Bangles sang a song called 'Walk Like an Egyptian' but I think it would be better if they had done 'Walk Like a Norwegian'.

What you do is put your foot down and then wiggle your hips imperceptibly to ensure you have grip before taking your other foot off the ground. I call it the Elvis Pelvis and it works. On Thursday I didn't fall over once.

This strange way of walkering may explain why there are no fat people in Norway. Not one. Though it doesn't explain why there are no cars.

No, really. On one night I stood outside having a cigarette in Lillehammer's equivalent of Piccadilly Circus and not a single vehicle of any kind drove by. Even more spookily, there wasn't a single parkered car to be seen either. It was as though Jonathon Porritt himself had flown over the town in a giant vacuum cleaner.

Or it could be because driving in Norway requires some special skills. If we had even a tenth as much snow, Britain would be lockered in 'ice chaos'. Police would advise motorists to stay at home and not make a journey unless you were delivering a kidney to the Queen herself.

Even the main roads in Norway are snow covered. The back roads are made up of what appears to be a rip-snorting wheel-twirling combination of ice, banana skins and Fairy Liquid.

You might imagine, then, that everyone in Norway would have off-roaders. They don't. In ten days I didn't see one, and that's because up there a Land Rover Discovery costs more than £100,000. So you buy a normal two-wheel-drive car … and cope.

And to make sure this happens you're limited to 4 mph and the roads are littered with forward-facing speed cameras that go off in a burst of blinding red light so intense it can strip all the paint off the front of your car. They don't take your licence for speeding over there. They take your sight.

I triggered one in the middle of a blizzard and it was like I'd driven through an acid trip. I was so disoriented I had to pull over and get a colleague to drive, and that was a shame because we were in the new Mercedes M-class. And I was rather enjoying it.

The old model was terrible. Designed just before BMW upped the ante with the new Range Rover and the X5, and built in Alabama by people more used to picking cotton than making complicated machinery, it emerged into the world badly built, lumpen, impractical and already old-fashioned. Small wonder that in *Top Gear*'s 2004 motoring satisfaction survey it came home in last place. The worst car money can buy.

Obviously Mercedes wasn't going to make the same mistake twice, so plainly the people making the new one have been told to stop singing 'Swing Low Sweet Chariot' and get on with some work, and the designers were told it was 2005, not 1956.

As a result the new car looks great, feels well made and when you climb aboard works like any other Mercedes, not a Massey Ferguson with electric windows.

There are, however, one or two things I should make clear before you run round to the local dealer brandishing a cheque-book. First of all it's no longer available as a seven-seater – boo – and then there's the cost. You will be asked to pay a minimum of £36,700 for the car and then, despite appearances, you will be charged an extra £1,320 for something called the 'off-road pro package'.

That really is like being charged £50 a head for dinner and then being asked to pay more for a knife and fork. And to make the prospect even more galling, the package includes various differentials, which is a good thing, and air suspension, which is not. You can't have the diffs without the air. Zis is not permitted.

If I were in your shoes I wouldn't bother with any of it and I wouldn't bother with the £270 off-road exterior styling package either because all you get for this is some underfloor protection, which you can't see, and a chrome radiator grille. Which will make you look like a drug dealer.

The worst thing about this car, though, is the gearlever. It's mounted on the steering column, a system popularised in America when teenage boys and girls needed to cuddle up at the drive-in. But ignored in Europe because we tend to get out of the car to watch films. And have sex.

It's annoying. Mercedes fits smaller cupholders to cars sold in Europe so why can't we have a European stick shifter as well?

It's not that the column stalk doesn't work. But it is an example of creeping American imperialism, one step further down the road for the San Francisco taxi driver who told me last year that 'pretty soon the whole world will play American football and soccer will die'.

The verdict, then, on the M-class is pretty much the same as my verdict on Norway. Efficient and good fun, but odd and too expensive.

Sunday 29 January 2006

This is the kind of gay I adore

Mazda MX-5

Of course, you can walk somewhere when your car breaks down, or if you're too drunk to drive it. You can also walk if you're only going a very short distance – to the bar, for instance, in a pub. But the notion of walking for fun is just risible.

Nevertheless, every weekend perfectly normal families go for a stroll to walk off their lunch. Others don beards and brightly coloured anoraks so they may be as one with someone else's piece of nature. As a result, the medieval peasant art of walking is now big business. And because it's big business the techno nerds have arrived.

For my recent *Top Gear* trip to the snowy wastes of Norway I packed a pair of old leather boots that have served me well over the years. Oh sure, they're a bit skiddy on wet rocks and have the weatherproofing characteristics of tissue paper. But they're manly and comfortable and stout.

The production team, however, assuming I'd have no outdoor shoes at all, bought me some modern alternatives. And God they were horrid. Big, orange and festooned with badges. The sort of thing you might expect to be murdered for in a Los Angeles jail.

Fashioned from Gore-Tex, which is apparently 25 per cent more breathable – than what, I don't know – they come with something called an advanced chassis and semi-automatic crampons, and have a preposterous name like the GTXX or V-Max. I might have put them on if you were holding my family hostage. Or if I woke up one morning to find I'd inadvertently become embroiled in a So Solid Crew video.

But the thought of voluntarily wearing something on my feet that had apparently been built on the same principles as a motor-cycle was just laughable. No way would it happen.

But it did. You see, after just one hour my stout old leather shoes had become soaked. I was wet. I was freezing. And I had no alternative. Begging the cameraman to steer clear of my feet I slipped into my new GTXX semi-automatic, extruded chassis Salomons.

The first problem was that to fit all the technology into the soles meant my height shot up from 6 ft 5 in to about 8 ft 3 in. But there was no second problem. These shoes were a revelation. Light, waterproof, grippy in all conditions and with lots of ankle support to keep me in one piece when I fell over on the ice. Which, in my old shoes, had been about once every half an hour.

What's more, my daughter says my new shoes are cool. So even though I now hit my head on doors, ceilings and even overhead power cables, I won't take them off. They're my new best friends.

If only all technology were so impressive. But it isn't. Take digital cameras as a prime example. With film, an astonishing library of the twentieth century sits in everyone's kitchen drawer. But with digital it sits in a computer's hard disk waiting to be lost when the damn thing crashes. Which it will, sooner or later.

Then you have flat-screen televisions. They're elegant and cool when they're turned off but switch them on and they don't work at all. The lip synch on mine is so out of kilter I only hear the news ten minutes after the subsequent programme has begun.

And of course some of the technology in cars now is just ridiculous. I recently swapped a Mercedes SL 55 for an SLK 55 and, yes, in many ways it's a big step backwards. The smaller car feels much cheaper, it lacks a properly usable boot, and while the performance figures appear to be the same on paper I do miss the urge of the supercharger when I'm in a real hurry.

But in one crucial respect the SLK is much better. It doesn't have air suspension.

And that means it doesn't do a little hop, skip and a jump every time it runs over a nasty little ridge or pothole.

In Norway I drove the new Audi Q7 off road, and while I shall reserve judgment until I've driven it somewhere more normal, I can tell you this already. The air suspension is rubbish. It turns all surfaces, no matter how smooth, into washboards.

Air suspension was developed because it gives backroom computer geeks a chance to fiddle, which they can't with a traditional mechanical set-up. With air they can make the car go up and down and they can fit sensors to ensure it stays level in the corners. They can tap away all night, writing programs that will make them look good at the next wiring conference in Palo Alto. And that's fine. But all they're really doing is making our lives just a tiny bit less comfortable.

And that brings me nicely on to the Mazda MX-5.

The old model was a phenomenon. The best-selling sports car the world has ever seen. Probably because it always felt just a teensy bit gay. Yes it was a modern-day and reliable incarnation of the old MG – they even recorded and then copied the sound of the British sports car's transmission whine – but you just knew that given half a chance this little car would be off to the gentlemen's public lavatories with its friends George and Michael.

That's why we all liked it so much. It wasn't threatening. Oh sure, some people said Mazda should fit a more powerful engine, but not me: I always wanted a detuned 1.3 litre – the Barbra Streisand version. A stripped-out, slowed-down, steel-wheeled alternative.

That, emphatically, is not what we've got with the new version. With its wider body and flared wheelarches it looks a bit more beefed up, as though they haven't evolved the old version so much as sent it to the gym. It now looks like it means business, like it might be more of a 'serious' sports car. A rival perhaps for the more grown-up, more heterosexual Honda S2000.

What's more, Mazda says that following customer demand for

space in the back to transport 'beverages', the boot is now bigger. Oh God, no. They've made a car for people who say 'beverage'. This doesn't look good.

But it is. Yes, it has all sorts of new-fangled techno nonsense like side airbags and traction control and an onboard computer. But this is installed simply to eke the last horse of power from each drop of fuel without upsetting every single EU noise and emission rule in the process.

In other words, what we have here is the automotive equivalent of my new shoes. Technology that works, hidden away behind a screen of good, solid engineering. It's digital but it feels analogue.

What's really brilliant is that despite the stronger body and the greater number of toys it weighs only 45 kg more than the old one. Computer geeks didn't do that. Engineers did.

And it was engineers who did the roof. Oh I'm sure there was pressure to fit an electrically operated soft top but this would have added weight. And when you power your roof down in traffic jams it makes you look like a berk. So what you get is a canvas top that can be raised and lowered, using just one hand, from the driver's seat. Power roof? You just don't need it.

And because they've kept the weight down the new car still feels gay, in both the new and the old sense of the word. The balance, the poise, the gearchange, the exhaust note; they're all spot on.

And the 2 litre model I drove was not so fast that it was scary but not so slow that it felt like a toy. Everything about the new MX-5 is perfectly judged so that what you end up with is a slightly more practical, slightly better looking version of something you loved anyway.

Sunday 5 February 2006

These Frenchies will never learn

Peugeot 407 Coupé

A couple of weeks ago my colleague AA Gill apologised to the nation for saying that Oman was on the edge of the Sahara desert. And then berated those who'd had the temerity to point out his mistake. Apparently when he gets letters saying he's ballsed up he laughs at them.

I don't. When I get a letter from a reader saying I've made a factual error my first reaction is rage. Then righteous indignation. And then, when my blood has cooled down a bit, I'm overwhelmed with a new emotion. Guilt: deep, tail between the legs, nose crinkling, hide under the furniture embarrassment.

Every week I come here with my tail feathers sticking up and proud. And it's a bit of a bubble burster when someone points out that I haven't checked my facts. That's like strutting around with a telltale wet patch on the front of your trousers.

That said, I recently wrote a piece saying that the Mercedes SL has air suspension and a chap called Khushal Khan wrote to say that it doesn't. He's right of course. But if I'd said it uses electro-hydraulics then I would have sounded boring. And I'd rather be wrong than dull.

Because in the big scheme of things, when I make a mistake, especially one I've made on purpose, the world keeps on turning.

Mistakes are a strange phenomenon. Because if a television presenter makes a mistake while on camera he'll get a £200 cheque from *It'll Be Alright on the Night*. However, if a doctor inadvertently makes a mistake while in the operating theatre, trust me on this, Denis Norden won't barge through the door with a clipboard and invite us to watch the 'hilarious' clip again in slow motion. 'And look at the patient when he starts to convulse, people.'

Once I invited a workman round for a swim in my pool. And that was fine. But when Michael Barrymore did exactly the same thing he had to leave his job and move to New Zealand.

But here's my point. It's now unlikely Michael will ever again invite anyone round for a splosh. What's more, after a poke in the eye from a reader two weeks ago I have now stopped referring to electrohydraulic or oleopneumatic suspension as 'air'.

This is because we're human, and humans learn from their mistakes. What's more, so do animals. Give a rat a choice of two tunnels, one of which leads to food and the other to an electric shock, and eventually he'll learn which is which. Peugeot, however, doesn't seem to be that clever.

When I first started writing about cars, the little 205 GTi was pretty much king of the hill. Volkswagen's Golf was falling off the rails, and as a result many switched to the wonderful French buzz-bomb. In a flash Peugeot went from being the maker of unbreakable taxis for the people of west Africa to the must-have accessory in booming Britain, as important as a Diana hair-do and a job doing something meaningless in the City.

Flushed with this success, the company kept on going, making a stunning four-wheel-drive version of the 406, which was named after a machinegun (it wasn't, I'm using hyperbole) and went like one too. And then the tiny 106 GTi, which gave me one of the most memorable drives I've ever had. Flat out from Carcassonne over the Pyrenees. Great part of the world. Great car.

And then they made a mistake. They decided to stop making exciting cars, a move that culminated in the arrival of the 607, surely the most dreary and underwhelming device in the history of mechanised transport. It wasn't like they'd gone back to their roots, making simple, tough cars to survive the simple, tough continent of Africa. It was as if they'd just given up altogether. It was like The Who releasing an album of humming.

You'd think that having failed so spectacularly they'd be keen to impress next time around, but they haven't. Examining the current Peugeot range is a bit like examining John Major's sock drawer. An endless grey world featuring nothing you would even want to steal.

The 107 is a Toyota, the 1007 is a joke, the 307 has the stand-out qualities of someone in a witness protection scheme, the 407 is the sort of car you might buy because you forgot you already had one, and the 807 would be the nastiest car in the world were it not for the aforementioned 607. I hardly ever bother reviewing these cars because I can't for the life of me think why anyone might be interested. Whether you want excitement, robustness, practicality, design flair, economy, speed, quality or just a set of wheels, you can do better somewhere else.

But then along came the 407 Coupé and I thought, a-ha, here at last is a Peugeot that someone might want. Because you've got expensive coupés from BMW and Mercedes and then not much else. Honda has dropped its Prelude. Toyota is about to abandon the Celica. Vauxhall never replaced the Calibra and Ford sold William Hague a Cougar then axed that too.

So what's left? Well there's the Mazda RX-8, which is jolly good if you don't mind spending as much on oil as you do on petrol, and that's about it. Yes, I thought, Peugeot has woken up at long last. It's seen a niche. The 407 Coupé will be excellent.

I was wrong. The first problem is the price. The GT HDi V6 version I drove costs a simply staggering £30,900 and then they have the bare-faced effrontery to whack on another £350 for metallic paint. This means the Peugeot costs about the same as a BMW 330 or a Porsche Boxster. It also means it costs a whopping £8,000 more than the Mazda RX-8. So it had better be good.

It isn't. The distance between the front wheels and the front of the car is about 18 ft (I'm exaggerating again), which gives the impression that you're looking at an anteater with a Peugeot sticking out of its bottom. That's certainly striking but I'm not sure it'll catch on.

Inside, things get worse. There's nothing to make you feel special. Oh, there's plenty of equipment and space but there's nothing to make you go 'wow'. And it's the same story when you put your foot down.

Yes, the big diesel drops lumps of torque into the mix but torque doesn't blow my ears off. Torque is what you get in an evenly matched rugby scrum. There's lots of grunt in there, but from the outside nothing appears to be happening. So it gives the car a lazy feel, like it's never really stretching its legs.

Perhaps it can't. The 407 Coupé weighs a significant 2 tons, and you can see why when you open one of the doors. They're so heavy I began to imagine that they might have been made out of Anne Diamond.

To see if I was missing anything I went on the Peugeot website and asked to look at the car in action. But to do that you have to register – presumably so they can offer you a bigger penis at some later stage – and then you are allowed to see exclusive content such as videos and, wait for it, an interview with the product manager.

Who would do that? Who would go to the bother of giving a big company all their personal details just so they can see someone from middle management talking a load of middle management bollocks? You'd have to be clinically insane, but then you'd have to be fairly mad to buy this car.

Yes, it's extremely smooth and comfortable, but that's like having two Jacks in a hand full of low clubs. You're still going to lose.

I fear then they're not making this car because they saw a niche. I suspect they're making it because they've always made 2+2 coupés. And they couldn't be bothered to stop.

Sunday 26 February 2006

Venus has trouble with her underpinnings

Volvo C70 T5 SE Lux

Last week research found that only 5 per cent of the countless recipes shown on television each week are ever copied at home by viewers. This is not surprising. You could give me the same ingredients that Gordon Ramsay uses and put me in the same kitchen with the same equipment, and even though we have exactly the same number of hands, fingers and noses I can absolutely guarantee that I'd end up with a plate full of over-salted, inedible mush.

Cooking is like painting. I have a brush and some eyes but everything I try to transpose onto canvas ends up looking like a dog. And it's the same story with DIY. My toolbox is littered with every conceivable gadget, but if I put something up it's not straight for a moment, and then it's on the floor all broken.

Ambition is no substitute for talent. A point I have been proving all week with my new photographic printer.

Being a man, I did not wish to consult those who know about such things. I simply got in the car and drove to PC World, where I bought the most expensive. It's an Epson Photo RX620 and it doesn't work.

I selected a picture on the computer, hit print and it came out sideways on an upright piece of paper. So I turned the paper round and tried again. And then again. And then again. This was annoying since a piece of top quality A4 premium glossy photo paper costs more, pound for pound, than gold.

Eventually, though, out came a lovely picture of the family taken by a passer-by on our visit to the Geysir in Iceland last year. Except that's not right. It looks like a lovely picture on the camera. It looks like a lovely picture on the computer screen. But what came out of my new printer was not lovely at all. It looks like we've all been boiled.

Now I know you can adjust this sort of thing using your mouse and a bit of software. So I bought something called the Corel Paint Shop Pro X version 10. It cost just shy of £60, and it doesn't work either.

All attempts to correct the redness of our faces resulted in more and more vivid hues until eventually my wife came and read the instruction manual.

It turns out the procedure is simple. You tell the printer what sort of paper you're using and how big it is. Then you give the information to the computer. Then you say whether you want 'landscape' or 'portrait', then you choose the quality level you're after, then you fix the red eyes, remove the blemishes, have a look at the preview and then, after just fifty-five minutes or so, out pops the finished product. Which is still crap.

Really and truly, I'm not a bad photographer. I understand about stop and depth of field. I know about composition and fill-in flash. Some of the pictures I've got back from Boots over the years have not been bad at all. But the stuff that's poured from my printer this past week looks like it was taken by someone who was being deliberately stupid, or who was Stevie Wonder.

And there you have it. I have the tools. I have the basic ability. But I lack that certain something, which means I cannot produce the sort of top quality digital pictures that you get from a professional.

And this brings me nicely to the door of the Volvo C70 T5 SE Lux. Possibly the most disappointing car in the history of the universe.

Like so many new cars these days, the Volvo C70 has a hard metal roof that slides electrically into the boot. That sounds great but there is a problem: the boot has to be at least as long as the roof, and because of that no car maker has managed to make a car of this type look right.

Peugeot, Renault and Nissan have made a complete monkey's breakfast of it, and even Mercedes hasn't got it quite right with either the SL or the SLK. Both are just too J-Lo chunky at the back.

Jaguar experimented with the idea of a folding hard top for the new XK but resorted to canvas in the end because they simply couldn't make the styling work.

Volvo, however, has cracked it because the C70 has a roof that folds in half. Swedish flat-pack furniture. And now, a Swedish flat-pack roof. Mind you, it is pretty complicated.

Certainly you should never operate this roof in public because it will cause those in passing cars to lose concentration and crash. And pedestrians to think you're showing off. But whatever, it means the car looks sensational with the roof up and, dare I say it, even better when it's down.

Inside, there is plenty of space in the back for adults, although I really can't recommend putting children back there when the roof's moving about. They could be sucked into the machinery and never seen again.

In the front, it's even better. Lots of space. Lots of light. Some genuinely stylish touches and quite the most impressive sound system since Jerry Garcia stopped being grateful and started being dead. It churns out 910 watts. This means you can still hear Whispering Bob Harris even if you're tooling along, roof down, at 150 mph.

This, then, is a car with a sky-high want-one factor. And with prices starting at £26,200 it's not that expensive either. Even though they charge an extra £25 for a switch to turn the passenger airbag off. How can a switch cost £25 when it isn't part of a nuclear missile or a space rocket? Whatever, on paper at least, the Volvo looks like a safer, more stylish, more practical and generally better convertible than anything at this level from BMW, Audi or Mercedes. I honestly thought I'd stumbled on a bit of a hidden jewel here.

But I couldn't help noticing that it had come from Volvo with my own desert island discs in the CD autochanger. Why do that? Could it be a distraction? A musical blanket to shroud some technical problem? Well if it was, it didn't work because this car felt so weird to drive that after just 200 yards I pulled over to see if I had a puncture.

The steering is absolutely lifeless when you're going in a straight line and horrid when you're accelerating, braking or going round a corner. Powerful front-wheel-drive T5 Volvos have always had torque steer but this is something else. This is diabolical.

You can hold onto the wheel if you like, but frankly you may as well hold onto your knees or your passenger for all the good it'll do.

Eventually I got used to it, in the same way that eventually you can get used to a headache. But I never had the confidence to open up the C70, to see what those 220 brake horse powers could do.

This was properly annoying because Volvo plainly has the ability to make this car work. They have the stylists and the engineers. But they built this car using parts from other, lesser Volvos. You can therefore think of it as supper made by Gordon Ramsay using only ingredients he could get from the twenty-four-hour petrol station.

Volvo is owned by Ford these days and I can't help imagining what this car would have been like if they'd accessed their daddy's parts bin. It could have had rear-wheel drive from a Mustang or a Jag. A V8 engine. Some Aston Martin steering. It could have been wonderful.

But it isn't. Volvo, plainly, has watched a television recipe for making a convertible. And then tried to copy it without going to the shops. Ingenuity got them to the table with something well priced that looks great. But I doubt you'll want to dig in.

Sunday 12 March 2006

It's the Terry Wogan of superminis

Fiat Grande Punto

The girl to my right at dinner last night was a Liberal Democrat. So she sends her children to school on the bus, dislikes titles and would like to get rid of the Queen because she's too expensive and the money would be better spent on muesli.

But because a nation needs checks and balances, if you got rid of the Queen you'd have to replace her with an elected president.

This went down well with the Liberalist. Of course the head of state should be elected. It's preposterous that we have to put up with a little old lady, or a man who admits he talks to vegetables.

Doubtless she imagines that the president we'd elect would be a sage old chap with a tweed jacket, the voice of Stewart Granger and the mind of Stephen Fry. Every day he'd thumb through the red boxes sent down from parliament, making wise observations and sensible suggestions.

But this wouldn't happen. If you think about it, America had 250 million candidates for president and was offered a choice of two. A man with the stupidest hair in Christendom and a blithering idiot who can't talk properly. It would be no different here.

At the next election there are three realistic options. An Old Etonian who's a communist, a dour slack-jawed Presbyterian, or an old-age pensioner. None has the voice of Stewart Granger. None has the mind of Stephen Fry.

When Londoners were offered a mayor, the best possible option was a man with out-of-control adenoids who keeps newts.

And the only Labour candidate found for the hard-up working-class voters in Dulwich and West Norwood turned out to be a woman who doesn't know whether she's £350,000 in debt or £650,000 in credit.

So what makes anyone think that the presidential candidates would be any better? They wouldn't. I can absolutely guarantee that the line-up would be an ethnically, gender-fair assortment that would make the candidates on *Big Brother* look sane and normal.

Or the job would go to a celebrity. No, really. Think about it. The good people of the state of California elected an Austrian bodybuilder who spent a career in film zipping through time and carrying very large logs. Ordinarily he would have stood no chance. But because he was Arnold Schwarzenegger he's now in the hot seat, putting countless petty criminals in a seat that's even hotter.

So we might very well end up with Lenny Henry. He ticks all the boxes. Black. Charming. Does loads for charity. And Dawn French would be a first-class first lady.

Then there's Paul McCartney. Obviously he isn't black but he is a scouser and that's the next best thing. Better still, he's internationally recognised, a keen vegetarian, a non-smoker and he has a disabled wife.

Or how about Nicholas Witchell? He's neither black nor a scouser but he is ginger. And is famously disliked by the royals anyway.

Maybe we could put the candidates in a televised office of some kind and give them matters of the day to discuss. We, the voters, would be able to see how they'd handle the Iraq crisis and what they'd do about foxy woxy. And how about using money from the voting phone lines to pay for the Olympic Games? Or some kind of badger sanctuary? The only danger with this idea is that you'd have to insert a token white middle-class person who, as we know from previous *Big Brother*s and celebrity-in-the-jungle programmes, would win. That'd mean we'd end up with Jack Dee as president (not such a bad idea) or Tony Blackburn. Or Carol Thatcher.

I wonder, then, would an Irish person be allowed to enter? I'd like to think so. It would make them feel better about the potatoes and Oliver Cromwell and we could also see the global politico-heavyweights of Bob Geldof and Bono enter the fray. Though I'm not sure we'd want a president named after a dog biscuit.

Whatever, if we do open the doors to Irishists, it means we could vote for Terry Wogan. Loved by millions. Cleverer than you might think. And after a 400-year career in broadcasting utterly unblemished by even a whiff of scandal. I'd vote for him.

So we'd end up with President Terry, which would be cheaper, slightly, than having a royal family. But would it be better? And that leads me, surprisingly, on to the new Fiat Grande Punto.

At the moment, small hatchbacks with a hint of grunt for long motorway journeys tend to cost around £10,000. A 1.4 litre Ford Fiesta Style is £9,295, a 1.4 litre Renault Clio Dynamique is £10,250 and a 1.4 Toyota Yaris T2 D-4D is £10,295. The new Fiat Grande Punto 1.4 Active Sport, on the other hand, is just £8,495. That's not far short of £2,000 less than the Toyota. So is the Punto inferior in some way? Not in the looks department it isn't. By a very long way, this is the prettiest of all the superminis, and the biggest. Which means it's also the most spacious inside.

Things are looking good, and they get better because not only is there a big boot, room in the back for children and space in the front for a small zoo, the interior is also a zany and funky place to sit. My test car had a pale blue dashboard, for instance.

Then there's the quality of the thing. Italian cars were always a bit like Italian tempers. Easily broken. But the new Punto has a substantial feel, a sense that nothing's going to fall off or come loose. The steering wheel is so fat you can barely get your fingers round it and the gearlever is the sort of thing that you'd expect to find on an American muscle car or a nineteenth-century railway locomotive.

Equipment? Again not bad. Certainly there are no obvious missing features that would explain the low price, except perhaps the lack of a boot handle. To open the tailgate you have to get into the car, push a button that is right in the middle of the dash and then climb out again. That would drive me properly nuts.

But not as nuts as the way the Fiat drives. Of course you don't expect it to be a ball of fire. But you do expect something to happen when you put your foot down, especially when you've just pulled out to overtake a slow-moving Rover 25 and there's a truck coming the other way.

Sadly, however, nothing does happen. You see, this is not only the biggest car in its class, but also by some margin it's the least powerful. As a result, 0–62 mph takes 13.2 seconds. And that, in the car world, is an ice age. I could forgive the Punto this shortfall if it had the usual Latin peppiness on country roads. But it doesn't. The electric power steering is too sharp and the brakes too snatchy. It's hard to make it flow. And the clutch bite is so sudden I did stall a lot too.

Other problems? Well, the stereo system couldn't receive Radio 2, the seatbelt warning beep was loud enough to shatter wine glasses, and if you put a can of drink in the cupholder and go round a corner it falls over. On balance, then, I'd have to say the Renault Clio is the better car.

Pity, because I liked the Fiat. I really like the styling and my wife thought it 'sweet'. But when all's said and done it's a bit like the idea of having Terry Wogan as president. Cheap. But not necessarily good value.

Sunday 19 March 2006

It's a mobile branch of the entertainment industry

Mercedes-Benz S 500

Can someone please explain what a scart lead is for? Designed to not quite fit in the socket, its prime function, so far as I can see, is to work itself loose and then fall into that unreachable vat of spaghetti that lives behind your television set.

If by some miracle you are able to find it again, you are then faced with the problem of putting it back. Hard enough when there's only one socket, but round the back of your home entertainment system these days there are usually 350.

The other day I called in a man to fix some aspect of my television and he found the last bloke I'd called two weeks earlier still round the back, still pushing wires into other wires in the vague hope that some kind of picture could be restored.

In the olden days I was a dab hand at electrical engineering, but now I am utterly at a loss. It is impossible – impossible d'you hear – to tune a modern-day television and if your Sky+ box breaks, which it will, every fifteen minutes, you cannot hope to effect a repair yourself. You must ring a man in Bombay who, after fifteen minutes, will put you through to a lady in Scotland who will tell you – I'm not kidding – to tap the interactive card on your fingernails before putting it back. And then . . . it still won't work. So you have to call out another man to join the last bloke who's still there helping the previous chap find the right effing scart lead.

In my house I have Sky+ in the big sitting room for when I'm watching what I call the home cinema. And what my friends call the VulgarSonic. And then in the small sitting room there's normal Sky that feeds various other TVs in various other out-posts. I do not know how they're all linked up. But I do know that if I press the red button to vote for Jack Dee or watch a weather forecast, the phone in my office makes some burping noises and then breaks.

Out comes a telephone engineer, who uses a sonic screwdriver to perform witchcraft and then goes away leaving us with a fully functioning phone system. But a plate of hash on the television. And when the man comes to fix that he breaks the phones again.

Only this time there's no burping noise.

Instead, and this is absolutely true, the home phone rings like clockwork every three minutes. Day and night. How can this be? How can we live in an age when your television rings your telephone 480 times a day? And there's nothing you can do to stop it.

I wish I was joking here. But I promise I'm not. When the engineer who'd been summoned to fix the Sky+ in the big sitting room left, the normal Sky in all the other rooms went down. And after the man who came to mend that went away, we lost signal to all the upstairs sets, and after the man who fixed that drove off the system in the big sitting room showed only blue and purple lines. And it was hard to call for help because the phone was talking to the television twenty-four hours a day. I simply cannot remember a time when all the televisions and telephones worked simultaneously.

Oh, and I nearly forgot. In case the Sky+ goes wrong again we now have a DVD recorder to go with the normal DVD player, the amp, the projector, the PlayStation and the hi-fi. That's six remotes, each of which has a minimum of twenty buttons. Fine. But if you accidentally sit on one of them you have no clue which one it was and what you should press to make everything work again.

Of course you stab away, going into menus and endless sub-menus until eventually you are so completely baffled by the electronic maze you have no option but to summon the man, who by this stage will arrive in a Maybach.

Then you have our kitchen. Not that long ago this was a simple room full of simple appliances. Pots. Taps. Cutlery. An Aga. The sort of stuff that would in no way bamboozle someone from the Stone Age.

Not any more. Now it is simply a room in the house where things are charged up. There are chargers for all the kids' Game Boys, for all our mobile phones, for our digital cameras and for various cooking things we neither want nor need. I've just been in there and we have, in one room, thirty-eight chargers – thirty-eight! And they're in such a tangle you can't work out which one does what. I spend an hour every night trying to breathe new life into my dying mobile by trying to plug it into a socket for a video camera we lost three years ago.

Things ought to be better in my office because there is wireless internet and a wireless keyboard. Fat chance. Twenty-three things need a plug socket in here and each of these twenty-three things needs to be connected to all the other things. That's 520 pieces of flex. And with an average length of 6 ft, that's more than half a mile of knotted wiring. Half a bloody mile.

And none of it ever works properly, which is why I approached the new Mercedes S-class last week with such fear and dread.

Let us take, as a tiny example, the driver's seat. You can make it go up and down electrically but in addition you can heat it up slightly, slightly more, or a lot. You can also adjust the support for your thighs, your lower back, your upper back, the bit in between, your neck, your head and your shoulder blades. I haven't finished yet. You can select how firmly you'd like the side bolsters to grip you in the corners and as a pièce de résistance, what sort of massage you'd like as you drive along. Slow and gentle. Slow and fast. Fast and gentle, or the Bangkok special, fast and vigorous.

Choose one and pressure pads in the seat itself inflate, deflate and move about as though the chair was full of Thai girls playing naked Twister. I liked it a lot. But think how much wiring is needed to achieve this. And then double it, because exactly the same options are available to the passenger.

And this is just the start, because then you've got the infrared camera that sees into the darkness way beyond the reach of the normal headlamps and projects the image on to a screen on the dashboard. Sadly, this doesn't work when the car is stationary. Mercedes says it's because the beam could hurt someone's eyes if they looked at it for long enough, but that's rubbish. I know perfectly well it's to stop anyone using the S-class for dogging.

Not that you need to dog in an S-class because this is the first car in the world to receive digital television. So you can watch pornography. While getting the full ladyboy.

Annoyingly, you can't watch television while on the move. I don't know why because it is impossible to crash an S-class. Sensors in the radiator grille note when the car in front is stopping and you're brought to a halt as well. But not so violently that the car behind smashes into your boot lid.

I really liked this feature, especially in stop/go motorway traffic. It meant I didn't need to look out of the window, which meant I had more time for playing with all the other stuff. The voice-activated controls for the sat nav (which knows where traffic jams are), the home cinema (I'm not joking) and the phone. The endless combinations of interior lighting. And the trip computer. I could even get it to scroll through the pictures on my camera, putting a slide show on the dash.

If you add all this up, along with the wiring needed for the engine and the computer-controlled suspension and the stuff needed to make sure you don't watch TV when you're driving, the result is 1,970 metres of wiring ... more than a mile of cabling. And here's the really annoying thing. It all worked. When I turned on the indicators, the phone didn't ring. When

I asked for a massage, the infrared camera didn't burn my dog's eyes out.

I am therefore seriously thinking of getting someone from Mercedes to come and mend my house.

And you? Well, if you want the most jaw-dropping piece of technology to be fitted with four wheels, you must have the S-class. And you must tick all the option boxes.

Of course, you may need to know first what it's like as a car. Well it seemed pretty faultless but I can't be sure about that. Unfortunately it's hard to think about fuel consumption or handling when you're watching the world whiz by in infrared and an imaginary Vietnamese girl is rubbing baby oil into your coccyx.

Sunday 2 April 2006

On second thoughts, this is a big mistake

Mercedes-Benz R-class

A couple of weeks ago the transport department, headed by Darling and ManLove, announced that they'd be opening a car-sharing lane on a busy stretch of motorway near Leeds. They argued that making people join forces for the trip to work would result in fewer cars on the road, a greener future for our baby children and 1,000 more wonderful years for our glorious leader.

Right. Well, if we're going to share cars then it makes sense to buy something with a large number of seats. I, for instance, run a seven-seater Volvo XC90 because you can cram kids in the back on the school run and this means their parents can stay in bed. How sociable and public spirited is that? Not very, according to Gordon Brown who, only two days after Darling and ManLove's initiative, announced that because I run a large car that's ideal for sharing I was to have my head kicked in by the taxman.

This seemed strange but there's a reason. Apparently when the Labour party came to power, it made a manifesto promise to cut the amount of greenhouse gas by 20 per cent by 2010.

To do this they'd have to get rid of every car, bus, train, factory, aeroplane and power station. And then they'd have to kill every cow, horse and sheep. And then they'd have to exterminate everyone in China and India. But no matter.

They made the promise, the voters believed them and they had to be seen to be doing something about it.

That's why Gordon Brown imposed his new tax on 'gas guzzlers'. The plan is that we stop buying off-roaders, the ice caps heal, the polar bears are saved and all will be well when Blair's 1,000-year Reich comes to an end.

Right. I see. So someone is going to walk away from a £70,000 Range Rover because of an £80 tax surcharge? Seems a bit far-fetched to me.

And now guess what? It obviously seems a bit far-fetched to the government as well, because just a week after the budget it announced that it wouldn't be keeping its promise to cut carbon dioxide emissions. In the same way that it hasn't kept its promise to sort out Iraq, the National Health Service, the education system, immigration, benefit fraud or anything at all.

So there you are. In the space of three weeks you are encouraged to do car sharing. Then you're handed a Range Rover tax for doing just that. And then you're told it makes no difference.

It's not just Range Rovers either. You'll be clobbered if you have a BMW 1-series or a Citroën C5. Which means nearly everyone with a reasonable car will be paying Gordon Brown to look like he's trying to achieve a goal that's simply not possible. And those who downsize to something more economical will find themselves banned from the new car-sharing lane proposed by Darling and ManLove. And this lot honestly think they'll get re-elected.

Jesus.

The best thing we can do is treat our leaders as bluebottles. There's no point waving our arms about and getting agitated because it'll make no difference. They will continue to buzz about being annoying. So let's just relax and think about this car-buying issue logically.

If you're part of a school-run syndicate, you need a lot of individual seats with individual seatbelts. But not a people carrier obviously, because this will give other road users the impression you have no social life and no exciting underwear.

The next obvious choice is a large 4×4, but this is not an option for the weak. That's because some people, usually on bicycles, bang on your roof as you go by and say they find your conspicuous consumption offensive.

What I want to do at times like this is bang on their cycling helmets and say I find their poverty offensive. But I'm made from stronger stuff so I turn the other cheek and run them down.

You may want to avoid this ugliness and go for a conventional estate car, which in many ways is wise and sensible. It'll be nicer to drive than any MPV or off-roader. It'll be easier to park, more stylish and much cheaper to run as well. But it'll only have five seats. And this brings me back to the Volvo XC90. The first car to have been designed by someone who had children, not an engineer who'd read about them in a book.

You get seven seats, as well as space in the boot for dogs and bicycles. And yet it is not much larger than a normal estate car. It's a triumph of packaging and yet it doesn't look like a mumsy MPV or a gittish Chelsea tractor. That's why it's such a smash hit, a de rigueur must-have accessory for every yummy mummy in the land. I'm on my second.

Next out of the blocks was Audi with the Q7, which is expensive, ugly, impractical and therefore irrelevant, and now we have the Mercedes R-class.

This car was listed as 'good' in the recent 'Good Car Bad Car' supplement. But because it is the policy of this column to correct mistakes as soon as possible I feel duty bound to tell you it isn't.

And this is why. It is billed as a crossover vehicle combining elements of an estate with the best bits of a 4×4 and it is a measure of Mercedes' success in muddling the two up that we managed to get our own wires crossed.

In the supplement it was judged as an estate, and was therefore up against the Audi A6 and Merc's own E-class. Here it may well be a winner, and first impressions were pretty good. But last week I drove one for 800 miles and realised that this wasn't an estate at all, it was a 4×4, and should be judged as such. And by this reckoning it wasn't pretty good. It was, in fact, rubbish.

The model I drove was a standard length, entry-level 320 CDI, which is about £42,000. Plus Bluebottle Brown's £80 punishment. This makes it nearly £10,000 more expensive than an entry-level Volvo and it's hard to see why.

Yes, Volvo's new diesel is no match for the creamy engine found in the Merc and yes, the XC90 wobbles where the Merc is smooth and flowing, but in 4×4 load luggers, handling, power and refinement must play second fiddle to the toys you get as standard and how much you can cram inside. The Merc fails on both counts.

First of all, just about every single gadget on my test car was an optional extra, which took it up to £46,000, and even then you get only six seats. This might be a bonus for an estate car but it's one fewer than most 4×4s.

It's the same story with boot space. With the third row of seats down, the boot is large. Bigger in fact than the Audi A6 or the E-class estate. But with them up there is no boot at all. What's the point of that? No, really. What is the point of a car that takes up four spaces all on its own, but has no space in the back for so much as an after-dinner mint.

Mercedes points out that for an extra £1,500 it will sell you a version that's 10 in longer, which makes it even harder to park. It argues that in this you get an extra 200 litres of boot space. But how much dog can you get into 200 litres? The front half of an Irish wolfhound? So what do you do with the rest? Leave it at home?

I have no idea how many litres of boot space is offered by an XC90 but I know I can get two labradors and a small bike in there. And I know it has one more seat than the Merc and I know it's cheaper, so why should I care if the engine's a bit rough?

The worst thing about the Merc, however, is that it's such a bore to drive. The larger engined R 500 (which was reviewed in 'Good Car Bad Car') at least has a burbling V8 to have some fun with. But in this version I went all the way to Co Durham and then back via London, Bedford and London again, and it never did anything remotely amusing. Except chew quite a lot of fuel.

It rode quite badly, failed to have the power for overtaking, gave me a hint of backache and was considered 'ugly' by those who saw it. I will therefore do what the government cannot do and apologise for being a muddle-headed nitwit.

This, contrary to my earlier reports, is not an estate, it is a 4×4. And not a very good one. You're better off buying a condom.

Sunday 23 April 2006

What a perfect way to make the girls go 'Eugh'

Lexus IS 250

Quite often, pink magazines full of advertisements for garden furniture and Jilly Cooper curtains call my wife to see if she'd like to become their motoring correspondent. 'We'd like you to write about cars from a female point of view,' they always say.

Right. I see. And what exactly is a woman's point of view when it comes to cars. The colour? Whether you break your nails on the door handles? How much space there is in the boot for babies? Puh-lease. My wife's argument on this point is sound. Women who are interested in cars are excited by exactly the same things that excite men. Power. Looks. Handling. And women who aren't interested in cars won't read about them, no matter what shaped genitals the author has.

So she sends off 1,000 words about a Caterham Cosworth, saying that it ripped her eyeballs out, set her hair on fire and left her with the same sort of ruddy glow she gets from a really good *Terminator* movie. This, as a general rule, is placed fairly quickly on the editor's spike.

If we look back over the years, my wife, a mother of three, has run a Caterham that she misses dearly, a Lotus Elise 111S that she sent back for sports exhausts because it wasn't loud enough, a BMW Z1 and a motorbike of some kind. Currently she appears to have an Aston Martin V8 Vantage.

Ask her about space in the back for kids or whether these things have convenient handles on which she can hang a handbag and she'll shove a hot conrod up your jacksie. She's not bothered. And it's an especially good idea to steer clear of fuel consumption, because if you bring this up she'll siphon a gallon from the tank and use it to burn you alive.

This is why I always give sexism a wide berth when writing about cars. Any suggestion that one model is better suited to men, or women, and I have to spend the rest of the day disentangling myself from the ironing board. Or begging to be let out of the Aga.

This is no great hardship because of all the 'ists' you can call me, 'sex-ist' isn't one of them. I don't run for the exits when a pilot comes on the PA system to say her name's Sandra, and when a lady doctor is examining my arthritic hips I've never once been tempted to say, 'Oh, and while you're down there . . .'

However, I am bringing some stereotypes to the table this morning because I have a question about the Lexus IS 250 SE. Have you ever seen one being driven by a woman? In fact have you ever seen any Lexus being driven by a woman? Apart from that girl in *Terminator 3* who nicked a 430 convertible – and she was technically a robot. I haven't. I've seen girls in Evo 8s and Ferraris and Astons. Once I even saw a girl in a Lamborghini LM002, which caused a faint but distinct stirring. But never in a Lexulator.

I'm sure that Toyota's marketing department will be reaching for the e-mail button right now to send me figures that show x per cent of Lexees are bought by women, but I bet that if these 'female' customers were examined more carefully, every single one would have an Adam's apple.

It's hard at first to see what makes the Lexus brand as uniquely male as a Leatherman or a hunter-killer submarine. The IS is a pretty car and we know from every single survey ever undertaken that no other vehicle on the planet is quite so well made.

Of course there are some things wrong with it. Space in the back is limited, the seats aren't overly supportive, the steering is way too sharp and the door mirrors are the size of barn doors. But since when did a woman ever complain about a mirror being too large? Perhaps, then, it's the rev counter that glows orange as you approach the red line. 'Noooooo' wailed my wife after she came back from the school run. 'I loved that. I made it orange the whole way home.'

What then? What feature does this car have that makes it so unappealing for women? My wife couldn't help. 'I just don't like it,' she said.

I did. Oh sure, it's not the fastest car in the world. In fact it has about as much power as my second serve. But this is not such a bad thing because of that super-sharp steering.

If by some miracle you're going too fast when you turn the wheel, you had better be awake, because everything can get awfully skittish, awfully quickly.

Also, the touch screen sat nav system was preposterously complicated. But you can solve this, if you're a woman, by reading the instruction book.

Me? I was too busy revelling in the quietness of the engine, the complete absence of wind roar, even around the six-acre door mirrors, and the well-chosen ride.

It's never too harsh that it shatters your bones on every speed bump and it's never so soft that it flops into the hedgerow on every bend. I also loved the sense that every button and every switch will outlive the sun.

Then there's the stereo, which has (a lot) more power than the engine, and the price. Take into account the list of standard goodies and this car costs not hundreds but thousands of pounds less than a BMW 3-series. It's better looking than a 3-series too. In fact it's better looking than a Mercedes C-class, an Audi A4 and a Jaguar X-type. Obviously, in this sector of the market, I'd take the Alfa Romeo 159 because that has a soul that the Lexus is missing. But if you don't want to be plagued with breakdowns, the IS 250 does appear to be a good bet.

And that brings me back to the original question. Why do you never see one being driven by a woman? To find an answer we need to get logical. Nobody who's interested in cars, whether they're a man or a woman, will buy a Lexus. They're just not zingy enough.

So they are only for people who are not interested in cars, people who simply want four reliable wheels and a seat. And this is where things split. Men are happy to go down the Lexus route whereas women are not.

To see if I could find out why, I did something unusual. I picked up the phone and rang a few girls who don't know one end of a dipstick from their left cheque-book. And all, curiously, said pretty much the same thing. 'A Lexus? Eugh.' 'They're perfectly revolting.' 'They're for people who play golf.' And best of all: 'They're all driven by the sort of person I wouldn't want to know.'

There's an inescapable conclusion here. Buy a Lexus and you are demonstrating two things. First that you are a man, and second that you are not interested in a car's power or handling. This, it seems, is not something women find attractive.

Think about this, before you say no to that Alfa.

Sunday 30 April 2006

It's a scream (yours) at 200 mph

Koenigsegg CCX

Top Gear's back on television tonight with a whole new look, a whole new base, a whole new feel and lots of new ideas that have never been seen on television. Well that was the plan. All through the winter we were racking our brains and burning the midnight oil as we thought up new ways to keep BBC2's most popular car programme fresh and entertaining.

First things first. We decided to build a studio and track in the Cotswolds but some local people objected on the basis that our reasonably priced car would cause 'pollution'. So we ditched that idea. And came up with a new one.

It's not that we're small-minded or petty in any way, but we've decided to stage a competition to find Britain's noisiest car. There'll be a number of heats, held every Sunday in the summer in the very village where people had objected to our plans. How clever's that? And to get round the problem of our studio looking a bit tired and familiar, we got a new one on the same site. This, we were told, was 50 per cent bigger than the old one, which caused us all to go down with a nasty dose of what I call Christmas Tree Syndrome.

This manifests itself in men who, when they go out to buy a yuletide tree, imagine that their house is much bigger than is the case. And therefore come home with something that's 14 ft too tall. So we filled our new studio with all kinds of static displays and decorative items that looked fantastic but, as we discovered in the pilot, left no room for an audience, which was bad, or cameras, which was worse. So we took all the flotsam out again and now, guess what? Our new studio looks pretty much identical to the old one.

So if you tune in tonight, it'll be the usual diet of cool wall, news, road tests, bickering and Richard Hammond's teeth. The only real difference is that I'm a little more bald and slightly fatter. Films? Well we road test the world's first convertible people carrier, which was awful, since we made it ourselves. We see which is faster, a car or a canoe. And I get to thunder about shouting 'power' in the subject of this morning's column. A Koenigsegg CCX.

A what? Well put simply a Koenigsegg is a Swedish supercar which, while crossing America on the Gumball rally, picked up the biggest speeding ticket ever issued: 242 mph. And that was the old, less powerful model. The CCX is much, much faster.

The company was started by a chap called Christian von Koenigsegg, who left school with the engineering qualifications of a duck but a burning desire to be a businessman. So, with a friend, he converted a room at home, bought a fax machine with his pocket money and registered a company.

Great, except the company he formed didn't have anything to manufacture or sell. The pair soldiered on for a while, staring at their dormant fax machine until one day Christian discovered the people of Estonia had nothing to spend their new money on. 'Aha,' thought our young Swede. 'This is a job for my fax machine.'

Immediately he decided that what the Estonians wanted more than anything was chickens. So he faxed a supplier in America and in months was a Baltic Colonel Sanders. And then he started buying carrier bags that had been produced with misprints, and selling those in Estonia too, where Tecso and Adsa were considered every bit as chic as Cocoa Channel and YLS.

At the age of twenty-two, Christian was a wealthy young man and decided to indulge a childhood fantasy for supercars – not by buying one but by getting out the pen and paper and building one.

The engine selected was an Audi V8, but as the car took shape Audi announced it would not supply any small company with its technology. So the team found an Italian racing company that made a V12. That went out of business, which brought Koenigsegg to the Ford V8. Then the factory burnt down. And all of Christian's hair fell out. Today I have more sticking out of my nose than he has on his entire body.

Even so the man soldiered on, bringing his agonisingly beautiful wife into the company and even employing his father, until in 2000 they launched the CC8. And then the CCR, and now with their own Swedish-made twin-supercharged 4.7 litre V8, the CCX. This is a very powerful engine. On normal petrol you get 806 bhp. But here's the good bit. If you tune it to run on eco-friendly biofuel, you get more than 900 bhp. So what we're looking at here is a car that's very much in the same league as the Bugatti Veyron.

Sort of. It's not hard to make a 250 mph car. You just need lots of power and a slippery body. But it is hard to keep a 250 mph car on the ground. And stop it. You need to spend a lot of money and time working on these things.

And while Christian has a few bob, he's not in the same league as VW, which went to the ends of the earth when it was developing the 1,001 bhp Veyron. This shows. Up past 190 mph, the back end of the Koenigsegg starts to weave and you get the distinct impression that if you go faster, the weaving will become so severe you'll be rolling through the Pearly Gates in a big Swedish fireball.

So you brake. And now the front end starts to weave too. And you're making a strange guttural noise that scientists would call the sound of fear.

Christian apologised and back at his mobile workshop fiddled with the brake balance, which improved things considerably. But I didn't dare head for the 200 mph marker again. To be fair, the *Top Gear* producer had insisted the car was brought to our track before it was properly finished. That's why the computers kept overheating, causing a monstrous misfire. In a few months these issues will be addressed.

Hopefully. But even if they aren't, you're just left with the supercar norm. The Ferrari Enzo needs a new clutch after three full-bore starts. And my Ford GT has not exactly been a paragon of reliability. I pushed its starter button yesterday and the only thing that started was the rear offside indicator. So that's back at the menders again.

So what have we got on the Koenigsegg that's good? Well it's a very pretty car, partly because it doesn't have any wings to keep it on the ground at 200 mph. And thanks to a new liftout roof panel there's acres of space inside for the American basketball players that Christian hopes will form the backbone of his customer base. It is also tremendously exciting to drive. The noise is hard to explain. There's a lot of it, and in some ways it sounds like an amplified version of that sound you make when you hit the brakes at 193 mph. A sort of AAAAAAAARGH.

Then there's the fire. When you lift off, huge jets of flame shoot out of the exhaust as unburnt fuel is ignited by the heat of the pipes. I liked this feature a lot. It'd certainly scare away the tailgaters.

Not that there'll be many since this superlight, all carbon-fibre car goes from 0–60 in a little over three seconds and will, I'm told, hit 250 mph. One thing, though: avoid trying your luck on corners. There's tons and tons of grip but when that's gone you will spin. There is no middle ground, no chance to solve the problem with a dab of opposite lock. Try to be cocky with this car and it'll kill you.

A lot of the excitement comes from this. Many of today's super-cars feel a little bit sanitised, a little bit smooth. Even a Pagani

Zonda is as docile and as user friendly as an ageing labrador. The Koenigsegg is not. It's a terrier with dobermann genes in its teeth. It's a supercharged great white, a fearsome beast, a killer, a man hunter.

There's a chance, though, that it may be the fastest car to go round the *Top Gear* track. You'll find out tonight. So will I.

Sunday 7 May 2006

Get one fast before they muck it up

BMW M3 CS

Many thousands of years ago, I was a member of the Ford Cortina 1600E Owners' Club (South Yorkshire branch). We'd meet once a month, in a car park, and would mooch about in the rain looking at one another's cars. Looking back on the experience, I really can't see why this should have had any appeal at all. I mean, yes, my car had a picture of Debbie Harry in the centre of the steering wheel, but other than that it was pretty much the same as everyone else's car.

Perhaps we thought that because we all had the same type of car we had a common bond, a platform on which lasting friendships could be built. But they were all miners. And when they lost their jobs a few years later they had to burn their cars to stay warm. So the bond was gone.

Today I loathe, with a furious passion, all car clubs. The notion that you're going to get on with someone because he also has a Mini is preposterous. Clubs are for people who can't get friends in the conventional way. They're for bores and murderers. The Ferrari Owners' Club is particularly depressing because they all have carpet warehouses in Dewsbury and creaking £10,000 rust buckets from the Seventies and Eighties.

Most turn up at events in Ferrari hats, Ferrari shirts, Ferrari racing booties and Ferrari aftershave and you can't help thinking: 'For heaven's sake, man. You've spent more on your apparel than you have on your damn Mondial.'

Anyone with the wherewithal to buy a proper, important Ferrari from the past sixty years is going to have better things to do with his time than drive to some windswept motor racing circuit no one has ever heard of and spend the day watching a bunch of Dewsburyites going off the road backwards in their botched and bodged 308s. Mind you, I'd rather swap saliva with someone from the Ferrari Owners' Club than go within 50,000 miles of someone who turns up to Aston Martin events. Because there are no cheap Astons in the classifieds – well, none that will actually get you to an owners' club meeting, or even to the end of your road – the members are a lot more well-to-do than their oppos with Ferraris. There are few regional accents, and lots of green ink.

All of them are stuck in the 1950s when for a few glorious years Aston Martin did manage to win a couple of not-very-important racing events. And all of them, you know, were attracted to the brand not because Aston made the best cars – it really, really didn't. But because they were made by British people and not 'darkies'.

The worst thing about an Aston Martin Owners' Club member, however, is not his politics, or his still burning flame of hatred for Harold Wilson. It isn't even his shoes, or his trousers. No. It's the way he refers to all previous Astons by their chassis numbers. And to the people who raced them by their nick-names.

'Do you remember when Pinky and Lofty drove xvr/ii-2? Course that was before bloody Wilson.' Sometimes, when they talk to me I find myself wondering what they'd look like without a spine.

Moving, slowly, towards the point of this morning's column, I must alight now at the BMW Drivers' Club, or whatever it's called, which used to host an annual event at the Nürburgring. This was an opportunity for them to turn up and show off their new short-sleeved shirts. I went once and it looked like a meeting of the Jim Rosenthal Appreciation Society.

Anyway, what they do, once they've examined one another's

leisure attire, is drive round the track and then get marked by judges for speed, accuracy and knowledge of the track. I came 197th out of 201.

Naturally, this was the car's fault. I'd taken one of the very first M3s, the left-hand-drive quasi-racer, which was great if you knew what you were doing, but a twitchy little bastard if you had fists of ham and fingers of butter. If you turned in to a corner with a little too much power, the back would swing wide – this was before traction control – and soon you'd be careering across the grass on your way to what Aston Martin Owners' Club people call 'the scene of the accident. Ho-ho'.

Unfortunately you'd also find yourself on the grass if you turned in with not quite enough power, or if you applied too much lock, or not enough lock, or the right amount of lock but a mite too quickly or a little too slowly. I hated that car with a passion.

Over the years, of course, BMW toned the M3 down to make it a little easier for nincompoops. But you know what, I've never driven a single one that I've liked. The last time I reviewed an M3 in *The Sunday Times* I said it was probably the worst car in the world. It was a convertible and the whole thing shuddered and shook over bumps. Plus, it had an early incarnation of BMW's flappy-paddle gearbox that was diabolical.

Friends kept telling me that the core of the car was sensational and that I was being put off by the trimmings. Yes, in the same way that I'd be put off eating a delicious shepherd's pie if the chef had sneezed all over it.

Subsequently I tried the CSL version on the Isle of Man. This had a carbon-fibre roof, a sequential gearbox, a boot floor made from cardboard and a big nostril in the front. It was very fast, and on the super-smooth TT circuit it was sensational. But on all other roads the ride was utterly brutal. So hard that it actually shook the tape off the heads of our television cameras.

And so it was that, never having driven a normal, non-sneezed-on M3, I tried Audi's new RS4. It was wonderful. Much better, I declared, than the BMW. And that would have been that until the new M3, with a V8, comes along later this year.

But then, last week, guess what rocked up at my house? One of the very last of the old M3s. They call it the CS because it has slightly faster steering than the ordinary model, along with slightly larger brakes and bigger wheels. But other than this it was standard. There was a proper manual gearbox, a roof, no iDrive, no sauce and no garnish. Finally, then, I was going to have to drive in the pie, sans phlegm.

Ooh, it's a handsome thing. The body seems to have been stretched over the wheels, in the same way that bodybuilders' skin appears to have been stretched over their muscles.

And inside everything is just so. Oh sure, the sat nav system is from the generation before BMW had even the first inkling how to make such a thing work, but the driving position, the moleskin steering wheel. It was all . . . just so right.

Not as right, however, as the way this thing drives. God, it's good. And it's even better when you push the little 'sport' button. This sharpens everything up even more, like you've given your horse a taste of the whip.

There's none of the early M3 skittishness and terror, and (sat nav aside) no stupid forays into technologies that don't work. It's just a beautifully balanced, forgiving and thrilling driving machine.

So, if you're after a car of this type, what to do? Wait for the new M3? Dive in now and get a CS? Or go for the Audi RS4? That's a hard one. I'm sure the new M3 will be a thrilling car. But I'm also sure it'll look like a big pile of dog sick, so we can discount that. That leaves us with the Audi and the CS.

And that gives us one of the most delicious choices in any corner of the motoring universe.

I'd have the Audi, for its engine. You might well go for the BMW, for its poise. And you know what? We'd both be winners.

Sunday 14 May 2006

A lucky strike to set Marks & Sparks flying

Mazda 6 MPS

If we travel back in time to 1973 we discover that the album chart in Britain was dominated by Elton John, Rod Stewart, Slade and er . . . Gilbert O'Sullivan. So, anyone seeking to enjoy some success in the music industry would probably avoid pinning their hopes on a cheesecloth bloke with a glockenspiel.

That, however, is exactly what Richard Branson did with Mike Oldfield and *Tubular Bells*. Was that skill? I don't think so.

Huge acres of newsprint are used up every day explaining that running a business is as complicated and as difficult as rocket science. It isn't. It's 3 per cent hard work and 97 per cent pure, blind luck.

I bring this up because I've just read a story in the Media section of the *Guardian* about a woman who took over the job of running ITV's daytime scheduling. Great. But within about five minutes Noel Edmonds had arrived on the other side with a barn full of boxes.

I have no idea what ITV runs at 4 o'clock in the afternoon. It's probably a fattish woman with a regional accent slamming doors and shouting 'I don't get it' as the bailiffs remove her three-piece suite. But it doesn't matter. The old and the unemployed have fallen in love with *Deal or No Deal*. And there's not a damn thing anyone can do about it.

Which brings me onto Noel Edmonds. I presume that over the past few years countless job offers have fallen through the man's letter box. I bet there were proposals to do shows about cheese, road safety, Keith Chegwin, and lots of ideas involving Mr Blobby. I bet there were also invitations to live in the jungle and eat Tony Blackburn.

But for some extraordinary reason he suddenly said yes when asked to do a quiz show that requires no skill at all on the part of the contestants. They aren't even asked to open their own boxes. And it earned him a Bafta nomination. So does this demonstrate that His Noeliness has some kind of crystal ball in his head? Or that he's a lucky bastard? Then you have Tony Blair . . . who isn't. He and his team work out precisely what he will say about forthcoming events, completely oblivious to the fact that the nation is being swamped with Hungarian paedophiles and that his deputy is bouncing up and down on a gobby secretary.

All of this brings me neatly to the door of Marks & Spencer's flagship store in Oxford Street. Or, as it's now called 'Your M&S'.

I'm not joking. To try and breathe a bit of life into what's seen as a rather lacklustre brand, they've changed the name.

Apparently, in recent years Marks & Sparks have tried all manner of things to stay afloat. They've dressed lots of sultry women up in lacy pants and put them in bus shelters.

They've told us all about their avocado and raspberry sandwiches and they've sought to reassure my mother she can still go there for a well-made, well-priced fawn cardigan.

But do you know something strange. I have never once, in forty-six years, ever bought anything from Mr Marks or Mr Spencer. Of course, people have bought me M&S pants and socks, but I have never been into one of the stores and come out on the other side with a bag of goodies.

Why? Well, I'm not sure what they sell, if I'm honest. I'm aware they do cardigans for ladies who are old, and thongs for those who aren't. But neither of these things appeal. And nor do their sandwiches. I tried one once and it was horrid. Like licking the butt cheeks of a sheep.

So that's that. Whenever I 'want' to buy something, I go to a Bang & Olufsen shop. And whenever I 'have' to buy something, I go to Selfridges. Marks & Spencer is not on my radar.

And changing the name to 'Your M&S' won't make a ha'p'orth of difference. In fact, if anything, it'll make me less inclined to go inside because it smacks of desperation. You can smell the fear in the boardroom. The sense that they've tried pushing the pants and the cardies and the sarnies and nothing's worked so now they're changing the name and, get this, writing it in a *Media Guardian* typeface.

Well, I'm sorry but that's like Noel Edmonds getting back into the world of television by changing his name to Ant'n'Dec. It's like Tony Blair getting out of his hole by saying he's now called David Cameron (which I sometimes think he has).

A name change is no good. So I offer a free piece of advice today to the chaps in charge of Marks & Your S. Have a very good look at the new Mazda 6 MPS.

At first glance, it appears to be nothing more than a rather lacklustre Korean saloon car. It even has the de rigueur Pacific Rim plastic radiator grille. A little something that bathes the package in an air of cheap nondescriptness.

Inside, it's a similar story. It's not ugly by any means and it isn't badly made or laid out either. But there isn't a single feature that causes you to stop in your tracks and say 'Wow'.

So if, for some reason, you didn't want a BMW 3-series, or an Audi A4, or a Mercedes C-class, or a baby Lexus, or an Alfa Romeo 159 or a Saab or a Volvo, there's nothing here to cause even a momentary flutter of the left eyebrow.

You will certainly be more tempted to have a look at the new Cadillac BLS. This does at least look interesting and it does appear to have been named after a sandwich. Don't be fooled, however, because although it's designed and built by Saab, in Europe, it is one of the stupidest cars on the market. The ride is hysterically awful, the steering is preposterous, there's no space and if you do some simple sums with the price, you find it's not that cheap either.

The Mazda is the other way around, not even remotely interesting to behold but when you turn the key and go for a drive it's . . . it's . . . it's just amazing.

Under the bonnet there's a turbocharged 2.3 litre direct injection engine that fires 256 bhp at the four-wheel-drive system. This means there's none of the torque steer you'd get from a powerful front-wheel-drive car. Put your foot down and bang. You're off.

Six seconds later you've exploded past sixty and shortly thereafter, on a wall of intoxicating exhaust roar, you're up past 140 and you're thinking: 'I really wasn't expecting this.' The Proton radiator grille and the complete lack of fuss and brouhaha give no hint at all that this is a magnificent driver's car.

It's more than that in fact. Because it's so plain, there's nothing to annoy you, no Lynx aftershave overtones, no Denim he-man voiceover masculinity. It's just a sensible, well-priced four-door saloon car . . . that goes like it's running on a cocktail of Tabasco and horseradish.

It handles well too, with nicely weighted steering and, sadly, some excellent brakes. I was rather hoping I could run into something which would have broken that idiotic grille. It really does spoil the look of what's far from an ugly car. And it's the only reason I'm not giving the MPS a five-star rating.

So there we are, a lesson for M&S. Mazda. For ten years they've been making some quirky niche cars like the MX-5 and the RX-8 and we've paid no attention to their mainstream efforts at all. But they didn't panic. They didn't change their name to 'Your Ferrari'. They just kept on, plugging away until some engineer had his lucky Alexander Fleming moment and hey presto, a tubular bell was born.

Sunday 21 May 2006

It's sex, but not as we know it

BMW Z4

When the BMW Z4 came onto the market many mocked its styling and jeered its designer. And I'm ashamed to say I may have been party to that mocking and jeering. While the proportions were rather good – it had a long bonnet and super-short bum – the detailing was hopeless. Just when a curve was starting to get interesting, an unusual crease zoomed into the equation, spoiling everything. It was a mess, a curious blend of organic bulbousness and trouser-press straight lines. It was almost as though it had been made by an origami expert out of Plasticine.

Then you stepped inside and, my God, it got worse. It was a cocktail of plastics that neither looked nor felt satisfying in any way. Then you discovered the designer was an American and you thought: well, that figures.

BMW themselves were obviously a bit worried, because when it came to advertising their new car they said only that it had the fastest-operating electric roof in the world. That was neither interesting nor, as it turned out, true. The roof on the Honda S2000 was faster.

To drive? Well it was far from BMW's finest effort, being a bit wooden and uninspiring. It certainly wasn't nice enough to overcome the woeful styling. Going ugly early is something that works in a Newcastle nightclub. But not when you're buying a car . . .

The thing is, though: it did work with the Z4. This was a car that, quite simply, came too soon. Because now, when I see one, I think it's a striking crisp and modern effort; much nicer to behold than the Mercedes SLK and a million times better than the push-me-pull-you Porsche Boxster.

So when I heard that BMW was going to let its motor sport division have a fiddle, it sounded like something truly wonderful would result. I love BMW's M cars, and when I heard the Z4 was going to get the M3's 3.2 litre straight six I was priapic with anticipation.

The best looking two-seater sports car with the best sporting engine of them all. Theoretically the best combination since someone said: 'I wonder what cranberry juice would taste like if you put some vodka in it.'

Now of course this theory sometimes doesn't hold up. You may recall the BMW Z8, which was a panty wettingly pretty car. And it came with the engine from an M5. That's a cocktail that sounds just as enticing and as appealing as Baileys with lime juice.

There's only one way to understand just how disappointing it was: you need to try Baileys with lime juice. Take a good slurp of Baileys and hold it in your mouth. Then take a slug of lime cordial and rinse them together as though you were using mouthwash. Sounds like a good idea, yes? The creaminess of the hen-night special with a fruity, tangy edge.

Yes, but sadly it isn't quite like that because the cordial causes the Baileys to curdle, pretty much instantly, so that within moments you have the most foul-tasting tennis ball in your mouth. What's more, it's too big to swallow so now you're gagging. And because your mouth is full, the vomit has to come out of your nose. This is not an edifying spectacle but it gives an inkling, I hope, of what it feels like to drive a Z8.

So would the Z4 M – as the new car's called – be more of the same? Or would it be an answer to the prayers of all those who find the Porsche Boxster too ugly, the Audi TT too homosexual and the Honda S2000 too Honda-ish? The performance figures look good: 0–62 is dealt with in five seconds and the top speed is, as you'd expect, limited to 155 mph. In other words the Z4 M appears to go just as quickly as the Mercedes SLK 55 AMG. Which is £8,000 more expensive.

However, there's a flip side to this argument. At £42,795 the new car is £19,000 more expensive than the cheapest Z4. Which is like building a ten-bedroom mansion in the roughest part of town. And let's not forget that the base Z4 is not that far removed from the Pifco Z3, which was more a hairstyling tool than a car.

It's tricky then. On the one hand £42,000 looks like good value. But on the other it looks like a hell of a lot. It wouldn't be so bad if the M looked markedly different from the standard Z4 – but you have to have a seriously chunky anorak to tell them apart. And it's the same story on the inside. Apart from a steering wheel so fat you can't get your hands round it – my wife liked this a lot – it was standard fare.

Still, I thought, in some ways I rather liked this business suit camouflage. It's what a BMW M car should be, lots of muscle hidden away until anyone tries to take it on. So I slotted it into first, dumped the clutch. And stalled.

While I applaud BMW for continuing to offer manual gear-boxes on their sporty cars – Aston Martin and Mercedes don't – I do wish they'd get their clutches right. They really are awfully bitey.

Whatever, I finally got it going and settled down into a big spiky bed of disappointment. The Z4 M is not what I was expecting at all. It doesn't feel or sound fast, and if you try to wring its neck the traction control system comes down on your head like an anvil.

I took corners at speeds that don't ruffle my SLK at all, and in the Beemer the little traction control light was winking away constantly. Either that's because it's overly nannied or it's a bad chassis. Either way, I didn't like it.

Then I stalled again.

The steering was a bit less direct than I'd been hoping for too, and worse still, when I lowered the roof I detected some traces of dreaded scuttle shake. This was awful. There's no way a Z4 M can be seen as a cut-price rival for the SLK 55, because it misses the mark on every level.

And then, on a trip down the motorway, I thought: 'Hang on a minute. This is jolly comfortable.' And it was. Early Z4s rode like their tyres were made out of bits of Edinburgh, but this one, the sportiest of the lot, was fairly soft and compliant. And quiet, too.

Sometimes with the Merc I daren't use full power because the racket from those tailpipes verges on being embarrassing. But in the Beemer all is soft and gentle.

And that's what this car is all about, actually. Contrary to what I'd been expecting, it's not a balls out, hunkered down M3. It's not a Patriot missile built to bring down the AMG Scud. It's a fast and comfortable cruiser; closer in spirit and character to the Jaguar XK.

On that basis I think the price is good, the looks are good, the hood is good, the engine is good. My complaints are few and small. As usual with BMW, I loathed the idiotic sat nav system, the fuel tank is far too small, and there's a bit too much buffeting when you put the roof down and go really fast.

This car, then, is not vodka and cranberry juice. And nor is it Baileys and lime juice. It's a well made, carefully prepared, slow and very comfortable screw up against the wall.

Sunday 28 May 2006

If you see it in your mirror, surrender at once

Volkswagen Transporter T30 TDI 174 Sportline

A couple of weekends ago the Countryside Alliance invited me to a fundraising concert. Of course, I'm not really very sure what the Countryside Alliance is, or does. In fact, come to think of it, I'm not sure what the countryside itself is, or does, either. But this was to be quite a gig.

Bryan Ferry was the warm up for a band that had a really rather amazing line-up. You had Eric Clapton, bits of Pink Floyd and a smattering of Genesis. The meat was then drizzled with a spot of Andy Fairweather-Low and served on a bed of Procol Harum.

Of course, for many, the big problem at such an event is what to wear. It's to raise money for the countryside so something tweedy would be in order. But it's a rock concert so nothing too dowdy. Oh and it's held outside in late May. So thanks to global warming and the drought it'll be pouring with rain and freezing cold. That's a tricky ask.

For me, though, the biggest problem was what to drive. I eventually settled on the new Mitsubishi L200 pick-up truck which, I thought, teamed rugged countryside practicality with a dash of urban flair. Oh, and it was black so everyone at the gig thought the drugs had turned up.

It was a wise and clever choice, but not a very nice or sensible car. A pick-up truck, to me, should be nigh on indestructible and designed by someone who only had access to a ruler, whereas the new L200 is all soft curves and brushed aluminium. Furthermore, a pick-up should only be sold in America.

In America, you see, there's no such thing as a Countryside

Alliance because there's no class-based struggle between a bitter-with-jealousy metropolitan elite and a few crusty old lords who have 120,000-acre grouse moors in Scotland.

In America everyone wants to be a part of the great outdoors. They like the idea of cutting down trees and shooting critters in the spine. Even the most sockless preppy from Georgetown DC is able and willing to slip out of his loafers at a moment's notice and into a hairy shirt for a weekend under canvas in the woods.

What's more, in America everyone wants to be a factory worker. They seem to find manual labour and engineer boots rather noble. Bruce Springsteen has more money than God but unlike Britain's rock gods, who wear tweed and Armani, he dresses like he's spent all day up a telegraph pole. Only in America could there have been a song called 'Wichita Lineman'. An ode to a man who spends all day long driving around a useless state, in a pick-up truck, looking for broken telephone wires.

Here, Dave Gilmour has never seen a BT engineer in Hampshire and thought: 'Yes. I envy your clothes, your hairstyle, your life and your wheels so much I'm going to immortalise you in a song.' As a result we've never been treated to a ditty called 'Winchester Lineman'.

Whatever; if you marry a love for the great outdoors to a sense that the 'working man' is a king, then you end up with a country where the bestselling vehicle is a pick-up truck.

Here, things are different. At the Countryside Alliance gig the car park was full of Kensington and Chelsea parking permits. No one there would have the first clue how to skin a rabbit but every single one of them could have walked blindfold from the cheese counter in Harvey Nicks to lunch at E&O in under three minutes.

That's because we're civilised and the Americans are barbaric. Civilised derives from 'civic', meaning 'of the city'. Barbaric derives from 'bearded', meaning someone who's 'in a wood and can't find any hot water to have a bloody shave'.

What's more, we have no real respect for the working man. He's very useful, of course, when your washing machine breaks. But you're not going to dress like him. Or talk like him. And you certainly have no ambition to drive the sort of vehicle he drives. Because that would be a van.

And that's the thrust of my point this morning. That the white van is in fact the British equivalent of the American pick-up truck. And the equivalent of the biggest, baddest, V10est, Dodgest Rammest of the lot is the Volkswagen Transporter T30 TDI 174 Sportline. Welcome, everyone, to Britain's fastest van.

If you thought like an American, this is what you'd want. Because then people would think you had a place in the country that you'd built yourself, and that for a living you fixed pipes. This would be every solicitor's dream machine. Eric Clapton would have one. Tony Blair would have a couple at Chequers.

So what's it like? Well it has a jolly big boot. I lowered my trousers until my bum cheeks were showing, went to buy some chicken feed and couldn't believe how much space was left over. What's more, unlike the pick-up truck I took to the Countryside Alliance gig, it is a secure area, so people can't help themselves to all your belongings at the lights.

Up front there is seating for three. One to do the driving, one to read a map and one to sit in the middle with his mouth hanging open, looking gormless. But in the VW there's a problem. There's no deep crevasse between the windscreen and the dash, which means there's nowhere to store your copy of t' *Daily Mirror*.

There is, however, air-conditioning, a CD player and leather upholstery. It's almost like being in a DFS store. Until you put your foot down.

Bloody hell it's quick. In no time at all the speedo is reading a staggering 120 mph. Then you're right up the chuff of someone in a Ford Focus who's doing forty, and this is where the VW really shines. You absolutely cannot see where the front is, so you can get really really close to the car in front without really knowing.

That said, the 2.5 litre engine, while powerful and torquey, isn't really very noisy. So while the driver of the Focus can see you – you're filling his rear-view mirror – he can't hear you. So he's less inclined to pull over.

In a normal van this would be an issue. But not in the Sport-line. This thing will do 0–62 in 12.2 seconds. It'll hit seventy in third. It is laugh-out-loud fast.

I must say when I first saw the alloy wheels and the chromed nudge bars I had a little chuckle. I thought it was a bit like writing 'turbo' on a microwave oven. And I allowed myself a smile when I noted it had traction control. But it really does go – and handle – like a car. Not a very good car, mind. But a car nevertheless.

So, do I want one? No. Not really. It's too big for most parking spaces, I don't own enough stuff to fill it, and while it's fast for a van it doesn't quite have the same overtaking ability as, say, a Golf GTI. Which also costs around £21,000.

If I were an American I'd have been proud of how it made me look like a son of toil. I could have driven around giving people in hard hats high fives. I could have loaded up the back with camping equipment and, like Norman Schwarzkopf, gone fishing with my kids. But I didn't do that either.

After I'd been for the chicken feed I couldn't think what else I might want to do with it. So it just sat in my drive, making me very happy. That I'm not an American. And that I'm not a van driver.

Sunday 4 June 2006

The poser's special just got potent

Audi TT 2.0T

Last year word began to filter through the fog of media gossip that a publishing company had commissioned some dirt digger to write a biography about me. I want you to stop and think about that for a moment. Imagine finding out that someone was going to write a whole book about you. They were going to talk to all your old friends and all your old enemies. They were going to meet up with your exes and find out what funny little noises you made at intimate moments.

How's that sound? Frightening. Well it gets worse because several months later a local farmer came round to say she'd found the contents of my wheelie bins emptied out in her garden. Why would someone have been going through my bins? And why did someone subsequently go to a great deal of trouble to break into my flat and steal my laptop? After a year there was a medical term for the state I was in. I was 'shitting myself'. I mean, we've all done things we'd rather stayed private. But here was a person with a publishing deal who, in all probability, knew what web-sites I'd looked at and what brand of baked beans I'd been eating.

Then, earlier this year, came joyous news. Having looked under every stone, the author announced to a diarist on the *Independent* that she'd binned the project. The relief was immense. And rather short-lived. Because she followed this up by saying:

'He's just too boring.'

Well, I was furious. But my anger was also short-lived because someone else has just published a biography about me and, having read it, I'm forced to agree. It seems I was born, grew up, got a job and had some children. And that's it. I am as dull as ditch-water. I am a herring gull among men. If you could look me up in a dictionary I'd be classified as 'common or garden'. If you look me up on Wikipedia, it really does say that I once drove into a tree: forty-six years old and that's all anyone can think of to say.

And so I have decided to start a homosexual motorcycle display team. We shall travel through South America, performing naked after taking vast quantities of high-grade cocaine. This, strangely, is an idea I got from the Audi TT.

What follows is a biography of this funny little car, so favoured among the squash-playing classes of EC1. People called Dom. People who buy their shirts at Harvie & Hudson. People who think *American Psycho* is the best book ever written. And not even slightly weird.

First mooted as long ago as 1995, the TT was nothing more than a four-wheel-drive Golf in a pair of sporty Lycra shorts. That's like putting Terry Wogan in cycling clothes and expecting him to win the Tour de France. It's not going to happen.

And it didn't. I remember driving it on the press launch way back in 1999. Actually that's not true. I remember getting very drunk on the press launch back in 1999. And then I don't remember anything at all. (See how crazy I was.) But I do remember people at Audi being very upset when I said the handling felt numb and distant. I was wrong actually. It turned out that the handling was in fact rather more than numb and distant. It was dangerous. And so, after some accidents and a spot of light death, the car was recalled, fixed and put back on sale. This should have been a kiss of death. But people, especially in Britain, just couldn't get enough of those cycling shorts. We just didn't care it had Wogan's heart and as a result we became the biggest market in the world for what I called the Titty.

As the years strolled by, more and more versions were introduced. Some had front-wheel drive, some had 150 bhp, some had soft tops and some had VW's amazing DSG flappy-paddle gear-box. But that numbness never went away. I can put my hand on my heart and say that I've never enjoyed driving any TT.

It was an affront, really, that a car named in honour of the 1905 Isle of Man Tourist Trophy race and styled with a Bauhaus look should be as inert to drive as a bucket full of argon.

The new one didn't fill me with much hope, either. Sure, it's based on the current Golf, which is a far better platform than the oil rig they used back in the late 1990s. But there was too much piffle in the blurb about styling.

'Oh God,' I moaned as I ploughed through endless pages on the elongated, more aggressive bonnet and the lower, longer, more aggressive stance. 'We can see all that. But what have you done to bring the damn thing alive?' Well I'll tell you what. They've done something because, while the exterior looks similar to the last TT, it is a different animal to drive.

The steering has a crackle and a fizz, so you're left in no doubt it is connected to the road. Likewise the engine makes a muted roar like it wants to be let off the leash and whipped a bit. And when you turn into a corner with your foot off the throttle, what's this … ? Why, it's the back end sliding round, ever so gracefully. It felt like I was driving Darcey Bussell.

This has been achieved with subtlety; a little spoiler that rises when you break the speed limit, a lower driving position for a better centre of gravity and, madly, a car made in two halves. The front is all aluminium, even the suspension, while the back is all steel.

It's not easy, mating these two metals, as anyone who's tried to wrench an alloy wheel off a steel brake disc will testify. But the effect is profound. Not only is the new car nine stone lighter than the old one, but also the weight distribution is just about spot on.

You can feel this when you're at the limit, I swear it.

I don't want you to think that I was hammering around in

the V6 quattro version either. The car I'm talking about had the entry-level 2 litre turbo motor and front-wheel drive. It was the £26,000 bottom rung of the ladder.

That said, it did have the flappy-paddle gearbox, which they now call S tronic. Why? What was wrong with DSG? That's like saying, 'I have a cat. But I shall now call it a dog.'

It also had the optional magnetic suspension. In essence, and try to stay awake at the back, the fluid inside the shock absorbers is filled with iron filings that move about and behave differently when they are exposed to an electric current. I'd love to meet the man who designed this, because I'm absolutely certain he would be a cure for insomnia.

Sadly I haven't driven the normal car so I don't know what that's like, but I do know that with those magnetically aroused iron filings the new TT corners well and, unusually for an Audi, rides brilliantly too. It's firm, but unlike the last model, never jittery.

Let's do some criticisms. Obviously the back seats are as useless as the poor sods who work in the factory making them. What's the point in wasting your life sewing something that will never be used? And imagine being the cow that gave up its life to provide the hide. Of all the pointless deaths . . .

The boot's not big either. But look, if this kind of thing bothers you, buy a Golf. More worrying is a slight lack of front-end grip. I tried the car back to back with the new Alfa Brera and while that car has several issues − a complete lack of brake horsepower being the most notable − grip wasn't one of them.

It turned in nicely to a corner and held on, while the Audi was slithering off into the bushes. I bet it could be cured by specifying better tyres. You should always do that. It really, really, really annoys dealers. The only other fault I can think of is the price. For £4,600 less you can have the still appealing but extremely thirsty Mazda RX-8.

I shall stop short of saying I loved the new TT. You can't love something that looks so similar to something you loathed. But I did enjoy driving it.

The changes they've made may appear to be small and subtle but the effect is enormous. Hence my foray into homosexuality, cocaine and motorcycle stunt work. It'll still be me; but I'll be interesting.

Sunday 11 June 2006

Breaking the law just got easier

Peugeot 207

Strange news. The government has thrown its considerable weight behind a new type of numberplate that can't be stolen.

Well, it can be stolen, but it takes three minutes to remove from your car and it will be broken in the process. As a result the thief can't attach it to his own vehicle and hurtle around the countryside clocking up points on your licence.

Nor can he fill up his car with fuel and then drive away without paying, knowing that the CCTV footage will direct the constabulary to your house rather than his.

All well and good, you might think from the comfort of your agreeable wing-back chair. But hang on a minute. Why is the government getting involved? They don't care two hoots if you have your car clamped by a psychopathic cowboy.

Truth be told, they don't care, really, if it's stolen. And actually, despite their sensible expressions and concerned noises, they don't even care that half of Bristol seems to have been stabbed recently. So why, all of a sudden, are they getting so excited by a numberplate that's hard to nick? You may be with them, of course. You may be one of the 33,000 motorists who had their cars 'cloned' last year and you may welcome any initiative that makes life harder for the thief and the vagabond. Well I'm sorry, but you're looking at this the wrong way round.

At the moment you drive about with the correct plates on your car, cursing every time you inadvertently trigger a speed camera or collect a parking ticket. You think it's not fair. You think you're being persecuted by an anti-motorist, pro-tax, *1984*-style government that's obsessed with infringing your personal liberty and emptying your wallet at every possible opportunity. You think all this because it's true.

So why not simply fit your car with the plates from another car? That way you'll never hear from the authorities again. Unless some other motorist who 'adopts' your plates triggers a speed camera in Bradford ... which again is no problem, because you can prove you and your car were in Dunstable at the time.

Only recently someone stole Terry Wogan's plates and then committed some awful atrocity while in Camden. It was a ram raid possibly.

Well of course it took Plod only four minutes to realise that Wogan does not sign off at 9.30 every morning and spend the rest of the day driving his Bentley around Dixons. So they let him off.

And by using his plates the thieves got away with it, too.

Are you seeing the problem yet? It's simple. If we all swapped plates the system would collapse, and it's genuinely hard to see how the state could put it back together again.

They'd need to get off the croquet lawn for five minutes and pull over every single motorist, and that presupposes they have a police force that isn't currently occupied filling in health and safety forms and refusing to climb ladders. And they haven't.

And that's why I have no points on my licence, and to his eternal mystification, James May aka Captain Slow has fourteen.

Let me give you an example. I was followed this morning by a swarthy-looking chap in an elderly Mercedes-Benz and I bet you any money he's never paid income tax in Britain, he's never paid car insurance and that the plates on his car are registered to an elderly doctor in Fife.

Plainly he arrived in Britain, looked at the way everything works and decided that by dispensing with the moral code he will never appear on the radar. So why should we? The rules of formal identity are only in place to persecute members of the law-abiding middle classes and, honestly, all you need to do to escape is change the six on your numberplate to a nine. And say, should by some miracle you ever be pulled over, that you've just been on a stag night, and that your mates mucked about with your car as a joke.

I'm not suggesting you go out and stab someone in the heart, or that you drive to London and throw petrol bombs at important public buildings. Changing your numberplate hurts nobody; it just means you'll never have to pay the London congestion charge again, or a speeding fine, or a parking ticket. And every single plan the government has for road pricing would be thrown into disarray.

That's why the government is so damned worried. You are not a free man because you are a number. But if you change that number you have anarchy in the UK.

If this does not appeal, but you still want to avoid parking and speeding tickets, simply pop down to your local Peugeot dealership and buy a 207.

It's not an ugly car by any means and nor is it especially pretty. It's just 'some' car that you buy like you buy curtain material: by the yard . . . You could drive this through the nave at Westminster Abbey and nobody would even look up. I bet you could drive past a speed camera at 100 mph and it wouldn't even go off. And yet behind the anonymous exterior this is an extraordinary car. You might imagine it's a replacement for the old 206 but actually it isn't. The 206 will soldier on, although as we know it'll no longer be made at Peugeot's Ryton plant near Coventry.

This is because the workers there paid taxes to Mr Blair who gave that money to the European Union who handed it over to the Slovakians who spent it enticing Peugeot to close down Ryton and build a new plant at Trnava. This means the Peugeot workers in Britain can now use their redundancy money to buy a 206 that's made in Slovakia thanks to the taxes they paid while they were working.

Or they can buy a new 207, which is much more expensive,

built in France and looks, so far as I can see, like the 206 did. Only a bit bigger. Small wonder the French never got their empire off the ground.

Of course, you may not care about the politics. You may have £10,000 burning a hole in your pocket that you wish to spend on a shiny new car. In which case you may want me to stop with the conspiracy theories and the nonsense of the EU and actually provide a road test in the rest of the space available.

Here goes. The 207 model I drove was the S version which had five doors and a 1.4 litre engine that produces some horse-power. It comes as standard with power steering, remote central locking, antilock brakes, air-conditioning, many airbags and — get this — body-coloured door handles. You know a car firm is struggling when they mention stuff like this.

To be honest, for this money I would have expected a wee bit more. Something to make me go 'wow'. Sat nav perhaps, or a trip computer I could find the button for. Or a ski jump in the boot. I also would have expected a better driving position.

It may be all right if you're a bit small and you wear flexible shoes, but in my sturdy brogues I went everywhere on the verge of cramp at 100 mph, or on my way to zero mph with my nose mashed onto the windscreen.

Apart from this (Mrs Lincoln), the rest of the car was all right. I liked the dashboard very much, though not the way it was reflected in the windscreen, and I liked the ride too. What's more, for a 1.4, it didn't half zoom away from the lights. Low gearing helped here. And yet on a motorway, at 85 mph, it was surprisingly serene as well.

Overall, I sort of liked it. I liked it nearly as much as the Renault Clio and the Ford Fiesta and all the other small European cars that this sort of money will buy. Then there's the 206 to consider. When that starts to pour out of Slovakia, it'll be much, much cheaper.

Here, then, is the ace up the 207's sleeve. If you buy one and are caught doing something naughty with it, simply tell the magistrate that you are a loony. He'll look at your car and be forced to agree.

Sunday 18 June 2006

Now the rich can buy a car just like you

Maserati Quattroporte

If you are poor, or fairly poor, life is full of exciting choices. Eating out, for instance. You've got KFC, Wimpy, McDonald's, Burger King, the local Indian, the Chinese takeaway and, for those special occasions, the Harvester. Things, on the other hand, are pretty bleak for those who have a substantial disposable income. Because where are you going to eat? I know of several hundred towns in Britain that have no decent restaurants at all.

It's the same story with houses. Those struggling at the bottom end of the property ladder can choose from a seemingly endless selection of starter homes. Whereas a completely tumbledown house near where I live went on the market recently for £500,000. And the last time I looked it was up past the £2m mark.

I can stretch this argument to cover clothes, holidays, haircuts, everything. And I can especially stretch it to cover cars.

If you want to spend £15,000 on a new set of wheels, it's like you're looking at the marketplace through a kaleidoscope of colour and choice. But for those looking to spend between £60,000 and £120,000, things are considerably more tricky.

'Pah', you might think, if you've just bought a second-hand Vauxhall Astra. You could buy a Ferrari for £120,000. And indeed you can. It'd be an F430 as well, which comes with just about the best chassis of any car made today and an engine that doesn't roar or purr. It howls.

Unfortunately, none of this matters because you won't actually be going anywhere in your Ferrari. It's too much like hard work, and after a while you will become bored with chiselling a dried-up fountain of phlegm from its flanks.

So, a Porsche 911 then? Of course, this has much of the Ferrari's appeal and performance but none of the Latin histrionics. It really is a car you can use every day. But it earned a reputation in about 1986 as a car for onanists, and even today some of that image still lingers.

To begin with, you might be able to convince yourself that other drivers are trying to dry their hands, for some reason, as they go by. But after a while you have to face up to the fact that they're not. They're calling you what Jonathan Ross referred to when interviewing David Cameron recently.

Yes, sure, you could buy a cheaper Porsche. A Coxster perhaps. But then you would be seen as someone who couldn't quite afford a 911. Or maybe you could buy a Cayenne. But then you would be seen as someone who has no taste or style.

This brings us straight to the door of Aston Martin, whose current and extraordinary success is, I'm sure, largely because of Porsche's image failings and the phlegm magnet that is a Ferrari.

If you buy an Aston Martin, you will not be spat at, you will not be given the bird, and you will have a very pretty car. Something you will have many hours to contemplate because, as a general rule, Aston Martins have a habit of not starting if you leave them alone for more than a couple of minutes.

I've lost count now of the number of people I know who bought a DB9 and then, having spent a few months watching it being ferried back and forth from the dealership, sold it again and rang to ask what they should buy instead.

It's a genuine problem. All Mercs, BMWs and Jaguars are seen as too downmarket, too common, too everyman. And all super-cars are seen as being too daft, too difficult and too daunting.

Sure, there are people out there who would offer to exchange some of your money for something they designed in a wet dream and built on an industrial estate. But really, I cannot recommend that you take them up because the cars they make will spend all their time either breaking down or crashing.

Bentley? Well yes, sort of, but each time I drive a Continental GT or a Flying Stirrup I can never quite get it out of my head that I'm in a Volkswagen Phaeton. It's like having a Bang & Olufsen stereo. You know that behind the Danish exterior beats a Philips heart. And that sort of spoils the moment.

The Range Rover Sport provided a brief respite, a place of refuge for car enthusiasts who wanted somewhere unusual to run and hide. But now we've noticed that a) it's even uglier than a Porsche Cayenne and b) every third person in the Prestbury, Wilmslow and Alderley Edge triangle has one.

In desperation, some of the country's super-rich are turning to the Americans for help, wondering out loud how life would be with a Corvette Z06 or a Roush Mustang. Or even a gigantic pick-up truck of some kind. Horrid, obviously, but what else is there to do? Buy a Bristol? Yes. Right. And then spend all day inside it, licking the windows.

I was considering the problem of what the rich might buy the other day while reading a copy of *The Week*. And there, on page twenty-three, was an advert that seemed to provide the answer. It was a simple, profile shot of a Maserati Quattroporte under a line that said 'What price exclusivity?'.

Hmmm. Now, in the past there was a very good reason why Maseratis were exclusive. Because they fell apart long before they ever reached the door of the factory. They were handmade, and handmade is just another way of saying the door will fall off. But the Quattroporte (it means four-door, by the way) was designed by Ferrari and is mass produced by Alfa Romeo. That's good.

Bonio has one, too, and while I'd rather saw my knees off with a rusty Stanley knife than meet the man, I will admit he's cool. So that's good too.

It is also ferociously good looking. Not from every angle, you understand. From some quarters it's too like a Vauxhall Cresta, and from the front it's too narrow. But from the side, especially on its new alloys, it's an absolute gem.

So I telephoned Maserati and asked if I could borrow one of the new £80,000 Sport GT models that comes with fat thirty-section low-profile tyres that I thought would ruin the ride. They did. But they looked good, so I didn't mind.

Other irritations? Well on a hot day, with five of us on board, the air-conditioning couldn't maintain a temperature without the fan constantly switching itself off. And then almost immediately on to full blast. And the sat nav wasn't very intuitive. And there were so many buttons it felt like I was at the helm of a nuclear power station.

But all the while, I couldn't help thinking: 'Yes, but this is it. This is the holy grail. It's the car the discerning car enthusiast can buy.' And it is, except for one thing. The bloody gearbox.

You probably think I'm becoming a bit of a bore about these flappy-paddle boxes but you really need to drive a Quattroporte to see the problem. Changes take for ever in auto mode, they're jerky in manual and if you try to time a shift at the red line, chances are you'll pull the lever at the precise moment it was going up anyway, so you'll go from second to fourth.

I haven't finished yet. If you try to pull away smartly from a junction, the car feels like it's going to fall in half, so violent is the jolt.

So you're sitting there in your U2mobile, swathed in leather as rich as you are, and you're spluttering down the road like you're trapped in the mind of a politician who's been caught lying on *Question Time*.

In a list of the five most rubbish things in the world, I'd have America's foreign policy at five. Aids at four. Iran's nuclear programme at three. Gordon Brown at two and Maserati's gearbox at number one. It is that bad.

What makes this so hard to bear is that I liked the rest of the car so much. I loved the silken clobber of its 4.2 litre V8 engine, the four-door practicality, some of the detailing and the ungoverned top speed of 167 mph. I liked the brakes, too, and the handling. It is, truly, a lovely car to drive quickly.

And, of course, it looks absolutely wonderful in the underground car park at your office.

If you don't like the idea of the paddle shift you can quietly phone your local Maserati dealer and tell it that you know an automatic version is in the pipeline. That's not an easy engineering job because it must go at the front, as opposed to the manual, which is at the back, but I know they're working on it. And in so doing, they may well end up with the only car the rich can realistically drive.

Sunday 9 July 2006

Broken down, you can admire it even more

Aston Martin DB9 Coupé

Last week while reviewing the Maserati Quattroporte Sport I made a bold claim. That if you left an Aston Martin DB9 alone for a few days its battery would become bored and die. This has made me feel guilty all week. Many people have told me that their DB9s refused to start after only a few days of inactivity, but being a proper journalist, schooled in the need for accuracy and proof, I felt it would be better to have first-hand experience of this phenomenon. So I devised a cunning plan.

I would borrow an Aston Martin press demonstrator that I would not use for a week.

Then, when the man came to pick it up again, we'd see if it started. Brilliant. The first road test where the car wouldn't go on the road at all.

Sadly, while I may have been schooled in the need for accuracy and proof, and while I like to think I'm a proper journalist, I'm still only nine years old. So the test lasted only three days before I thought 'sod this for a game of soldiers' and went for a damn good thrash.

I'm sorry, but having a DB9 on the drive and not driving it is a bit like having Keira Knightley in your bed and sleeping on the couch. If you've got even half a scrotum it's not going to happen.

This, then, is what I have to say to those who claim their DB9 won't start after a couple of days. What is it that you were doing that was more fun than being in it? No really. Unless your job is to be the fly on the wall in a Hooters changing room, I can't imagine that you have much of an answer.

My job this week is to review the new Lexus 350 Something Or Other. It's been outside all week, sticking pins in my conscience every time I walked past it and climbed, once more, into the Aston. Unprofessional, I know. But the DB9 does that to you. It assaults your heartstrings with a soothing balm of warm mango juice.

The only consolation is that unlike the previous examples I've tested, all of which had a paddle shift auto box, this one had a lever sticking out of the floor. It was a manual. It's not a very good manual, if I'm honest; it's heavy and cumbersome and feels like it may have come from a combine harvester. And it's attached to the engine via a clutch that has 3 ft of travel and a bite zone that has the exact same width as an ant's front left leg. You stall this car more often than you don't.

But when you don't, I have to say it's a joy. Having the gears and the clutch means you have total control over the revs and how far through the bonnet you could jettison all those valves. There's no Blair-matic computer overlord.

I even got it into my head that the new(ish) gearbox had somehow improved the turn-in as well, and the steering. But then, using an old-fashioned journalistic technique called 'picking up the phone', I discovered my test car was fitted with a £2,495 sports pack.

Hmmm. Fitting a 'sports' pack to a 6 litre V12 GT car. Isn't that a bit like fitting a 'pretty' pack to the aforementioned Ms Knightley? A bit pointless.

What you get for your £2,500 is altered steering, uprated springs and a softer front antiroll bar. And what this means is a harder, more firm ride but a quicker response to driver commands. Sadly, though, it also means some of the heaviness is gone from the steering. I used to quite like that, the sense you were manhandling the car rather than just sitting there, driving it.

There's more too. A standard DB9 makes sense. It's a grown-up, more relaxing, more comfortable and more expensive version of the baby V8 Vantage. But give a DB9 a hard ride and a manual box and visitors to an Aston showroom are faced with the agony of choosing which they'd rather have. Me? I'd rather have the salesman tie me down and tickle the soles of my feet with a feather duster.

So quite by accident we arrive at a proper story. Which Aston Martin should you buy if you're the sort of person who likes to crack on a bit? The manual DB9 with a sports pack? Or a standard Vantage? I dislike making choices. Children's schools. ITV or BBC. Swings or roundabouts. Even going out for dinner in Chipping Norton requires a nightmare hour of pen sucking. Should it be the Indian? Or the Chinese? Or Whistlers, for a spot of deep-fried brie? Last weekend it was the Goodwood Festival of Speed and the Charlbury music festival. So which was it going to be? I could have ended up going to neither because I couldn't make my mind up.

I think all men are like this. It's why war takes such a long time to finish. And so the notion of deciding to buy an Aston Martin rather than a Ferrari or Porsche, and then arriving at the showroom to discover there's yet another decision to be made – aaaaargh. Let me see, then, if I can help.

Practicality? Well yes, the DB9 has rear seats but no mammal yet created, not even when God was on the LSD trip that gave us the pink flamingo, could fit into them. That said, the boot is pretty generous but it can't match the hatchback versatility you get from the Vantage. Oh and because the V8 is smaller, it's easier to park.

In terms of styling, however, the DB9 still has it. You could walk round it, squint, go cross-eyed, do whatever you want but you won't find a single angle from which it looks even slightly wrong. The Vantage is slightly less successful. Stand directly in front of it and it appears to have no wheels.

That's one-all, and then we get to the noise. And of course the Vantage's V8 makes a hell of a racket. For sheer volume, nothing short of a big bike can bring so much din to the road network. But it sounds a bit synthetic, a bit manufactured. The DB9's V12 exhaust roar is also contrived, I know that. But it's better. Deeper. More menacing somehow.

Inside, the DB9 wins as well, chiefly because, when you turn it on, you don't get a message on the dash saying 'Power. Beauty. Soul'. Every time that happens in my wife's V8, I want to vomit.

I suppose at this point we should examine the price difference. The Vantage is £79,995. The DB9 we're talking about here is about £109,000. That's a big gulf and on paper at least that isn't really explained by the performance gap.

Both do 0–60 in 4.something seconds and both will top 175. But if you look behind the spec sheets, a different picture emerges. The V8 feels like it's struggling to be fast whereas the DB9 makes it all seem so effortless. This means that in the Vantage you're always having to work the box and hammer the brakes, whereas in the DB9 you can just sit there with your hair on fire listening to Ken Bruce.

I think then that if you bought the Vantage you'd spend large chunks of your time with it wishing you'd spent the extra £29,000 and gone for the DB9. When I first wrote about this car, oh ages ago now, I described it as perfect and I know some of you who've had flat batteries are cursing me for that.

But I won't back down. There is, as Mr Bacon once told us, 'no excellent beauty that hath not some strangeness' about it.

And the strangeness of a DB9 with a flat battery is that you have longer to sit around looking at it.

Sunday 16 July 2006

It's the best, but there's a big catch

Porsche 911 Turbo

So, where are you going for your holidays this year? Tuscany? The Dordogne? Spain? The list of possibilities is seemingly endless. But it's not as long as the list of places you don't even consider. Yakutsk, for instance, or Algeria. I bet you never really thought about Haiti either, or Iran. But topping the list of places I bet you're not going to is Germany.

Don't you think that's a bit weird? I mean, most of the places that don't stack up as tourist resorts fail because you'll be shot or because you'll come home with an interesting new disease. Neither is even a remote possibility, however, if you take the family to Munich.

And there's more. What is it that Tuscany has that Bavaria lacks? There are mountains, lakes and the promise of many cloudless days sitting around a swimming pool. You can even find a bottle of local wine that will make you just as drowsy as the stuff you get in Italy.

And then Bavaria really gets cracking, because there's no possibility of running into John Mortimer at the greengrocer's. You won't be woken at 6 a.m. by a teenager on a 4cc motor scooter, and you won't be troubled by strimmers on a Sunday because this is Germany and that sort of thing is banned.

What's stopping you from going, I imagine, is not the country itself but the people who live there – the Germans. But if we look back over the summer of sport, it's hard to see why this should be a problem.

I mean, did you see that ape the Spanish sent to Wimbledon?

What, apart from basic bone structure, do you have in common with him? And then there was the World Cup. The Italians all looked greasy and disgusting, the Portuguese were worse, and the French appeared to be Algerian, whereas the Germans, to be honest, looked like us. Except for the glaring fact that they could actually play football.

Yes, you might be thinking, the Germans do look like us but they are not like us because they have no sense of humour. Really? So when was the last time an Italian made you laugh? How many times have you left a French restaurant with your sides rent asunder? And where's the comedy in taking a donkey to the top of a bell tower and hurling it over the side? The Germans, on the other hand, do have humour. It's just tuned a little differently from ours. To prove this, I shall now tell you a German joke. A man is out shooting rabbits with his friend. He takes aim and misses, slightly to ze left. So he reloads, aims again and misses by the same margin to the right. He then puts his rifle away. 'What are you doing?' says the friend. 'Well,' says the man, 'on average, ze rabbit is dead.'

To us, this is about as funny as soil. But tell it to a German and you'd better make sure the St John Ambulance people are on hand, with oxygen. If this joke had been written earlier, our boys could have read it out at the Somme and millions of lives could have been saved.

So why do they find it so hilarious when we don't? Well, that's simple. Our humour is based around cruelty whereas there it is based around maths (and farting, obviously).

This becomes obvious when you look at the new Porsche 997 Turbo in the 911 series. You'll note it's the 997, which means it's one newer and one better than the 996. But it isn't one better at all. It's millions better. If I'd made it, I'd have called it the Porsche Jesus Christ Almighty Would You Look At That Bastard Go.

Of course, it's the same basic shape as all previous 911s but the engine is completely different. In fact it's completely different to any engine we've ever seen before because the turbos have variable vane technology. This means they work like small boosters when the revs are low – good for immediate response – and rockets when the revs are high.

The upshot is 473 bhp, which doesn't sound like much. But if you put your foot down, I promise, all thoughts of a power shortage will be gone immediately. Because this car doesn't accelerate. It teleports. Bang, and you're in the next space and time continuum.

The figures suggest there are faster cars, and on a track there are. The Ferrari 430, for instance. There are cars, too, that are more fun to drive; the Pagani Zonda springs to mind here, and the Ferrari again for that matter. But on a normal everyday road, where a Zonda's massive rear flanks don't fit and a Ferrari's low nose keeps graunching, you can exploit all of the Porsche's power and torque all of the time. In the real world nothing could hang on to the tail of a Turbo. Nothing.

And of course, being four-wheel drive there's immense grip even when it's raining. And better still it's well made so it won't go wrong as often as its Italian rivals. And it has four seats and sat nav and a phone and all of the things you'd get in a Mercedes or an Audi.

Oh, and let's not forget fuel consumption. Because of the variable-pitch turbo blades it has a Wesleyan attitude to consumption and, as a result, doesn't even attract the gas guzzler tax in America.

As a technical exercise, then, the 997 Turbo is hugely impressive. And yet I wouldn't buy one any more than I'd go on holiday this year to Baden-Baden.

Some of this is down to the styling. The Porsche Turbos from the late Seventies were pretty, almost dainty little things. And they were simple. The 997 is none of that. It is small compared with most supercars, but it doesn't look it, and it's been blunderbussed with trinketry.

Every panel, every small corner, every nook and every cranny is fussy and overdone. And on my test car the brake callipers were yellow. I'm sorry, but how complete does your life have to be for you to worry about the colour of your brake callipers? I know of no one apart from David Bowie who wakes every morning to think: 'Hmm, I'm good looking, rich, a rock star and crikey, I'm also married to a supermodel.'

Inside there was a problem too. My car had the optional sports seats, which have electrically adjustable side supports. Fine, but even on their widest setting they're still too small for those who haven't seen their feet in a while. If you're not David Bowie, stick with the standard seats. They're fine.

The seats, however, and the brake callipers are only small reasons why I wouldn't have the 997 Turbo. It isn't even the Onanist City Boy image that still clings to the car. No, for me, I would steer clear for exactly the same reason you will not be taking your holidays in Dortmund. There's no passion.

Just last week I drove the new Lamborghini Gallardo Spyder. It was, of course, a preposterous car, loud and shouty where the Porsche is smooth and unruffled. Jarring and stiff where the Porsche is comfortable and controlled. It isn't as fast as the Porsche either, despite being £33,000 more expensive. And yet the Lambo grabs you by the heart and the Porsche just doesn't.

Even though the 911 is the better car, by hundreds of miles, I'd buy the Gallardo. But then I'm a man who's having two holidays this summer. One in the Isle of Man. And one in Botswana.

Sunday 23 July 2006

At long last, that hybrid hocus-pocus has a point

Lexus GS 450h SE-L

Last week a man in the *Top Gear* audience gave me some wire. It didn't appear to be the best present I'd ever received until he explained what it was for. 'It's so you can connect your iPod to your mobile phone,' he said.

Now I'm a man who likes a gadget, so I thanked him profusely and turned to go. Then I thought of something. Why would I want to connect my iPod to my mobile phone? What would they possibly have to say to one another? It would be like slotting George Bush into the back of Hillary Clinton. Fun, in a 'look at that' sort of way, but a bit pointless.

Which brings me on to the BlackBerry. I'm told by those who've invested that this is the biggest leap forward for mankind since the invention of fire, and that when you've had one for a week or so you'll wonder where you've put it. Because losing it is like losing your mouth and your ears.

For those who think a BlackBerry is a fruit, let me explain. It's a mobile phone that can also receive and send e-mails. This means that no matter where you are on the planet someone can always get hold of you to ask if you'd like a bigger penis.

But this is not its biggest fault. Have you ever been out for a drink with someone who has one? Sure, they're in constant contact with the office, which is great for them, but they're not in constant contact with you. Every time you get to the interesting part of a story the BlackBerry chirps and you can see they're not listening any more. They're willing you to hurry up and finish talking so they can whip it out and see if, this time, it's not somebody wanting to offload a bucketful of Viagra.

Go out with someone who has a BlackBerry and you'll not get a single word out of them. Because it will be chirping or whining or playing the theme music from *The Persuaders*. And they'll be texting with one hand and sending an e-mail with the other and it'll be like talking to someone who has an unreachable itch and a daughter who's just been kidnapped. Their mind won't be on what you're saying.

If you have a BlackBerry you may be physically out with friends but mentally you are at work. This means you can never have fun. You can never relax. Soon, then, your friends will stop wanting to see you and then you'll die, quite early, from stress.

Another way of dying quite early – though this time with an axe in the back of your head – is to get a researcher's job on *Top Gear* and be found by me, using the Wikipedia website as a research tool. Oh, it sounds great, like the BlackBerry and a wire that connects your mobile to your iPod, but it doesn't work.

To prove this I recently checked the entry for Jeremy Clarkson and after just a short time thought, 'Wow. When can I meet this guy?' He sounds like a riot, a cross between Nick Van Ooestrogen and Genghis Khan. He's killed hundreds of cyclists, murdered all of northern Scotland, eaten a barn owl, and at weekends he goes out and rams trees for fun.

Apparently all the entries on Wikipedia can be updated by anyone. Which means there's nothing to stop you going on there are saying oh, I don't know, that Bonnie Tyler is a man.

Or try this for size. Wikipedia says the Toyota Prius looks like and performs like a normal car but delivers 50 per cent better fuel economy. That's not true. A Prius doesn't look or perform like a normal car and it will do only 45 mpg – far, far less than you'd get from a Golf diesel, say. I harbour a belief, founded on an admittedly limited grasp of science, that if you removed the electric motor and the batteries from a Toyota Prius, you'd save so much weight that it would become more economical and therefore even kinder to the environment.

But saving polar bears, of course, is not the point of a hybrid car. The point is not to save the planet but to be seen trying. I saw a Prius in California the other day with the registration plate 'Hug Life' and that's what the car does. It says to other road users, 'Hey, I've spent a lot of money on this flimsy p.o.s. and I'm chewing a lot of fuel too. But I'm making a green statement.' Think of it, then, as a big metal beard, a pair of open-toed sandals with wheels, David Cameron with windscreen wipers.

And that brings us onto the subject of this morning's road test – its big brother, the Lexus GS 450h. Unlike the Prius, which is a stand-alone model that looks like nothing else on the road, the Lexus hybrid looks exactly like its normal brothers. So if you buy one of these you're not making a statement. In fact, while driving up the Bayswater Road this week, a gnarled and furious cyclist who'd been inconvenienced by my presence leant through the window to give me a piece of his warped and bitter mind. And before I had a chance to draw his attention to the hybrid badging, he was gone. If I were a real environmentalist I'd be a bit pissed off by this.

This car, however, does work the other way round. It works for normal people. I, for instance, liked it a lot.

It's not the fuel economy. Lexus makes many bold claims, saying that by combining petrol and electric motors it'll go to the moon and back on a single drop. It won't. It'll do the sort of mpg you'd get from any large diesel.

Nor am I all that bothered about its carbon dioxide emissions, because I don't have a company car. If you do, however, then the savings are big. It's £2,500 a year less than a comparable Audi.

Does this mean it's saving the planet? Hmmm, I'm not so sure. Its 3.5 litre V6 engine is fantastically clever, combining direct and port injection. So I wonder how miserly it would be even without the electric motor and the batteries and so on.

Let me put it this way. On electric power alone, this car has a range of just 1.2 miles. Providing you don't exceed 20 mph.

It starts silently and for the first few inches it's on batteries. But then the big V6 kicks in and doesn't really shut down again until you're home. Hybrid? Yeah, in the same way that my Ford GT would be a hybrid if I put a child's windmill on the roof.

The only good thing about the electric motor is that it provides extra power when you mash your foot into the carpet. And I'm not sure that was the point.

So where's the appeal? It's not that fast, the CVT gearbox is as unusable as all other CVT gearboxes and the ride, beefed up to cope with the extra weight, is harsh in normal mode and bone-shaking if you hit the sport button.

And you will hit the sport button because a lot of the Lexus dash is quite confusing. It even has a device that tells you which way to turn the steering wheel if you wish to miss an obstacle.

These, however, are all quite small faults. And they're balanced nicely by the styling, the quality and the sense that you really are in something a little bit different. But the one thing that swung it for me is that if you take this huge, gas-guzzling super saloon into London you don't have the faff of paying the congestion charge. Because it's a hybrid, it's exempt.

Since Uncle Ken introduced the charge a couple of years ago I haven't driven into central London once. I can't be bothered to talk to recorded messages. Life's way too short. But with the Lexus I drove up and down Piccadilly all day.

It was great. It drove like a normal car and looked like a normal car, so people didn't think I was a lunatic green person. I even did a couple of U-turns for fun.

Of course, if you never go to London there are better, more comfortable cars. But if you do, the Lexus is something very unusual. Technology with a point.

Sunday 30 July 2006

Look, Bishop Killjoy – I've found the holy grail

Ford S-Max 2.5 Titanium

A couple of weeks ago the third most senior bishop in the Church of England announced that it was a 'sin' to jet off on foreign holidays and drive a gas-guzzling car. Yup, the Bishop of London, the Right Reverend Richard Chartres, said tourists and school-run mums were being 'selfish' for making global warming worse.

Quite how he arrived at these conclusions we don't know. I've checked and he has no known scientific qualifications. So far as I can tell, he read history before taking a job in Sainsbury's. His hobby is advising men on how to wear dresses.

So, is eco-vicaring the lunatic ramblings of a lone maverick in a dog collar? Or is it now official church policy? Well, when reporters contacted the Archbishop of Canterbury, Rowan Williams, for his views on the matter, he agreed that he too had a beard. And that yes, not having a beard was selfish.

I suppose we shouldn't be surprised by this. Few organisations know quite as much about selfishness as the Church of England. They preach to their increasingly small congregations about the iniquities of homelessness, and then lock up their churches at night to make sure tramps can't get in and nick the communion wine.

They tell us about the need for tolerance and to forgive those who trespass against us, but won't let homosexualists into the pulpit because that sort of thing is a sin too. And so is being a woman. And so is greed, of course. The sort of greed that turned a simple belief into one of the richest institutions in the world.

Then there are those who practise bell-ringing for two hours a night. Is that not a bit selfish; imposing your hobby and your vision of traditionalism on everyone within five miles? Some of whom may well have come from cultures where guns, not bells, are the soundtrack of village life.

Would these people therefore be on the moral high ground if they were to shoot a bell-ringer?

In the sort of multiculturalism the church likes so much these days (so long as you're not a poof) then yes. Presumably they would. I'm sorry. I know it's Sunday. I know many of you have deeply held Christian beliefs and you don't like to see them being criticised.

But for the same reasons I don't like to see cars being criticised, especially by some jumped-up shelf stacker who has absolutely no idea what he's on about.

That said, I am approached by an increasingly large number of people these days who believe that their off-road car might be causing the lovely summer we're having. This, for some reason, is making them feel guilty.

Well, I don't know what's causing global warming. I've read several reports saying it's the Land Rover Discovery and that you must immediately part-exchange it for a windmill.

But then I've read an equally large number that say global temperature variations are cyclical and that choosing to become an automotive vegetablist won't make the slightest bit of difference.

I don't know which are right because my only qualification is a bronze swimming medal. What I do know is that those who wish to change their Land Rover Discovery for something else have a bit of a problem. What? Writing in the *Telegraph* recently, Annabel Heseltine made a very good point; that the law requires children in the back of cars to fasten their seatbelts. And that if you have four children, you therefore need four back seats. Which means that G-Wiz electric car won't really do. And nor will a people carrier . . .

When I was a young man in London I had a very large overdraft and no real sense of how it might ever be paid off. Occasionally I'd look into the future and think, how do people manage? I am living in a shared house and I cannot afford the basics – cigarettes and beer.

So how do you cope when you have a wife who can't work because she's at home looking after two small children? How can one wage packet sustain four people, four holidays, four sets of clothing, four new pairs of shoes? And how does anyone ever have enough money to buy a washing-up bowl? No, really, I used to see them in hardware stores and wonder how boring and complete your life would have to be before you'd even think about buying such a thing. And that really is where I stand on the people carrier.

They're for people with no imagination, people who can't think of anything better to do with £17,500. Buying a Renault Scénic is like buying a passport into the grey, sterilised world of upper middle age.

So if you need lots of seats because you have lots of children, it has to be a 4×4 of some kind. We have the Volvo XC90. You may prefer a Disco. Either way, it shows you are still packing a bit of meat. That you haven't yet reached that stage in life where what you crave more than anything is 'an early night'.

And then along comes the Right Reverend Richard Beardface to say that you're a sinner and a heretic and that you should be placed in a wicker man and burnt while Britt Ekland prances around a nearby hotel room naked as a jaybird.

So what's to be done? Well, at last there's an answer in the rather beguiling shape of the Ford S-Max. It's a people carrier but they've named it after a slang word for heroin. And that sums it up rather well.

You look at the exterior styling, the 18 in alloy wheels, the raked windscreen, the low roofline, and you think, yes, it might well have seven seats in there but who could possibly fit on them? Richard Hammond? You're in for a shock. There's tons of space for me behind the wheel and tons of space in the middle row too, which is made up of three individual seats, all of which slide and tilt independently of one another.

In the boot there are two more seats that rise – easily – from the floor and behind them you have a boot that is big enough for a medium-sized dog. And under this there's another boot that is big enough for a small overnight bag.

Or you can fold all the seats in the back away and end up with a cargo area that's big enough for a standard house door.

So then you stand back and think, how in the name of all that's holy (not poofs, in other words) did they get all that in there? The answer is to be found when you try to park. The S-Max may appear to be compact and sporty but it's only a whisker shorter than the Volvo XC90.

It is, however, much better looking, and much cheaper. The range starts at just under £17,000 and is still only at £22,000 when you get to the five-cylinder turbocharged 143 mph 2.5 Titanium.

Which is what I drove. I was expecting a characterless unibox but I was wrong. It was great to look at and cheap and more versatile than a decathlete's trusty Leatherman. I'm not saying it's a sporty car in any way, but it goes, handles, steers, stops and most importantly rides way, way better than you could hope for. And on top of this, it did 30 mpg, felt very well screwed together and came as standard with air-conditioning, electric everything and automatic headlamps. Which were second world war search-light bright, incidentally.

This, then, is the holy grail. It's an MPV you buy because you like it. Not because you need it. And because it appears to be small and has no four-wheel-drive system, you'll be able to park it outside church, knowing the vicar won't come along and chop it up with his special nine-bladed eco-sword.

Sunday 6 August 2006

Don't all point and laugh at once

Nissan Micra C+C Essenza

I had to drive in convoy through central London last week behind the *Top Gear* producer in a bright yellow Porsche Coxster. Or Gayman, to give it its official name. You might imagine this would be quite a thrill; driving through one of the most vibrant and amazing cities in the world in an egg yellow Porsche. And indeed you'd be right. It was quite a thrill. But only for me, in the car behind.

Very often in car magazines reporters will claim the car they've been driving caused a bit of a stir as they motored along, but this is only to make the job of road testing seem more important than is actually the case. It's almost a cry for help. 'Hey, I'm not a nerd. Everyone loves cars.'

But the fact is that here in Britain you could drive a polka-dot Rolls-Royce through the Queen's legs and no one would look up.

One bloke in *Autocar* claimed recently that a Lamborghini Gallardo caused 'absolute mayhem' when he parked it in a Tesco car park. But I assure you it didn't. You get 'absolute mayhem' when you drop a cluster bomb in the residential area of a big city. What you get when you drive a Lamborghini into a British supermarket car park is called 'studied indifference'.

However, if you have a yellow Porsche Coxster it turns out that people will turn round and point. And then they'll nudge their friend, who'll point too. And then they'll both have a jolly good laugh. Twice people leant out of their vans to call my producer friend a student of onanism.

And then there's the reaction he got from people in proper Porsches, by which I mean the 911. They laughed, too. Because turning up in the big city in a Coxster is like turning up to Elton and David's white tie and tiara party in a rented DJ.

Of course, from behind the wheel you are blissfully unaware of the hysteria in your wake. Because of the limited rear visibility you simply can't tell that you've turned London into a scene from a Smash commercial. You're sitting there thinking, I look good. I feel sharp. I've spent £43,930 on a mid-engined sports coupé. What a tool . . . you look.

What you're doing is strutting through town with your flies undone. You're commuting to work with your skirt tucked into your knickers. The Coxster? It's like congratulating someone on the forthcoming arrival of their baby only to find they're just fat.

The poor think you're a git for having a Porsche. The people with proper Porsches think you're a git because you actually don't have a Porsche at all. The Coxster, then, is the most embarrassing car in the world, except for one thing . . . it's beaten, just, by the Nissan Micra C+C.

I honestly don't know where to start with this one. So let's begin at the meeting where I presume someone decided that what the world needed most of all was a Nissan Micra with a heavy and complicated folding metal roof.

Now we all know that meetings don't work.

All of them − with no exceptions − are a complete and utter waste of everyone's time. Show me someone who goes to a lot of meetings and I'll show you someone who doesn't have a proper job.

All the great inventions and great leadership choices come from the mind of one egomaniac who then gets the job done. Everything after the initial idea is formulated can be achieved by e-mail.

Meetings are where good ideas get watered down and bad ideas are forced along because no one ever has the courage to stand up and say: 'What the bloody hell are we doing here?' You may have seen an item on *Top Gear* recently where the three presenters were roadies for the Who. At the editorial meeting that sounded brilliant. 'Imagine. We all get lost. Our vans break down. And the band have to go on stage the next night and do an acoustic set because we broke their amps. Ha, ha, ha.'

Of course, someone pointed out that we couldn't actually do any of that because 80,000 people had bought tickets and the Who weren't going to let them down just because three apes from a pokey motoring show on BBC2 wanted a laugh. So obviously we couldn't get lost. And we couldn't break their equipment and we couldn't break down either.

Collective thinking, however, decided that it was still a great idea. And so it went on television. And it wasn't.

I suspect this is what may have happened with the Micra C+C. At some point there must have been a meeting where someone explained that the cost of the motors needed to power a folding metal roof had fallen in recent years. And that as a result it would make economic sense to fit such a thing to even the smallest car. Yes, even the Micra.

Wow! Imagine that. Our fun'n'cheeky bite-sized'n'cute little shopping car could have the security of a metal roof when it's raining and then on sunny days the roof could glide electrically into the boot. Brilliant! However, I refuse to believe it took very long for the big flaw in the plan to rear its head: specifically, the roof wasn't actually going to fit in the boot.

Instead of canning the project, though, they made the separation point between roof and windscreen much further back than is either ideal or aesthetically satisfying. And obviously this still wasn't enough so they had to enlarge the boot by fitting what can only be described as an aircraft hangar on the back.

The result is one of the ugliest cars ever made. I'm no fan of the normal Micra but at least it is sort of sweet. The C+C isn't. It is enough to make your dog sick.

And to make matters worse, because they've located the separation point so far back, smaller drivers, who sit near the wheel, are still effectively under cover even when the roof is down. Oh and the rear seats are big enough only for transporting amoebas.

So yes, Nissan has indeed ended up with a convertible hatch-back. But the cost of fitting a folding metal roof has rendered the car utterly useless. It's ugly, impractical and, at £15,250 for the top model, bleeding expensive.

It gets worse. Because of the motors needed to make the roof work, and because of the strengthening beams fitted to compensate for the loss in structural rigidity, the C+C is about two million tons heavier than the standard car, which has an effect on both performance and fuel economy. Oh, and it's a price not worth paying either because despite the strengthening beams it still has the worst scuttle shake since the old Ford Escort XR3i soft top.

To sum up, then, it's ugly, impractical, very expensive, slow, not terribly economical and unpleasant to drive. The only good thing is that it's made in Britain. But so is the Mini Convertible, and that's much better.

The worst thing about this car, however, is the deep, stomach-churning embarrassment of being seen in it. I'm used to being pointed at and abused when out and about but I'd say the Nissan caused the insults to double in number. And because there was no roof, I saw and heard them all.

One sunny Sunday I had to plan a very special route to a friend's house for lunch. I wasn't interested in getting there quickly, or safely, only in not driving through any built-up areas.

Someone, at some point in this car's development should have had the courage to pull the plug. Unless of course I'm wrong and the plan wasn't to build a convertible hatchback at all. Maybe they sat down in Japan and said: 'Hey, guys. I hear

Porsche are doing a yerrow Coxster. It's supposed to be the most embarrassing car in the world. Do you think we could beat it?' They have.

Sunday 13 August 2006

Ice-cool cutie, you stole my heart

Lamborghini Gallardo Spyder

In the whole of human history it has been impossible to buy a Lamborghini unless you are Rod Stewart. They've always been just too silly, strutting around in their leopardskin underpants asking all and sundry if we thought they were sexy.

The company began making industrial heaters but quickly the proprietor realised that this was a waste of his name. If you're called Stan Arkwright you can make industrial heaters, but if you are called Ferruccio Lamborghini you need to start making cars with guns on them, for Rod Stewart.

As cars go they were pretty hopeless. The Miura took off if you asked it to go faster than eighty, and the Countach was as wieldy as a meat locker. The clutch was set in concrete, the steering wheel was nailed to the dash, and the air-conditioning had all the vim and vigour of an arthritic punkawallah.

But there's no getting away from the fact that it went grrrrr a lot, and looked spectacular. Did we think it was sexy? As a car, no. But as a poster on a wall it rang rings round even that tennis girl scratching her bottom.

Porsche would sell you a precision instrument. A powerful cutting tool with zero flex and the unbreakability of carbon-granite.

Lambo, on the other hand, just painted its cars orange and fitted doors that opened upwards.

After the Countach went away we got the Diablo, which could get from 0–60 . . . once. And then you'd be covered in a thin film of what used to be the clutch. And after the Diablo came the Murciélago which, so far as I can tell, was designed specifically to appear at parties, backwards, in a cloud of tyre smoke shouting 'Mine's a tequila'.

But then, one sad day a few years ago, Lamborghini was bought by Audi.

All of a sudden the Lambo boys were coming to work with plans to make a car that had space rockets and torpedo tubes only to find their fierce new headmaster was saying: 'No, boys. No more flying before you can walk. You can't fit gamma-ray rear lights until you've made the clutch work properly.'

The result was the Gallardo. The One Cal Lambo Lite. It looked like a Lamborghini with all the mad bits sanded off. But it went like no Lamborghini before. Because it actually went, even when it was raining.

Plainly the fierce new headmaster was pleased with their efforts because now he's let his boys go a bit mad again, cutting the Gallardo's roof off, squeezing a bit more power from the engine, and fitting orange seats. And I won't beat about the bush. It's my new favourite supercar.

Of course, there are several mistakes. The spoiler, for instance, rises from the tail when your speed climbs past 80 mph. And unlike any other car with this feature there's no override button. So if it's up it's a case of: 'Hey, everyone, look at me. I'm speeding.'

There's more. If you push the seat all the way back the leather rubs against the firewall and squeaks. And while it comes with the same central command unit that you find in an Audi A8, half the features aren't available. Like a phone, for instance. Or iPod connectivity.

Then there's the speed. Or rather the lack of it. Yes, you get a 5 litre V10 engine that produces 520 bhp and 400 carbon dioxides, but even so, if you have the roof down the top speed's a yawn-making 190. What's more, despite the four-wheel-drive system it could only get round the *Top Gear* test track in 1.25.7. That's three seconds slower than the old Ferrari 360 CS.

Partly this is down to the extra weight of the Spyder – it's a bit of a porker – but mostly I blame the Pirelli tyres. They are stunningly good for the first two or three hard laps but afterwards – and I've noticed this on Astons and Ferraris as well – they lose their bite completely. And you end up in something with the handling characteristics of a Hillman Avenger.

You're probably better off with the Bridgestones. Which don't bother giving you much grip in the first place.

So why, you may be wondering, am I so fond of a squeaky car with no phone, no iPod connection, too much body fat, tyres that last less than three minutes, and the real world performance of a BMW Z4? I'll tell you why. Because it's got orange seats. And because it is so pretty. And because when you go above 3500 rpm it makes a noise like a punctured sumo wrestler. And because you sit so far forwards, which makes it feel like you're on the nose of some giant, snarling power-crazed animal.

But you're not. You look at the pictures and you imagine it's another whopping great supercar with hips like Marilyn Monroe. But actually it's tiny, as near as makes no difference the same length as a Ford Focus.

Better still, it comes with a device for raising the nose when you get to a speed bump, and air-conditioning that actually works, and the roof's electric, and after a little while you find yourself thinking crikey, it's a supercar without the superstar tantrums. I could use this every day.

And then if you're not very careful you'll find yourself in the Lamborghini showroom deciding what colour goes best with those orange seats, and laughing at the price list. £400 for a 'journey pack'. Which turns out to be a cupholder. Ho, ho, ho.

I couldn't believe it. I am not Rod Stewart. I don't wear

leopardskin pants. And yet there I was wondering if I should have the 'comfort pack', which is soft suspension. Yes, probably, so long as there's no way a passer-by could tell.

Some of you at this point will think I've gone mad. And that if I want a mid-engined supercar I should go for the Ferrari 430, which is faster and much better. True, but Ferrari these days are just a bit too up themselves for my liking.

I don't like the way Jean Todt sits on the pit wall every other weekend looking like his dog just died. I want to shake him and say: 'Look, man, you're running the Ferrari race team. Lighten up. Go and set a fire extinguisher off in Ron Dennis's trousers or something.'

And I don't like the way they won't allow their cars to be featured in the Gran Turismo racing game. And did you notice how, at the end of the Pixar film *Cars*, a Ferrari appears flanked by two Maserati Quattroportes?

You just know that this was a scene dreamt up not in Hollywood but in the legal headquarters of Fiat SpA. '*Si*. You can use our image and our likeness, and we grant permission for Meester Schumacher to have a speaking part, but if you do not feature some Maseratis as well it would break our hearts – and your legs.'

Frankly, the producers should have used a Gallardo, because you get the impression no one at Lamborghini would have noticed. They'd have been round the back of the bike sheds, smoking and wondering if their next car could have breasts.

Ferraris are serious cars for serious people who drive around wearing a serious expression. The Gallardo can do serious, too. It has Audi electrics and Audi engineering. But as you career towards the next bend on a wave of extraordinary sound, half blinded by your own upholstery, you'll be making the noise of a howler monkey and wishing you were naked.

Let me put it this way. I took the Gallardo backstage at a recent Who gig and it looked right, sitting there among the rock stars and the roadies. It looked as right, in fact, as a Ferrari looks on a windswept track day in Cheshire.

For the first time ever, then, you can buy a Lamborghini. And I think I might.

Sunday 20 August 2006

I've had more fun in a road digger

BMW Z4 M Coupé

Many years ago I was approached by a television executive whose name I can't remember. Anyway, he'd been to stay with Griff Rhys Jones, or maybe it was Vic Reeves. Or it could have been someone else.

That's not the snappiest intro of all time, I admit, but stick with me. You see, whoever it was had rented a JCB for the weekend and was so busy moving piles of soil around his garden that he'd refused to come inside for meals or drinks.

'It gave me an idea for a show which I'd like you to host,' said the television exec. 'Pro-celebrity digger driving! We could get teams to pick stuff up and put it down again. BBC1 7 o'clock. How about that!' I nodded sagely to show that I was listening, but what I was actually doing was eating the inside of my own mouth to stop myself laughing. And as the pitch unfurled I had to swallow great lumps of flesh to keep my face straight.

No, really. I'd have ended up with Keith Chegwin on one team and some bird from a Flake advert on another, moving mud under the supervision of two fat Irishmen with bum cracks like the San Andreas Fault.

So, having listened for a while, I promised the executive that I'd give the matter some thought, went outside and, despite the pain from two lacerated cheeks, fell to my knees and wept with convulsive, life-threatening hysteria. The sort that you think won't stop until every blood vessel in both your eyes has burst and you're blind.

Last week, though, it did stop because I had to rent a digger to clear away a dead seal and now I know exactly why Griff Rhys Jones, or Vic Reeves or whoever it was, had been so captivated. And why pro-celebrity digger driving is undoubtedly the next Big Thing for television.

The best thing about diggers is that, to begin with, they appear so daunting. I have sat on the flight deck of the space shuttle and in the pilot's seat of the Blackbird SR-71 spy plane, both of which are straightforward compared with the dash of an earth-moving machine. There are so many levers, so many opportunities for making a terrible hash of it.

Viewers would love it; the sense that at any moment Keith Chegwin is going to get his head cut off.

And to make matters worse, the Volvo I rented sits on two tank-type tracks that are tiny. It therefore looks like an elephant balancing on one leg. There's a feeling that if you go down any sort of gradient, or load the bucket with anything heavier than a pillow, it will topple over.

And when you're inside, getting to grips with what does what, you really do feel like you're attempting keyhole surgery while riding a unicycle.

To begin with things went badly. With a cry of 'Watch this', which is the international precursor to all big disasters, I swung the bucket through a 180-degree arc, straight into the shin of my ten-year-old son. The impact was so enormous he actually flew for a greater distance than was achieved by Orville and Wilbur Wright.

Plainly the digger was more powerful than its small and ungainly dimensions would have onlookers believe. And so it turned out.

My initial plan was to fill in a pond of stagnant water. With spades and elbow grease this would have taken a couple of men eight hours. The digger had it done in twenty minutes.

So then I thought I'd level an awkward piece of garden. This was done in half an hour. And I was left with a pile of mud that needed to be moved.

I cannot fully explain the joy of picking up a full shovel load of soil and then, by teasing the levers this way and that, swinging it to the chosen dump spot without spilling a single pebble. It sends a shiver down my spine just thinking about it. You might say that the earth really did move.

What I loved most of all, though, was that after just a few minutes, and a few accidents involving your children (or Keith Chegwin), you quickly get the hang of it. Of course you do. It's designed for road workers to use, and mostly they're not that bright.

And to keep the adrenaline flowing, you never lose the sense that it's always on the verge of falling over, crushing whatever part of your body has flopped out of the window. Two or three times it lurched alarmingly, causing my head to smash into various nuts and bolts that poke from the bodywork. Plainly, Volvo's obsession with safety in its cars does not extend to its plant.

However, you soon learn to predict when these lurches might happen and how you might use the hydraulics to keep you upright. I became so fascinated by the process that after I'd moved all the soil I picked it all up and put it somewhere else. Lunch passed. Supper passed. Night fell and I was still out there, playing landscape chess with a semi-tamed, desperately unstable wild animal.

I urge you with all of my heart to rent a digger. And to spend a weekend picking up your entire garden and putting it back again.

Sadly, I'm unable to be quite so enthusiastic about the limited edition BMW Z4 M coupé – a hard-top, hardcore version of the Z4 M convertible. The idea's good enough. I reviewed the soft-top car a few weeks ago and thought it quite comfy, more a rival for the Jaguar XK than a Honda Fireblade. So the notion of beefing up the suspension and adding a roof to create a stiff road-going racer – yes, that sounds grand.

Hmmm. The first problem is that its back end appears to have been styled by someone who wasn't concentrating. The old Z3 M coupé was deliberately ugly, like the bastard son of Gérard Depardieu and a bread van, whereas this new one's just plain, like a supermarket checkout girl.

The second, bigger problem is one of expectation. It's a long-nosed, short-tailed, two seater in the mould of, say, the old Austin Healey. You know it's been stiffened up and you know it has the engine from an M3. You can see the fat tyres and the four exhaust pipes, and as you sit there gripping the almost absurdly thick rimmed steering wheel, you are expecting greatness.

And it doesn't come. Drive it normally, on reasonably smooth roads, and it feels like a normal Z4 M, only with a hard roof and an ugly backside. And you can't see why you might want to spend nearly £42,000 on such a thing.

Then you find the sort of twisting, bumpy back road that the Ramblers' Association would like to see governed with a 3 mph speed limit and you think: 'Yes. Here we go.'

But it won't. Oh sure, the engine's a masterpiece but the traction control light flickers constantly, suggesting that the suspension is so stiff the rear wheels are actually airborne half the time. So it lurches and pitches and is generally pretty horrid. Couple this to brakes that are too sharp, a clutch that requires practice and a steering system that's been toughened up – but not enough – and you're left with something rather underwhelming.

It's probably the first disappointing BMW M car I've ever driven.

If you want this sort of car, the Porsche Gayman is an obvious rival. It goes harder but is deeply embarrassing to be seen in. So what I'd do is buy the soft-top Z4 M instead. Or if you want something really fun for the weekend, buy a digger.

Sunday 3 September 2006

My favourite car?

That's a tricky one

He appeared to be completely normal, just an ordinary man with two eyes, a nose and a pair of trousers, tootling up the motorway at a reasonable 70 mph. And yet he obviously wasn't normal at all because he was driving a Lexus SC convertible.

This means that at some point in the recent past he'd spent a not inconsiderable £54,778 on a car which has the ride quality of wood, the style of a burns victim and all the excitement of being dead. Plainly, then, he was a mentalist.

Further down the road I saw a fat woman who also carried an air of human-ness about her. But she too was obviously a certified window licker because she was driving, in public, in a three-cylinder Hyundai Accent diesel. She would no doubt argue that it's cheap. Absolutely. But so is self-immolation.

The Accent diesel performs with the gusto of a light breeze and corners with the relish of an oil rig. It is, I think, one of the three worst cars money can buy. And remember, it's made by people who think *One Man and his Dog* is a cookery programme.

I wanted to bang on her window and explain the error of her ways. I wanted to point out that today, more than ever, there is simply no excuse for buying a rubbish car because the market-place is awash with stuff that's really good.

Normally, at any one time, there's only one car on sale that really gets its hook into the soft flesh of my brain's sillier bits. Sometimes there are none. I seem to recall that in the late Eighties things were so bad that I went for a couple of years without owning a car at all. And then along came the Escort Cosworth.

Now, however, there are probably twenty or thirty cars that I'd gladly buy, cars that I want to buy, cars that keep me awake at night as I toss and turn wondering which one would be best . . .

My current favourite is the Lamborghini Gallardo Spyder. Lamborghinis have always been 10 tons of style with no substance at all. But in recent years Audi has put a bit of Araldite in the mix and now you could nearly convince yourself that this noisy and shouty mid-engined drop top supercar with bright orange seats is a sensible exchange for 131,000 of your pounds. Plus another £600 if you want a cupholder.

It is expensive. Too expensive really for what you get in terms of technology, but when you first put your foot down, and those tail pipes start to trouble seismographs in faraway places, and the four-wheel-drive system starts to post power to whichever one of the fat tyres has the most grip and the whole thing starts to come alive, then all of a sudden £131,600 doesn't sound so bad any more.

Of course, each of us needs a slightly stupid excuse for buying a supercar that you can never use. Mine is: I keep banging on about what fun supercars are to own and drive. So it's only right and proper that I should put my money where my mouth is. My children agree with me on this.

But then the next night I come over all Maserati-ish. I loathe the flappy-paddle gearbox that comes as standard and ruins the Quattroporte, but I know a traditional automatic is in the pipeline and I'm sure that this will remove the bung that, to date, has stopped me buying one.

It may be a four-door saloon and it may have a few styling cues from the 1972 Vauxhall Cresta, but nevertheless I challenge you to park this outside your house and then walk to your front door without turning round for one last look before going inside. It has, what's the word . . . presence.

But then for a similar sort of outlay − £83,000 − you could have an Aston Martin V8 Vantage.

In fact the only reason I do not have this car is that my wife has one, and it would look greedy, having two.

The only reason you might shy away is because you prefer the looks of the DB9. Tricky one, that. But tricky in a delicious can't-choose-between-the-summer-pudding-and-the-crème-brûlée sort of way.

The DB9 is £25,000 more expensive and it's hard when you drive the two back to back to see why that might be so. The V12 is creamier than the savage V8 but in terms of performance there's little to choose between the two. Of course the DB9 has back seats, but unless your children are conjoined in some way, or they came out of your wife as torsos, then they won't fit anyway.

And then there's the bigger, prettier car's Achilles' heel. If you were to list the three top things you never hear people say, you'd have at number three 'I wish I had a smaller penis', at two 'On balance, Tony Blair's done a good job', and at number one 'I bought a DB9 and I've had no trouble with it at all'.

No, really. If you leave a DB9 alone while you pop into the shop for some biscuits, some electrical item on the car will burrow into the battery and eat all its amps. DB9s never start. Whereas my wife's V8 has been totally bulletproof.

So it's the Vantage, then, but hang on a minute, because what about the new Jaguar XKR. It's faster than the Aston, more powerful than the Aston, more practical than the Aston, considerably less expensive than the Aston, and while the Aston looks good and makes a tremendous noise, the Jag's not what you'd call a shy and retiring minger.

As I lie awake at night agonising over such things, I sometimes wonder if it isn't best to stick with the Mercedes SLK. Or what about the bigger, more practical SL, which is so perfect the only updates they've lavished on the 2007 model is a bit of chrome round the spot lamps and a bit more on the key ring.

Then there's the BMW M5. All that power, all that handling,

all that comfort, all those doors, and all for the surprisingly low price of £63,500.

See what I mean? I passionately want all of the cars we've looked at so far and the list goes on and on. I also want a Volkswagen Phaeton, a Rolls-Royce Phantom, a Corvette C6, a Vauxhall Monaro, a Porsche Carrera GT, a Zonda F, an Alfa Romeo Brera and an Audi RS4 convertible, or a hard top, or an estate. I'm not bothered, just so long as it has that astonishing 414 bhp V8 motor.

I'm also acutely aware that I have never owned a Range Rover and that now is the best time ever to take the plunge. Partly this is because the current model with the supercharged Jag engine is very good but mostly it's because in a Range Rover today, with all this eco-jingoism, you feel like a naughty schoolboy.

As I drive around in that lofty, leathery seat, I feel like I'm behind the bike sheds at school, having a fag, and then a cigarette.

You aren't actually hurting anyone or anything, except the fag a bit, but only at first, but you have that sense of swimming against the tide. It makes me feel all warm fuzzy.

It does not make me feel as warm fuzzy, however, as the king of the hill, the engineering summit, man's hobnail boot in the face of nature. The Bugatti Veyron. Like the Lamborghini it's little and feels well made but unlike the Lambo it does 252 mph. This makes it officially 'very fast'. Also it costs £830,000, which makes it officially 'very expensive'. That said it is also a bargain, since it costs VW £5 million to make each one.

Would I give up a kidney to have one? Yes. Without a doubt. And I'd throw in my left leg as well.

Which of course is all very well, but none of the cars mentioned here is of much help to the fat woman in the Hyundai Accent diesel. She only has a budget of, say, £9,000 and that's not a tenth of what's needed for, say, a Maserati Quattroporte. No worries. If she wants faster, more comfortable and more economical transport than her Accent, then she should try a pogo stick, or a space hopper or an Oyster card. Or she could buy a Fiat Panda. Better still, she could get out there and rob a bank.

Inside Jeremy's dream garage

Lamborghini Gallardo Spyder
Aston Martin V8 Vantage
BMW M5
VW Phaeton
Rolls-Royce Phantom
Corvette C6
Vauxhall Monaro
Porsche Carrera GT
Pagani Zonda F
Alfa Romeo Brera
Audi RS4
Bugatti Veyron

Sunday 10 September 2006

I'm sorry, this is absolutely gross

Overfinch Range Rover SuperSport

Please try not to be too alarmed and distressed by the extra-ordinarily vulgar exterior of this car. It is much, much better than it looks.

It is a Range Rover Sport which, in essence, is Benidorm with windscreen wipers. If you were to crash a Cheshire wife-swapping party into a DFS Boxing Day sale you'd come out on the other side with something like this. It is ghastly. Very possibly the least cool car that money can buy.

And unlike the proper Range Rover, its quiet and dignified big brother, it doesn't seem to have a point either. I mean, how can you have a Range Rover 'Sport'. That's like having a Tractor GTi. Or a Space Shuttle Diesel. And has anyone else noticed that from the back it's also rather ugly?

Anyway, to make it that little bit worse the Range Rover Sport has been painted in the sort of strident and vibrant shade of blue that simply doesn't exist in nature. And inside it has beige carbon-fibre trim nailed to just about every flat surface. To make it that little bit heavier, I presume.

I simply cannot remember driving any car that provoked so much mirth from other road users. All the way round the M25 people were slowing down for a better look and all gave the same verdict. A resounding, open-mouthed thumbs down.

Imagine how that would feel if it were your car. How would it feel to drive along leaving a trail of hysteria in your wake? Pretty bad I should think.

And I haven't got to the body kit yet. This was so monumentally awful that the car, ghastly and uncool as it was, did its level best to shake it all off. I'm not joking. As I drove along a whole chunk just fell away.

The boot lid broke, too. Of course you might think this would be no big deal, because the Range Rover Sport has two. But when one breaks the other won't open either. So that was that. I had to tape it down with gaffer tape and that made people laugh even more. Driving along in a stupidly blue nasty car with the boot taped down and bits of the body kit missing? Jogging naked through a church service would be less humiliating.

The thing is, though, that because the boot lid wouldn't shut properly I could hear clearly the noise coming from the four exhaust tailpipes.

And it was extraordinary. Under hard acceleration it sounded like a lollipop stick rattling in the spokes of a bicycle, and then on the overrun it popped and banged like the big V8 was being spoon-fed with caviar through golden carburettors.

It was a beautiful sound, a wonderful sound. A sound to warm the cockle of your follicles. So what, you might be wondering, was it doing coming from the back of a Range Rover?

Well, this is no ordinary Range Rover. (You can say that again.) It is in fact an Overfinch Range Rover and that, for those who know their off-roaders from their onions, will elicit a quiet nod of approval.

Overfinch is a little-known company that, for the past thirty-one years, has been taking out the Range Rover's V8 and replacing it with a Corvette's 5.7. That's like replacing a lamb chop with a big old rump steak.

The result is dramatic. I once staged a drag race between an Overfinch Range Rover and a 2 litre Ford Focus. And even though the Overfinch was towing a Ford Focus on a trailer, it still managed to win. If I'd ever owned an old Range Rover I'd have had it discreetly Overfinched; no question about it.

But then one day BMW bought Land Rover and replaced the old British Leyland V8 with a smooth, modern, clean 4.4 from its own parts bin. And that rather knackered the Overfinch boys. Because replacing that with a big American lump of pig iron would have been like replacing a Gordon Ramsay oyster risotto with a Big Mac.

Then it got worse, because Land Rover was bought by Ford, who now fit the Range Rover with a supercharged 4.2 litre V8 from Jaguar. And again we find ourselves asking the question. Why replace this with a Corvette's wood-burning stove?

Why indeed? So what Overfinch does is keep the engine but fiddle about with the peripheries. It increases the boost pressure of the supercharger, changes the air filter so that the engine can breathe in more easily, and fits a better exhaust system to aid breathing out. And then, inevitably, its computer nerds set about the on-board ECU, remapping it completely.

The result is an extra 52 bhp, bringing it up to 447 bhp, and an extra 80 lb ft of torque, bringing that up to 485 lb ft. It's fast. Easily fast enough to get away from the wave of hysteria that its body kit and paintwork have provoked.

And it stops, too, because it's fitted with six-piston cross-drilled discs at the front and four-piston cross-drilled discs at the back.

For me, though, the biggest, and nicest surprise was the result of fitting those gigantic 22 in wheels and painted-on low-profile tyres. I saw them and thought yes, very nice, but they are going to totally destroy every single bone in my body. They don't. The grip is improved, the steering feel is improved but the ride comfort seems to be totally unaffected.

And now we get to the really good bit. You don't have to have the paintwork – which costs a whopping £6,995 – or the body kit. In fact the only reason they were fitted to my test car is because Overfinch thought they might stand out on television. Sorry, guys. There's no way I'd film it. Partly because no one's TV could cope with the vividness, and partly because *Top Gear* goes out before the watershed and that body kit would make children cry.

Here's the deal, then. If the man from Overfinch tries to sell you any form of cosmetic alterations, just say no. The proper Range Rover cannot be improved and the Sport is beyond redemption. Tell him that you only want him to work on the engine, exhaust and brakes. To get what I had will cost £11,280 and is worth every penny.

More than this, I kept thinking 'hang on a minute'. The Range Rover has the same basic engine as the new Jaguar XKR so presumably these modifications will work on that too. They'd transform it.

Britain lacks really good tuning companies. Germany, Japan and especially America are awash with people who'll take your off-the-shelf car and convert it into something really very much better. See the Roush Mustang for details. Or the Brabus Mercedes SL.

In Britain, however, the art doesn't really seem to have caught on. There are boys with their hats on back to front painting their Citroëns turquoise and that's about it. Why? It is in our blood to tinker. We are a nation of men in sheds.

We are not, however, as Overfinch has proved with its work on the Sport, a nation of artists. Style should be left to the Italians.

Sunday 17 September 2006

My mission: to prove this car is not perfect

Audi RS4

Show me someone who's utterly contented with their children's school work, their houses, their cars and the places they choose to go on holiday. And I'll show you someone who's a damn sight happier than me.

Once, I thought I'd found the 'perfect car'. I was driving through an agonisingly pretty bit of Italy, on the most glorious summer evening, in a Ferrari 355 and I remember turning to the camera and saying: 'I think I'm experiencing motoring perfection here.'

So I came home, bought one and quickly found that actually it had the driving position of a Seddon Atkinson dustbin lorry, a sticky throttle linkage, and that if you wanted to service the engine it had to be taken out of the car. This cost eleven billion pounds.

Perfect? It was nothing more than a rung in the ladder of constant improvement that has brought us today to the Ferrari 430. And that isn't perfect either. It looks like a trout that's just won a cider drinking contest.

I'm never quite content with anything. I went on holiday earlier this year to a smashing hotel in the Caribbean that had just about all the bases covered. Except it was full of rather too many people who spend rather too much time donating to the Labour party.

Then there's the view from the back of my house. It's wonderful. Faultless in every way except that away off on the far distant horizon there's a telegraph pole. And that's all I see when I look out of the window. Everyone else sees the glorious Cotswold countryside. I see the pole.

My eye seeks out the imperfections in life and glosses over the good. The first time I walked down New York's Fifth Avenue I was disappointed that the buildings weren't taller. When I first met my wife I thought her lipstick was a bit too red. Nothing in my life is ever quite right.

I'm currently reading a book called *The Power of the Dog* for the second time in a week. Why? Because on the first pass it appeared to be utterly blemish free, faultless. And to my mind that can't be. So I'm reading it again to find the little mistakes, the passage that's a bit too long. The squeak of dialogue that doesn't ring true.

I did that when I went to see what is still my favourite film: *Local Hero*. First time round, I thought it was wonderful. Second time I thought Jenny Seagrove's webbed toes were a bit silly.

Then you have the greatest quotation in human history, uttered when Neil Armstrong stepped onto the moon. But it's not quite right, is it? Because if it was one small step for man, then it must have been one small step for a mankind. And that doesn't make sense.

All of this, as I'm sure you've guessed, is leading me to the Audi A4, a perfectly reasonable saloon car, spoilt for me – naturally – by a styling crease that runs down the flanks. You don't notice this, however, on the RS4 because it has massively flared wheelarches shrouding huge low-profile tyres. You know, just from looking at it, that it's going to be very, very fast. And it is.

It was designed to be a rival for the old BMW M3, but if anything they overshot. The BMW had a 3.2 litre six-cylinder engine. The Audi was given a 4.2 litre V8. The BMW came at you with 343 bhp. The Audi churns out a remarkable 420.

Of course a new BMW M3 is waiting in the wings and that will have a V8 too, but for now Audi's running the only game in town and it's a game, I guarantee, you'll want to play. I drove an

RS4 last year in the south of France – which is a stunning part of the world spoilt by too many Russians – and I loved it.

It was the first Audi for fifteen years with steering that feels connected and suspension that doesn't shake your hair out. And then there's the engine. Oh God, the engine. It's a masterpiece, as peerless as the Koh-i-Noor.

I hurled that car up mountain passes at speeds that boggled the mind and I enjoyed every minute. Except for the minutes when I was stuck behind Dutchmen in caravans. But there weren't too many of those because with 414 bhp on tap, and four-wheel drive to put it on the road, you can overtake in gaps smaller than a stripper's knickers.

That said, it wasn't perfect. The optional bucket seats were so massive that there was no legroom in the back at all. None. So you were being asked to spend £50,000 on a four-door four-seater sports saloon that couldn't take four people.

You have the same problem in the even more expensive RS4 convertible I was using last week. Even though it had normal front seats the space in the back was so pitiful there wasn't even room for my children, and the boot's pathetic too.

However, while this may be an issue in the saloon, where practicality is the raison d'être, it doesn't matter at all in the soft top because, as I've said many times, the only person who ever looked good in the back of a convertible was Hitler. Everyone else just looks embarrassed. Or, in the RS4, squashed. And a bit frightened.

As with the saloon, the whole experience is dominated by the engine. It sits in the mix like Nelson Mandela would sit in a room full of accountants. And I love it. I love the noises it makes – you want to have the roof down just to hear it more clearly – I love the even spread of torque, but most of all I love the power.

Jaguar uses a supercharger to eke 400 bhp from its 4.2 litre V8. But with no extra assistance at all Audi gets 414 bhp. And it's delivered through all four wheels so there's no unpleasantness;

you push the throttle and you go past 60 mph in 4.9 seconds and on to a limited top speed of 155.

And that's just the start, because on the steering wheel there's a little button marked S for sport. A lot of car makers fit various models with sport buttons these days, and all claim they sharpen up the suspension and change the steering. Really? Most of the time they seem to do nothing more than ignite a 'sport' warning light on the dash.

Not in the RS4, though. Its S button changes the throttle control mapping and renders the car almost completely undrive-able on the road. It's a button you should only press when you're on the track or when no one is looking. Pushing it is like the moment when Kevin Bacon pushed that button to stir the oxygen tanks on Apollo 13. Suddenly you're flirting with gimbal lock . . . whatever that is.

I left it well alone and sat back to revel in a car that goes like double cream, sounds like God snoring, and is every bit as poised and controllable as the old BMW M3. That is extremely high praise.

The nose heaviness of previous fast quattro cars has been eradicated by fitting aluminium front wings and mounting what's already a small engine backwards. Oh, and the four-wheel-drive system sends 60 per cent of the power to the rear wheels, which is really where you want it. I liked the way this car looks, I liked its quality, I liked the way it was civilised, roof up or down, and I liked the intuitive way all the controls work. Even the sat nav.

Of course, it isn't perfect. It can't be. Nothing in my world is. But I'm genuinely struggling to think what might be wrong with it. I'm therefore going to do what I did with *Local Hero* and *The Power of the Dog*. I'm going to keep on testing it until something crops up.

So, I'm going outside now. I may be some time.

Sunday 24 September 2006

Looks like a Bentley, drives like a duvet

Chrysler 300C CRD Touring

Ever since man discovered he had a penchant for war, there has been rivalry between the services. This is all to do with pride and tribalism and, generally speaking, it's a good thing.

However, when a leaked e-mail from an army officer describes the RAF as 'utterly, utterly useless', you get the distinct impression that this is far beyond good-natured teasing. You have visions of him lying in a ditch desperately calling for air support and hearing nothing over the radio but the sound of a Harrier's starter motor whirring uselessly.

The problem, of course, has nothing to do with the people who fly or service the planes. And everything to do with those grinning buffoons in Westminster who've spent the past five years unable to see what's going on due to the fact they're all deep inside George Bush's bottom.

You read about billions being shaved from the budget and squadrons being merged to cut costs and, frankly, it doesn't mean anything at all. Not when you've just been startled out of your skin by a Tornado that has flown between your chimney pots at 4 million knots.

However, I've done a bit of checking and it seems the RAF can field five strike attack squadrons that must share sixty Tornados. Then there are the offensive squadrons, which have twenty-six Harriers and some Jaguars, which may as well be Sopwith Camels. And that's it.

In total, with the air defence Tornados, they have just 150 aeroplanes that can actually do fighting. The Luftwaffe has more than twice that. So do the cheese-eating surrender monkeys. In an air war we'd struggle to beat the Bubbles. Of course 150 fighting planes is fine when all we have to worry about are a handful of mad Irishmen, but since Mr Blair realised that his retirement fund relied on being popular in the land of the brave, we're now fighting what seems like half the world.

It is an extraordinary scandal and what makes it just so shiversomely hideous is that Blair and Brown and all the other useless fools who preside over our wellbeing know full well they can get away with it.

Strip the NHS of funds and pretty soon you'll have a bunch of nurses on television sobbing. Decimate the fire brigade and immediately the streets will be full of men in donkey jackets, standing round braziers. But the forces? You can squeeze their gonads until their eyes pop out and still they won't moan.

When asked recently if the British Army could cope, its new top man General Sir Richard Dannatt replied: 'Just'. He can't come out and say: 'Are you joking?' Because this is not the army way. Even though he's waging war on two fronts using US helicopters that shoot themselves down and Sea Kings that have a top speed of four if it gets hotter than 57C – which it does in Iraq, a lot – he still has to stiffen his upper lip and tell the world that everything is tickety boo.

It's not just the top brass, either. Back at home, quietly, soldiers may tell their loved ones that things are pretty bleak. But have you ever heard one say so publicly? Were they at the Trades Union Congress in their apple-green short-sleeved nylon shirts banging on the tables demanding more money and better equipment? No they weren't. They were out there, far from the television cameras, in a shit-awful part of Afghanistan fighting with pointed sticks.

I do hope Blair can sleep easily at night knowing that his lecture tour pension fund is being paid for by the blood of a thousand British soldiers and airmen. And I hope, too, he realises that if the RAF really is 'utterly, utterly useless', it's all his fault.

It makes you wonder how on earth a bona fide lunatic managed to achieve such a position of power and influence but, actually, lunacy these days is all around us. It sits in the editor's chair at the *Daily Mail*. It runs the United States. And I found a shining example of it only the other day as I stopped in a petrol station to fuel an Audi Q7.

'Ooh,' said the man at the next pump, 'I've just ordered one of those. It comes next week. What do you think?' I could have been kind. I could have made his day. But I wasn't in the mood, so I told him straight: 'It's one of the three worst cars I've ever driven.'

Well, he was flabbergasted. But not as flabbergasted as me when he went on to say that he was buying the Audi as a replacement for his Aston Martin V8 Vantage, which had broken down.

I see. So you bought an Aston and you were 'surprised' when it wasn't quite as reliable as granite. That makes you mad. And now you've replaced it with something that could be nailed to the side of a cathedral to ward off evil spirits. That makes you a swivel-eyed loony.

I first encountered this gargoyle of a car earlier in the year as we were filming the *Top Gear* winter olympics, and though it felt pretty nasty I decided to withhold judgment, since doing a biathlon in a car isn't terribly representative of how it might be used in, say, Driffield.

Well, I've now used it in London, Bedfordshire, Northamptonshire, Oxfordshire, Surrey and Hampshire and can reveal it's no better in any of these places either. It's far too big to fit comfortably on any road other than an American interstate, but inside it's surprisingly cramped. Think of it as an Aga. As big as a post office van but stumped when presented with a Christmas turkey.

Certainly you get a lot more room in a cheaper and much better looking Volvo XC90. You get more of everything even in the new Ford S-Max.

And then there's the question of 'feel'. The Q7 feels just like a normal Audi. And that's fine in a normal Audi. But it's a big SUV and it should give off a sense that the Tonka toy exterior styling is in some way replicated on the inside, so that when your children fight and bite and kick, none of the fixtures and fittings will be damaged.

The Q7 really is 'utterly, utterly useless' and I was all set to keep on kicking it until all the available space on these pages was used up. But then, lo and behold, I was presented with a car that is even worse. The Chrysler 300C diesel estate.

Worryingly, it looks rather good. There's a huge radiator grille that puts you in mind of a Bentley Arnage, and the squared-off muscly body sits on tall tyres that hint at not only a great deal of power but a comfy, cosseting ride. A decent salesman could make a fairly good fist of whipping up your enthusiasm on the inside as well. The back seats fold down easily, the load opening at the back is cavernous, there's a separate storage area under the boot floor away from muddy paws, and there's lots of standard equipment.

For £27,275 this looks like the bargain of the century and a brief test drive will do little to dispel that notion. The diesel engine is so unclattery that I had to get out to check the badge. And despite the size it's terribly easy to drive. The only thing that might put you off is the limited rear visibility, but apart from this you'd be hard pressed to find anything wrong. Don't worry, though. I have. Lots.

You need to think of this car as one of those home-brand council house stereos that you find in department stores. It's cheap, but it's cheap for a reason, which becomes abundantly clear when you turn it on. It's rubbish. So it goes with the 300C. Chrysler, which is owned by Mercedes these days, is at pains to point out that this car is not – as I've previously claimed – based on the old Mercedes E-class. They say they considered this idea but dismissed it.

Pity. Basing it on a well-proven car would have been a better idea than basing it on a crème brûlée. God, it's a wallowy old hector. You have absolutely no sense that you're connected to the road in any way. Imagine, somehow, fitting an engine to your duvet and you start to get the picture. Of course this might not bother you but the ride comfort will. Despite the wallow-matic suspension and the tall tyres, it crashes and jolts where a normal, proper European car glides and hangs on.

Then there's the sat nav screen, which is so bright it's like driving into a second world war searchlight, and the difficulty you'll have while parking and the sheer ghastliness of the half-timbered steering wheel.

Yes, it's cheap, but so's the RAF these days. And that doesn't work either.

Sunday 1 October 2006

Something nasty under the bonnet

Volkswagen Phaeton

If you believe the anti-speed campaigners, Britain is full of young tearaways in souped-up Citroën Saxos driving down the pavement at 150 mph killing millions of babies. And then being sentenced to three minutes' community service.

This argument seems to be winning support. There's a mood abroad in the land that speeding drivers who maim and kill other road users should be sent to prison for 2,000 years. And if the prisons are full they should have huge 6 in nails hammered into their heads.

Yes, we're told, we should treat speeding in the same way that we treat drinking and driving. And doubtless you're nodding in agreement.

Right. So how come you parked in your flowerbed last night? Because while it's very easy to say you disapprove of drinking and driving, it's even harder to get home from a dinner party in the sticks. So like millions of other middle-aged, middle-class motorists you cross your fingers, stick to the back roads and hope for the best.

I'm afraid it's the same story with speeding. Because while the image of a speeder is a nineteen-year-old in a turquoise Saxo, we all drive too quickly. Pretty well every single one of us, pretty well every single day.

And how would you like it if you were coming back from a hard day at the office, perhaps not really concentrating, to find that a child has run into the road? You do your best to stop but you were doing 40 mph and there's no chance. So the child dies.

Imagine how that might feel, to know that you have killed a child and that you have utterly destroyed the lives of its family. And then along come the police, who announce that you were driving without due care and attention and that as a result you will go to court.

Will a long prison sentence cause you to drive more slowly in future? What? More than the fact you've killed a child? I doubt it. All it will do is quench the natural and understandable parental thirst for revenge. And rob your children for many years of a father.

Anti-speed campaigners argue that a car is every bit as much a lethal weapon as a gun, and that's probably true. However, while a gun is designed specifically to kill, a car is designed specifically to take your rubbish to the tip and your children to school, If you kill someone with a gun, the chances are you meant to. If you kill someone with a car, the chances are it was an accident. And accidents can only be prevented by something we don't have at the time. Hindsight.

So what's to be done? Well instead of campaigning to outlaw excess speed in all its forms, which means campaigning against all of us, we need to target the offensive against those who drive stupidly.

But even this isn't quite as easy as it sounds. Last week I was following a Renault up the M40 during a streaming wet rush hour. Through the blur of the wipers I could see the tail-lights dissolving into impenetrable spray for mile after interminable mile. Trying to overtake the car in front, then, was completely pointless.

But that didn't stop our friend in the Renault from trying. He was glued to the van in front of him, veering from side to side and braking every few seconds as the gap narrowed from a foot to three or four inches. Then he'd go by on the inside and begin his assault on the next car in line.

I began to believe he might be a psychopath, or that he had

discovered some pressing need to kill himself, so I actually took a note of his registration plate. It began FG55. He knows the rest.

And at this point those of an anti-speed persuasion would urge me to report him to the police. But hang on a minute. He wasn't speeding. At no point, in traffic like that, did he ever exceed sixty. Yes, he was driving like a lunatic, but even here there's a problem. What if he's just had a call from his wife to say she was in labour? What if his child had been taken ill? You may say that's no excuse but I remember well the night my mum phoned to say my dad was very ill. Had I driven up the M1 at the speed limit I would not have seen him before he died. Because I went somewhat faster than seventy I made it in time to give him a hug and say goodbye. Would you have denied me that? We know from official Department for Transport figures that breaking the speed limit is responsible for only 5 per cent of road accidents. It's rare that I call for balance, but that's what we need in the debate on road safety.

It's one big grey area, and that brings me, after a long and rather humourless time – sorry about that – to another grey area where all is not necessarily as it seems. The Volkswagen Phaeton. The dullest way on earth of doing 155 mph.

Recently, India Knight tried to argue that men drive fast to impress women. The Phaeton is proof that she's talking nonsense.

From the outside it appears to be the sort of car your old geography teacher might drive: bland almost to the point of invisibility. You can't impress anyone with it because it's nigh on invisible.

But underneath this extraordinarily ordinary body it's a Bentley Continental GT. Same four-wheel-drive system, same architecture, same incredible attention to detail and, if you go for the electronically limited 155 mph 6 litre W12 engine, the same sort of power plant as well. But I didn't go for the W12, which is one of my ten favourite cars. I tried the diesel.

So you climb into this exquisitely finished car, adjust the supremely comfortable seat, set the air-conditioning just so, and sit back to admire the eye-scorching simplicity of the controls. And then you turn the key.

You expect the softest of purrs. But what you get is the sound of a Third World building site. What's more, to make this jolly big car move, you have to give the accelerator pedal a fairly hefty shove. The result is a car that feels as lively as a fire station. This engine is fine in the off-road Toe Rag. But is emphatically not fine in the Phaeton.

Of course at this point dieselheads – who are like petrolheads only with dirty fingernails and nothing interesting to say – will claim that a little extra noise and a slight unwillingness to set off is a reasonable price to pay for all the benefits. To which I say, okay then, what benefits? Please don't come at me with fuel consumption because this is a 5 litre V10 diesel. Parsimonious it is not, and what's more it produces more carbon dioxide than a whole flock of cows. And nor is it anything like as fast as you'd hope.

Diesels normally deliver large amounts of mid-range torque and the VW V10 is no different. There's a whopping 309 bhp as well. But somehow this brutality doesn't make itself felt on the speedo, so you bury your foot in the carpet even more and now the fuel consumption is even worse and there's a roundabout coming and whoa, heavens above. The brakes are only just up to the job of stopping you.

And there we are, straight into another grey area. Those who buy the big petrol engine will be accused of antisocial speed-driven lunacy whereas those who buy the diesel will be applauded for their environmentalism and their slowness. But which is easier to stop, a rabbit or a brontosaurus? If you are a child, thinking of running into the road, make sure you do so in front of the petrol version, not the diesel.

Almost all cars are ruined by the fitment of a diesel engine. In the same way that all wines, no matter how fine, would be ruined if they were served with a splash of crude oil. But the Phaeton is ruined more comprehensively than any other.

This is a car built to be the last word in discretion. It is a car designed to be as silent and as efficient and as focused as a contract killer. So putting a diesel under the bonnet is like putting James Bond in a pair of wellingtons. The whole point is lost.

Sunday 15 October 2006

Oh baby, you're just a rotten tease

Audi S6 Avant

When I was eighteen years old, my bank manager wrote to say he was disappointed that I had a £3,000 overdraft. This made him look like an idiot, because opening an account for an eighteen-year-old boy and then being 'disappointed' when he runs around town vomiting cash into various pubs and clubs is like going to see a film starring Steven Seagal and being 'disappointed' that it's terrible.

If an octogenarian billionaire comes home from work to find his pneumatic twenty-two-year-old bride playing hide-the-sausage with the handyman, he cannot claim to be 'disappointed', because surely, if he had any brains at all, he'd have seen it coming. If you employ a man who knocks on your door asking if you'd like a new tarmac drive, you cannot be disappointed when he sets your precious roses in 3 ft of solid concrete and then sends a nightclub bouncer round with a bill for £400 million.

I once went on a holiday to Tuscany and was annoyed to find when I got there that the villa I'd booked had an American family living in it, and that I'd have to spend two weeks in the spare room of a house two miles away. And then I was very annoyed that the owner turned out to be the head of the local Communist party and that he'd decided I needed to be lectured from dawn till dusk on the failings of capitalism. In Italian.

'*Voglio uccidere i cestini di Thatcher di Signor e la marca fuori dei suoi capelli pubici*,' he would rage endlessly, as I trudged up the road to the house where I should have been staying to ask the Americans if I could make use of the pool I'd paid to use.

But was I disappointed? No I was not. Because thanks to my bank manager's disappointment, I'd booked the holiday on the cheap through an east London PO box that I'd seen in a small ad. I therefore knew before I set off that it couldn't possibly end well.

Disappointment is a word for people who don't think ahead; people who get themselves into fool's mate when playing chess, people who buy a Hyundai Accent. It's why I'm loath to use it.

And yet, in the motoring arena, I have to use it all the time because there's no industry in the world capable of building up so much hope and then failing to deliver. You look at a company's background, its expertise, its finances and the ingredients that are available to it, and you assume it cannot possibly produce a bad car. And then it comes up with the BMW Z8.

How did that happen? It had the underpinnings of an M5 and a body so beautiful I had an ache in the pit of my stomach when I first saw it. But it drove like everything had been attached to everything else with spit and two crossed fingers. It was awful.

Then there was the Ferrari 360. This came after the glorious 355 so we were all expecting more of the same, only better. But what we got was a twitchy little bastard with the face of a gormless frog.

And now we have the new Audi S6 Avant, which is fitted with the V10 engine from a Lamborghini Gallardo. When I first heard that this was being planned, I was – I'm ashamed to admit – priapic with anticipation. Audi had recently demonstrated with the RS4 that after years in the suspension wilderness, it had finally got to grips with the twin peaks of ride and handling.

Ally this to the traditional Audi qualities of good, understated style, exemplary quality, tons of estate-car practicality and that Italian supercar engine and you can see why I'd become a human tripod.

The only thing I didn't know is what sort of car the S6 would be. Would it be a hunkered-down, super-sharp road rocket with exhausts like oil pipelines, five-point harnesses and tyres that had a lower profile than paint? Or would it be a true Q-car, a real wolf in sheep's clothing? Smooth, quiet and dignified on the outside but with tons of quiet power in reserve. I began to slobber like a dog as I toyed with what path I would have taken if I'd been in charge.

What we've been given, however, is neither of these things. What we've been given is an ocean-going turkey, a lemon the size of Steven Seagal's ponytail, and possibly the biggest disappointment in all of automotive history.

First of all, there's the engine. Yes it's lovely – no question about that. You've got a high compression ratio of 12.5:1 for glorious reserves of torque, you've got direct fuel injection, continuously adjustable camshafts, and the ten pistons have 5.2 litres of space to move around in. Yum yum.

It's a peach on the road too, always subdued, although under hard acceleration as you near the 7000 rpm redline there's a whisper of bass. It's so faint it could be drowned out by Bob Harris but it's there all right, reminding you that beneath the body of this station wagon there beats a thoroughbred horse.

Fine. But it produces only 429 bhp. That's just a gnat's more than you get from the V8 in an RS4, and it's nearly a hundred less than you get in a Lamborghini Gallardo. Why? Audi owns Lamborghini so it's not as if the Italians have 'lost' a hundred horses as some kind of latter-day payback for losing the war. And it's not like the Audi boffins were wary of what happened the last time a mass-production car was given a monster engine . . .

The Lancia Thema 8:32 was a four-door saloon fitted with the 3.2 litre engine of a Ferrari 328. That didn't work because you can't expect a front-wheel-drive car like the Thema to be able to handle the power of a Ferrari V8. And so it turned out to be. But the S6 has four-wheel drive and could easily handle the full force of the Lamborghini V10.

So what's gone wrong? Well, the Audi engine factory is

designed to produce engines with a 90-degree Vee, but the Lambo's engine has an 88-degree Vee. Ergo, if they were going to make the engine in an Audi factory, it had to be changed. That means the S6 has only 429 bhp and that, in turn, means that every time you put your foot down, you feel a) cheated and b) like the car you've bought was designed by accountants.

You also feel like you're not really in control because it has quite the sharpest throttle response of any car I know. It will only set off at full pelt, which is a nuisance when you're having to contend with a gearbox that works like it's on cannabis, and steering which – I feel sure – is made from old driftwood.

And then we get to by far and away the worst thing: the ride. They call it 'S line', and it doesn't take too long to work out what the S might stand for. Clue: four letters, begins with S, ends in hit. Which is odd because it really isn't one.

It's not firm in a controlled way. It's firm like the matron in a Carry On film. It's firm to the point where you start to laugh at its complete inability to ride with grace or panache over absolutely anything.

I would love to meet the team who designed it, because I do not believe that anyone who has ever driven 'a car' before could possibly have fitted this and thought it might do. Their bosses should certainly dig out their CVs and do some deep background investigation, because they're either imposters or they're secretly working for BMW.

I can't be bothered to go on, frankly, because it doesn't matter how much I like the styling or the quality, or wonder why you might want to spend £400 on an electric boot lid that closes at the speed of glacial drift; everything is overshadowed and ruined by the suspension, and to a lesser extent by the steering and the throttle linkage – which is as fast as the boot lid is slow.

Perhaps they wired them up the wrong way round?

With a tiny, tiny set of tweaks and a lot of mass sackings in the suspension design department, the S6 could be turned into something quite breathtaking. The ingredients are all there. But what you are being offered for £56,600 is actually well beyond a 'disappointment': it is actually utterly, utterly useless.

Sunday 22 October 2006

Okay gorgeous, let's pretend that little bit didn't fall off

Jaguar XKR coupé

Did you see that television series about the Galapagos Islands? God, I want to go. It looked like the most perfect place on Earth. Iceland with the thermostat turned up, and lots of animals to laugh at.

But of course there's a problem. If you want to see a flock of those blue-footed boobies, or a seal playing a hearty game of bug-the-sea-lizard, you have to spend four years in various different airports, followed by a dose of jet lag so horrid that each eyelash will weigh more than a caber.

I'm afraid this is always the way. Every dream has a drawback. You may fancy the idea of owning a Ferrari Enzo, but after three fast starts it will need a new clutch and at every roundabout you'll have the problem that you won't be able to see what's coming. So you'll have to use the Force, which is fine if you are a Jedi Knight, which of course you aren't.

So okay then. You while away the hours dreaming of owning a small cottage by the sea. Great. But the reality of a second home is that you're always 75 miles away from a clean pair of under-pants.

Then you have those people who turn up on *X Factor* every week saying that what they most want, what they really want more than anything else, is to be famous.

Now of course fame does have certain advantages . . . but there are obvious disadvantages too, such as for instance the fact that every time you go to a public convenience people will whip out their camera-phones and try to take photographs of your gentlemen's area. This becomes wearisome.

And consider this: if you are even mildly famous, people will feel they have the right to come up to you in the street and tell you you're fat or ugly, or that you're no good at your job.

Try to imagine what that feels like.

Now hold that thought and imagine how it feels if you spend the rest of your time surrounded by agents and managers who do nothing but shower you with the rose petals of flattery. This sends you bonkers.

In extreme cases, fame can even mean you end up with a small African baby called Dave.

It also means you can't lie when you're in a taxi. One of the great gifts of anonymity is being able to tell the driver that you're the world's first homosexual astronaut, or that you're employed by Stevie Nicks to adjust her gusset when she's on stage. But when you're Nicholas Parsons you just can't do this.

What's more, you can't ever shake off fame – it's not like dandruff. So if you decide one day that you've had enough, that you don't want people to take pictures of your privates any more and that you don't want an African baby called Dave, well that's tough. You will always be 'the bloke who used to be Peter Purves'.

And that gets me back onto the scent of this morning's theory: the sure-fire certainty that all of life's pleasures are tainted with a dollop of unpleasantness. Chocolate tastes delicious but it makes you fat. A moustache masks your inadequacies as a man, but it makes you look like a nitwit. And a powerful car will be fun to drive, but it will smash up your skeleton every time you drive over a bump.

I mean it. Someone, somewhere, has decided that any low-slung, sleek looking car with a big, thrusting engine must be 'sporty', so it has to have suspension that's made from pig iron and rocks.

This is idiotic. If you take a careful look at the sort of people who buy low-slung, sleek looking cars with big thrusting engines, some – for sure – are footballists who won't mind the discomfort of a rock-hard ride. But most, I reckon, are slightly paunchy middle-aged men and women who are way past the days when it was either acceptable, or indeed possible, to sleep on the floor after a party.

People with enough money to buy and insure fast cars are usually of an age when their own chassis are starting to fall prey to osteoarthritis, or even osteoporosis. Which means that if they run over a pothole they need to be isolated from the bump or their hips will come apart and their ribcage will turn to dust; you cannot bring a car safely to a halt if this sort of thing happens.

It's one of the reasons I'm so intrigued by the Lamborghini Gallardo Spyder, because here is a car with a shouty V10 engine and bright orange seats, which you can buy equipped with what's called a 'comfort pack'.

In other words, you can have the speed and the looks and the noise, but you don't have to come home every night with your legs held onto what's left of your torso by nothing more than skin.

It's also why I have fallen so very badly in love with the new Jaguar XKR. It sits on fat, low-profile tyres and has aluminium gills so you expect it to be as hard as a sideboard and as unforgiving as an enraged barbary ape.

But you'd be wrong, because it is wonderfully soft and compliant. Getting out of, say, an Aston Martin V8 Vantage and into an XKR is like climbing off a kitchen chair and getting into bed.

Yes of course the Aston is a sharper drive; it turns into corners more aggressively and hangs on more tenaciously, but when do you ever drive on the limit anyway? And even if the answer is 'sometimes', the Jaguar is still remarkably good. Despite the softness, it is very, very competent in the bends.

After a few laps of the *Top Gear* test track I actually felt that it had been deliberately set up to look good in our power-sliding shots. I know of no other car that's so easy to kick out of shape and hold there until the tyres burst. I absolutely loved it.

I also loved the creamy-smooth automatic transmission, the remarkably spacious boot and the fact that I really could get two of my children into what look like ridiculously small back seats.

The new XKR then, is a car you can dream about that doesn't really have a spike in the middle. It won't make you fat. It doesn't make you go blind. And you don't have to have an African baby called Dave.

Sure, the supercharged engine doesn't provide as much power as you'll get from a Mercedes or a BMW. And yes, the interior does look a bit weedy for what is actually a £70,000 package. So yes, you might be tempted to buy German instead, and that's just fine. But don't come crying to me when you run over a catseye and find that your left leg falls off.

And oh how I'd love to end it there, on a note of jingoistic pride. But sadly I cannot.

Because the first car I tested suffered from a flat battery. No big deal, you might think, except that with its keyless entry system, there was no way of opening the door to get in, and with an electric handbrake no way of moving the car either. And then the rear parcel shelf fell off . . . and the Bluetooth wouldn't work.

Fortunately the second car I tested was much better – to begin with. But then its sat nav went on the blink, and the passenger airbag warning light came on. And then the rear parcel shelf disintegrated in that one, too.

A spokesman for Jaguar insisted that both cars were pre-production models and that all the faults will be fixed before the cars go on sale.

The parcel shelf, apparently, was a last-minute addition after it was found that if you drove over a sharp bump with luggage in the boot it could bounce straight through the rear window. I'm assured that tougher clips have been specified.

And the sat nav? It overheats, and so it's been decided that the system used on cars specified for Middle Eastern countries will be fitted here in the UK too. 'Don't worry,' he said. 'We're on top of things!' Of course he's bound to say that, but I hope he's right. It would be a shame to think I had found a dream with no dark centre, only to discover that it's actually as volcanic and as unpredictable as the very thing that kicked us off this morning – the Galapagos Islands.

Sunday 29 October 2006

It's the new champion of Formula Plonker

Renault Clio Sport 197

Even though Fernando Alonso, the mono-browed young fish-nicker, did not acquit himself well this year, endlessly complaining about how the team wasn't treating him properly and how the stewards were fixing races in Michael Schumacher's favour, I did feel rather sorry for him as the grand prix circus reached its ear-splitting climax in Brazil.

First of all, he was beaten in the race by Felipe Massa, who behaved as though he'd been wired up to the national grid. And because he was a Brazilian, in Brazil, the Brazilian television director decided that the fish-nicker should be largely ignored.

To make matters worse, this had been Michael Schumacher's final race before he headed off to Switzerland with nothing but his dogs and his chin for company. And that's all anyone was talking about. Not Fernando's second world championship, but what life might be like in F1 without the Hun.

Boring, I reckon, though not everyone agrees.

Martin Brundle, the F1 commentator, said recently that he struggles to think of any great Schumacher overtaking moves. Really? Well what about that last race, when he went from last place to fourth? What about the way he drove so aggressively he frightened Giancarlo Fisichella not just out of his way but clean off the track?

And what about the time at Silverstone when he was stuck behind Damon Hill? For lap after lap, on the approach to one particular corner he drove on the wrong side of the track, cleaning away all the dust and the marbles, so that when he finally made his move he had all the grip in the world.

That was the great thing about Schumacher's racing – he used intelligence. Ross Brawn, his technical director at Ferrari, said that even when he was on a hot lap, he could converse about clouds on the back side of the circuit and whether they might bring rain, whereas other drivers could only ever grunt.

Then you had the time when he finished second despite being stuck for half the race in fifth gear, and the Spanish Grand Prix in 1996 when, in torrential rain, he lapped almost the entire field. Sometimes he must have thought that he was the only human in a field made up entirely of incompetent playboy blind people.

Ah yes, say the detractors, but what about the times when Schumacher has been most unsportsmanlike? Stirling Moss says the German's career will always be blighted by the way he parked his car on the circuit at this year's Monaco Grand Prix.

I'm sorry. Am I hearing this straight? Because I fail to see the difference between this and the sledging that goes on in cricket, or the punching in a rugby scrum.

The mere fact that Michael actually thought to park his car, and therefore bring out the yellow flags and thus prevent anyone from qualifying faster than him, shows yet again that he's more intelligent than anyone else out there.

When I first met him, way back in the days when he had a mullet and he was racing for Benetton, he was a shocker. Ford, his employer at the time, had asked him to road test a Mustang for *Top Gear*, so he did, coming out of the pit garage at Silverstone, getting into the car, and refusing to put a microphone on. The reason for this became clear shortly afterwards, since he also refused to speak.

But then many years later, while making a show called *Speed*, we contacted Schumacher to ask for written permission to show some of his so-called unsportsmanlike moves over the years, and he agreed. He had mellowed.

Sort of. Because I will never forget his final race in Brazil, and that extraordinary charge from last to fourth place. Can anyone think of any other driver out there now who would have the skill and the aggression, and the determination, to do that? I can't.

Losing Michael from Formula One is not like losing your arm or leg. It's like losing your torso. It's like removing America from the world map and hoping that somehow Spain can fill the void.

It's another reason why I feel sorry for Fernando. Not only was he largely ignored as he won his second championship, but he had to go home knowing that next year the best Formula One driver in the world will be sitting at home in Switzerland.

Still, at least the turbot thief can move on to a new team next year, content that he has left at least one legacy from his time at Renault – the Clio Sport 197.

Obviously Renault isn't prepared to pour millions of pounds into Formula One if there's no payback to be had in the show-room. So this little car is the result.

Look at the back end and you'll find a Formula One-style diffuser under the rear bumper. Brilliant. The idea is that as you drive along a low-pressure zone is created underneath the car, sucking it onto the road and giving more grip. It means you don't need a spoiler, which gives grip in the corners but sticks into the air flow on the straights, slowing you down.

What's more, if you look behind the front wheels you will spot two vents that direct air that would normally be trapped under the bonnet down the side of the car, further improving its aerodynamics.

If you were to be told all this in a Renault showroom I feel sure that you'd be impressed. It may only be a three-door 2 litre hatchback, but hey, if you squinted a bit and maybe grew a small piece of facial hair under your bottom lip, you too could be the second-best Formula One driver in the world.

Actually I'm not so sure. You see, I'm willing to bet all of Richard Hammond's pay packet that if you removed both the gills and the diffuser from the Clio it wouldn't make the slightest bit of difference. Oh, I'm sure computers in a wind tunnel could spot a percentage-point shift, but from behind the wheel, in your brogues, not a chance.

In fact, by trying to give this 134 mph car a Formula One feel, they might just have made it worse, because the twin exhausts leave no room under the boot floor for a spare wheel.

I suppose at this point I should explain that, as a car, the hot Clio isn't bad. It rides well, clings on nicely in the bends, looks great and has a delightfully torquey engine.

But fitting a 2 litre hatchback with all this pseudo-F1 stuff is like fitting your washing machine with a front wing. It makes you look a bit of a plonker.

There's more, too. I'm beginning to think that the days of the hot hatch might be coming to an end. I've always been a fan: the idea that you could have a powerful engine in an easy-to-use shopping trolley was great. But these days they're too expensive to insure and rather too showy for comfort.

Take the Golf GTI as a prime example. The latest version is brilliant, but when did you last see one on the road? I think, therefore, that with the Clio 197 Renault has used the second-best driver in the world to create some unnecessary additions to a type of car we don't want any more.

Don't worry, though, because I have a plan. Instead of trying to put more speed into a small car, why don't the car makers try to insert something we'd appreciate a whole lot more: more comfort and luxury.

Renault is well placed to do this because back in the Eighties it made something called the 5 Monaco. It looked like a conventional Renault 5 but it was kitted out like a Maybach with leather and luxuries oozing from every pore.

Nobody does this any more, and they should, because – think about it – in this day and age, which would you rather have, an on-board DVD system or a rear diffuser?

Alonso, I feel sure, would want the diffuser. But what would the best racing driver in the world want as he heads off into retirement?

My case rests.

Sunday 5 November 2006

Have yourself a red-blooded time without riling greens

Alfa Romeo Brera Coupé V6

These days green activists try to quash reasoned debate on the environment by claiming that all of science, and all of the world's experts, are on their side. But here's an Inconvenient Truth. They aren't.

There are many scientists, really properly good ones with really properly good qualifications, who maintain that man's impact on the environment is minimal. There are even more who say we just don't know.

Then you have Danish egghead Bjorn Lomborg, who studied a vast range of eco reports before presenting his findings in a book called *The Skeptical Environmentalist*.

Let us take the Exxon Valdez tanker crash as an example. After it happened men with sandals came on the television to call the accident an environmental catastrophe. We saw shots of sticky guillemots in their death throes, and, of course, we knew it was all our fault for driving 4×4s and turning up the central heating whenever it gets a bit chilly.

But Lomborg presents an interesting fact that wasn't covered by the news reports. Yes, 250,000 birds were killed by the spillage, but this is also the number killed each day in America from collisions with plate glass. In Britain alone 250,000 birds are killed every two days by domestic cats.

Sadly, though, the true impact of man's activities on the environment are almost always swept away by headlines suggesting we'll all soon be 'consigned to the dustbin of evolutionary history'. Not in a thousand years, but maybe by teatime if we don't watch out.

Then you have the Kyoto protocol. This is seen by most people as a political device that would save the world if only George Bush and his oil-rich neocon advisers in the White House would sign up. But Lomborg disagrees.

Kyoto calls for industrialised nations to cut carbon dioxide emissions by 30 per cent below what they would be by 2010, but, as Bjorn says, this would only postpone by six years the temperature we'd reach in 2100. So to reach the Kyoto goals we'd be spending anything between £100 billion and £350 billion each year and then we'd have to pay the costs associated with global warming anyway.

In other words we'd spend all the money we should be using to feed the poor and heal the world's other problems so that we don't have to rehouse 200 million Bangladeshis. Only to find that in 2106 we're going to have to rehouse the Bangladeshis anyway.

A big story? You'd have thought so, but it simply doesn't get a look in. If anyone dares to suggest that global warming isn't man's fault, or that it won't be such a bad thing, or that technology will save the day – like it always has done – you will be ignored, or you will be hauled onto the Jeremy Vine show so that George Monbiot can call you a lunatic.

Some of the green propaganda is driven by a post trade-union vision of world equality. You'll note they never attack fat lazy northerners who won't get off their arses and fit loft insulation; only middle-class mums with 4×4s and families who use cheap airlines to get to their second homes in Provence.

Then you have plenty of other greenies who need funding for their research and they know it'll all dry up if they announce that everything's fine.

This is probably why, in 1997, the World Wide Fund for Nature announced that two-thirds of the world's forests had been lost for ever. When questioned, it admitted that the report on which this was based had never existed. In fact, the truth is that there are many more forests in the world now than there were in 1950.

But of course, it was swallowed whole by the media, who have an endless appetite for bad news, and now we have the world's governments leaping on the bandwagon too, because they've realised that they can capitalise on our guilt with a raft of new green taxes. And George Monbiot is on hand to dismiss as a madman anyone who dares complain.

You know in your heart of hearts that the world is constantly changing, that continents move and that ice ages come and go, but you're being browbeaten by a slick and unstoppable industry into believing that because of your car, and your central heating boiler and that cheap weekend break you took last year to Prague, the gods are angry and that unless you pay Mr Blair another £5,000 a year they will visit upon you a plague of locusts and a storm that will last for at least a thousand years.

So, and this is an inescapable fact, there is about to be a complete change in the sort of cars we buy. This happens only once in a while. In the Seventies we all had four-door saloons like the Ford Cortina because Britain was a depressed communist state and no one had any imagination. Then came the hot hatch-back, which afforded us the practicality of the saloon but with the power of an E-type Jag. And then that was replaced by the Chelsea tractor.

Now the onslaught of miserablism from the greens means that four-wheel-drive cars will be vandalised the instant they are left alone, so you will need something else. But what? Well obviously this doesn't work if you have a school run to think about, but if you just have a 4x4 as a style statement, might I suggest you replace it with an Alfa Romeo Brera? I should stress straight away that it is not the fastest car in the world. The 2.2 (front-wheel drive) has the performance of a plant. The 3.2 (four-wheel drive) I tried is better, but even so whenever I mashed my foot into the carpet I sometimes thought, 'Oh no! It's broken.'

But examination of the data shows it to be a heavy car that takes seven seconds to reach 60 mph and about a week to reach a hundred. A problem? For me, yes, but if you are used to the performance levels of, say, a Shogun, the seven seconds to sixty is going to feel like you're stapled to the front of a Eurofighter. So you'll be just fine.

You'll be fine with the comfort, too. It rides beautifully and despite the tall tyres handles nicely. Actually 'nicely' is the wrong word. It is exceptionally good.

Less successful is its interior. There's not much space in either the back or the front, and this being an Alfa Romeo nothing does what you expect it to do. If, for instance, you wish to turn down the radio you push a knob on the steering wheel which is marked with a telephone symbol. And everything is written in Italian.

So why am I recommending it? Well, there are two reasons. First, as you drive along you can feel the Alfa-ness of this car, the little tingles and the droplets of feedback that you don't really get from anything else in this class. If you truly like cars, you will truly love the Brera.

And with it being so slow, you'll have plenty of time on every journey to appreciate this.

But there's another bigger reason. The way it looks. Styled by Giorgetto Giugiaro — a man I hate because I can never remember how to spell his name — it is one of those cars that forces you to turn round after you've parked it up at night, for one last look before you go inside.

The car I drove was red, and that's wrong. In black, with tobacco seats, this would be one of the sexiest cars made. The triple headlamps, that flowing, tapered arse, the lean-forward stance, and best of all the sense that while it's Italian and unusual and exotic, it's not a silly-money showoff's toy.

Prices start at £22,800, and even for a 3.2 litre V6 with all the toys on board, you'll still be charged less than £30,000. There's nothing here to fan the fire of green fury, there's nothing to make you feel guilty. You haven't bought a car to drive around in like your hair's on fire, you haven't bought a car to lord it over all and sundry at the lights. You're not a yob. You're not a bore. You've bought something for one reason only: because it's beautiful.

I think that could be the next Big Thing.

And what makes the pleasure so doubly satisfying is that you have a four-wheel-drive car, yet no one can tell.

Sunday 12 November 2006

Think of it as the Golf GTI before it got fat

Volkswagen Polo 1.8 GTI

When you buy a washing machine, does it ever cross your mind that the water could be injected into the drum a little more quickly, or that the spin cycle could be turbocharged in some way? No? Well what about your lawn mower? Ever thought of chrome plating the blades or supercharging the two-stroke? Really? You've never felt the need to fit blue underfloor running lights or add a whale-tail spoiler? Of course not, and rightly so. There is a very good reason why you leave your household goods alone; because you have a sense that they've been designed to be as good as possible, and that if you start tinkering you're going to make them worse.

I bet, therefore, that your toasted sandwich maker is exactly as it was when it came from the shop – still in its box, even. And I'm also willing to bet that you have not modified your car in any way, either.

Obviously this doesn't apply in America, because any nation that can't make a cup of coffee and is utterly confused by the recipe for 'a pot of tea' is going to struggle pretty badly when it comes to something as complex as making a car.

So if you have a Buick or a Chevrolet, then even a four-year-old child with a Fisher-Price screwdriver set could make dramatic improvements. If you have a Pontiac Aztec, you may as well wheel it to a spot under your kitchen worktop and attach it to the plumbing, because it would make a better washing machine than it does a car.

That's why America is awash with small tuning companies to

whom all car enthusiasts turn when they've bought a car from GM, Ford or Chrysler.

What's more, Americans always think they can do better. It's why they try to tune and customise shows like *The Office* instead of just buying ours.

Here in Europe, however, things are different. Yes, there are tuning companies – Overfinch for example – who do good work. But as a general rule we steer clear of trying to make improvements because we have a sense that when it comes to the business of making cars the car makers are better qualified than some bloke who rents an arch from Network Rail.

I looked at a new Jaguar XK8 last week that had been modified by a company called Racing Green. It looked tremendous and the performance figures were impressive too. But I noted the enormous wheels and the low-profile tyres and couldn't help thinking: 'If they work, then why didn't Jaguar fit them in the first place?' More worrying are those who try to change a car's performance using nothing but a laptop.

You may not know this but the engine in your car, providing it isn't a Riley or something else from the days when black people were funny, is controlled by a computer with simply awesome power.

It reads the humidity, checks the weather and notes the ambient temperature. It sees where you have your foot on the throttle, what gear you're in, whether you're going up a hill or down the other side, and when it has all the information it needs it refers to a 'map' and thinks 'Okay. If it's this hot, and the car is in this gear, and the throttle is in this position, the "map" says I must inject precisely – to the nearest atom – this much fuel into the cylinder.'

And if you have a four-cylinder engine turning at 4000 rpm the computer is referring to the map and making these infinitesimal decisions 133 times a second.

The map is drawn by clever people who live with their

mothers and do not know what daylight looks like. It is designed so that the engine uses the smallest amount of fuel while providing the cleanest possible exhaust and the maximum amount of power.

The map, then, is a series of compromises and if you, too, are the sort of person who lives in the dark and likes to hack into defence computers and start world war three, you can access it with a simple laptop and make changes.

Great. But it doesn't always work. Recently, at the MPH show in Earls Court, we needed to change the handling characteristics of the new Jaguar XKR. On the slippery floor there was too much understeer and any attempt to kick the rear end out with a bootful of throttle resulted in one rear wheel spinning uselessly.

Naturally I suggested hitting it with a hammer, but no. A man plugged a laptop into the car's computer and with each strike of the keyboard he made the handling just a little bit worse. Each time he made alterations to the map, trying to improve one thing, something else would cease to exist altogether.

I've seen this before, at various Formula One races, and when very high performance cars are delivered to the *Top Gear* test track. People in corporate short-sleeved shirts try to cure misfires, and a million other maladies besides, by plugging the car into a laptop and giving the map a new set of compromises. It never works. Ever.

The misfire may be cured but the downside is that when you start the engine it immediately sucks all of the sky into its cylinders and then bursts. Or it shoots so much carbon dioxide out of the back that the temperature shoots up to a million and we all die.

I'm not saying that car companies always get it right. They don't. But they're more likely to get it right than you. And that brings me on to the Volkswagen Polo GTI.

This comes with a 148 bhp version of the turbocharged 1.8 litre twenty-valve engine that produced 237 bhp in the old

Audi TT. So why not simply change the map and, hey presto, you have a 237 bhp Polo. Wow. With something like that, you could bend time.

Hmm. I advise caution, because while the engine is certainly strong enough to handle 237 bhp, the car isn't; something you will discover about half a second before you hit the tree.

If Volkswagen thought that the Polo could handle 237 bhp, then it would have 237 bhp. They've decided that 148 bhp is about right, and I agree.

In many ways this little car is the spiritual successor to the original Golf GTI. Back in 1981 that cost £5,700, which in today's money is around £13,000 − £7,000 less than the current, much bigger Golf GTI.

The Polo is not only closer in size to the original hot Golf but at £14,810 closer in price too.

And spirit. It has few of the fancy add-ons that have all but killed off the hot hatch as a volume seller these days. Apart from a lower ride height, and a honeycomb grille, it just looks like a small car that happens to have a big engine. And I like that.

I liked the handling, too, the sense that you can go round any corner at any speed. And I liked the power. Yes, there's a bit of turbo lag, but if you stir away at the gearbox that's eliminated and you're left with a little car that's genuinely nice to drive.

It's also surprisingly practical, well equipped and easy to park. And it's easy to mend, because of course the wing on a Polo GTI is exactly the same as the wing on a normal Polo.

The only problem is that if I wanted a fun little car I'd rather have a Mini − a car where you really can save money and get better performance with a bit of after-market tuning.

An £11,000 Mini One does 0–60 in 11 seconds and has a top speed of 112 mph. A Mini Cooper, with exactly the same engine, does 0–60 in 9 seconds and has a top speed of 126. How? Simple. The 'map' is different.

So instead of buying a £13,000 Mini Cooper, go for an

£11,000 Mini One – which is exactly the same – and then pay someone with an Oedipus complex a hundred quid or so to change the map.

I hope that, for once, I've been of some use this morning.

Sunday 19 November 2006

For once, I'd recommend the slower version

Audi TT V6 quattro

The road that connects Oxford to my house in Chipping Norton is called the A44 and it's really lovely. There are long straights to build up some speed, there are tight, well-cambered corners and there are long, sweeping bends through which you can feel the car playing 'dare' with the laws of physics.

I should imagine that even in something like a Golf GTI you could cover the fifteen miles without too much bother at an average speed of 100 mph.

But, of course, the local highway bureaucrats have decided that the speed limit should be half that. Just 50 mph. They even send a civil servant in a van to a special pig perch every so often so he can photograph the disobedient.

This is extremely dangerous. Because it means that some people do indeed drive at 50 mph. And that means those who can't see any reason for the 50 mph limit have to get past. And this means that at any given moment in the day or night, over half the traffic on the A44 is actually driving on the wrong side of the road.

Time and time again I come round a blind bend to find someone with wide eyes and a goldfish mouth heading straight towards me as they try desperately to get past someone in a 50 mph Hyundai.

So far I have been lucky, but one day I shall have a head-on accident and I shall be killed. And everyone will blame the idiot who flouted the law, even though it was the law itself that caused the accident.

If I were in power I'd put a minimum speed limit of 60 mph on that road. And arm the civil servant in his van with a rifle so he could shoot anyone who was failing to comply.

Now at this point you're probably expecting me to launch into yet another polemic on why speed doesn't kill (see Richard Hammond for details) and how it in fact makes you cleverer. But no. Instead of explaining why people go fast, I want to take a look this morning at why some people don't.

I don't mind if you stick to the speed limit. That's fair enough. You have probably given your wife nine points and she's refused to take any more.

No. I want to know why some people drive up the A44 not at 50 mph but at 40 mph or even 32 mph.

Obviously some of them are in tractors and that's fair enough as well. We need the oilseed rape and the linseed that farmers grow to fuel our cars and feed our cows, so they will be exempt from my slowcoach cull. No. I'm talking about people who wilfully and deliberately drive slowly when there really is no need to be doing so. These people always have a half-mile tailback of exasperation in their wake, and since their cars have mirrors they must surely know this. So what are they thinking as they trundle along at 32 mph? If they cared for the safety, wellbeing and happiness of other road users, they would pull over from time to time and let everyone pass. But they don't. They never do. They know they are holding the world up. And they simply do not care.

So what kind of people are they? Well, obviously they have such dull and empty lives that they don't mind wasting time by driving everywhere at half speed. They're bored at home so they may as well get in the car and set off.

And they don't much fancy where they're going either, so they feel they may as well dawdle so that they can get there as late as possible. For these people, being in a Vauxhall Corsa at 26 mph is the most interesting thing they will do all day.

Show me someone who drives slowly and I'll show you a catastrophic bore. Someone whose life is empty, shallow and pointless. But there's more to it than that.

They are also deeply unpleasant. Like bell ringers, they wish to impose their beliefs and their way of life on everyone else. They are people with an antisocial personality disorder, manifested in amoral behaviour without empathy or remorse. And that's the dictionary-definition of a psychopath.

This, then, is a useful tip for the police. The next time someone goes on a random shooting spree, hosing down innocent men, women and children and then making good his escape, please do not look for someone driving away at high speed in a flash car. Look instead for someone in a chocolate-brown Nissan Micra doing 28 mph. You don't believe me? Well, think about it: how many racing drivers have been done for murder? None.

And now try to picture Saddam Hussein doing 200 mph in a Koenigsegg. You can't, can you? Or Michael Ryan, or Robert Mugabe. And then consider Hitler, whose automotive legacy was the VW Beetle – absolutely the slowest car in the world. Remember the M25 murderer Kenneth Noye? Remember what car he stepped from before he stabbed that kid to death? Was it an M5 BMW? Nope. It was a diesel-powered Land Rover Discovery, and this proves my point. Slow drivers – they're all exceedingly dull and they're all murderers.

Which brings me, quite naturally, to the new Audi TT. I reviewed the 2 litre front-wheel-drive version a few months ago and I liked it very much. So you'd expect me to rave about the much faster four-wheel-drive V6 I've been using this past week. Hmmm, well ... the base car develops a murderous 197 bhp, whereas the V6 delivers a creamy and interesting 247 bhp. But you'd be surprised at how similar the two feel in terms of outright get-up-and-go.

Yes, the V6 gets from rest to 62 mph in 5.9 seconds but the

base car is there just half a second later. And it's a similar story at the top end, where the V6 can do 155 mph – just 6 mph more than the front-driver.

And it's the same story with handling. Of course the V6 has four-wheel drive, which affords you a lot more grip, but curiously the front-driver is more rewarding and actually better to drive. It certainly is if you spec it up with the optional electromagnetic suspension, without which the V6 felt – dare I say it – a little crude and jiggly.

And then we get to the gearbox. It was a standard six-speeder and it was the first gearbox I've come across since the mid-1980s that just wouldn't behave itself. To get first gear you had to go into second gear first, then shove it forwards hard. Failure to do this resulted in no gear at all, or – on two occasions – much to the consternation of the chap behind me, reverse.

Of course, you can get round this by instead specifying the DSG system – the only flappy-paddle gearbox in the world that works – but go for this and electric suspension and that £29,000 bill is going to climb alarmingly. What's more, compared with the Alfa Romeo Brera I reviewed a couple of weeks back the TT is fairly impractical. Yes, you can get a child in the back of the Audi, but if you slam the tailgate after he's in there you'll fracture the poor thing's skull. I know this for a fact . . . And there's more. Because if a child is small enough to fit in he'll have to have an EU booster seat, and that won't fit in.

It sounds like I'm having a downer on this car, and that's probably unfair. It looks fantastic and I think you'd be proud to own such a thing. The engine is good, too, and the quality of fit and finish is wonderful.

The thing is, though, that the Brera with a V6 and four-wheel drive is even more desirable and even more beautiful to behold. And if your heart is set on an Audi, the normal 2 litre version offers just as much, for £5,000 less.

Weirdly, then, I'm recommending the slower version. But if you find yourself on the A44, please don't use this as an excuse to actually drive it slowly.

Sunday 26 November 2006

They're fighting the last war – in slow motion

Land Rover Defender 90 Td5 Station Wagon

A couple of years ago my wife decided that although she had some horses, the other twin peak of country living was missing. So, she declared, we must rush out immediately and buy what everyone calls 'a proper old Land Rover'.

I do not understand the appeal. It offers what's best described as Sealed Knot motoring, giving its devotees an idea of what life might be like if they had to go about their daily business wearing a full suit of armour. It's like an automotive Aga: big, heavy, cumbersome and completely ill at ease with itself in the modern age.

Having said that, Richard Hammond is a big fan of old Land Rovers, though because he's only 5 ft 1 in tall his is fitted with Cuban heels in the shape of elongated red springs and some high-chair struts.

The F-reg car that my wife bought for £4,000 was much better than that. It had silent air screamers on the front wings, which, as air passes through them, emit a shriek that's audible only to any deer or bears that might be in the road up ahead. It also had tyres on it that were wider than anything found on a Lambo, and even more knobbly than the Singing Detective's face.

Apparently it had once belonged to the Swiss army, which was also tremendous. It meant it couldn't have seen much action.

And because of its military pedigree it had full camouflage paintwork, super black tinted windows, an SA80 clipped to the dash and a 20 ft aerial at each corner. It also had a metal roof that could be removed in as little as two days, providing you had six friends to help you, and a small crane.

Mind you, this was not the biggest drawback. No, the biggest drawback was the fact that under the bonnet it had a paraffin stove. It was – and I'm not exaggerating here – the slowest car ever made. And so, when it was charged with the task of towing a horsebox laden with Evo-Stick and Araldite – or whatever it is my wife's horses are called – it would barely move at all.

Once, on a not-too challenging hill outside Chipping Norton, it just stopped. Honestly, there was more horsepower in the trailer.

This caused many rows. Last year, for instance, I set off in it on December 10 to buy a Christmas tree and I didn't get back till April.

I hated that car. I hated the heavy steering, and the fact that every time you closed the door it smashed your shoulder into several small pieces. I hated the lack of legroom, and the way the 1.5 horsepower paraffin stove managed to make more noise than the Hoover dam.

Passengers, too, were worried about the sharp edges in the cabin, which they reckoned would be a serious issue in a crash. Chance would be a fine thing; you need to have some speed to have an accident, and our Land Rover wouldn't even go fast enough to get the air screamers working. Not that this was a problem, because even if you came round a corner at full speed, a tortoise would have time to amble out of your way.

Eventually I won the day and my wife agreed to swap this stupid car for one with an engine. A big one.

You can buy V8 Land Rovers. They were made from time to time and for various foreign markets. But they are rare and consequently expensive.

Don't despair, though, because there are plenty of Land Rovers lying around, and plenty of old V8 engines. So we simply bought the two entities – for next to nothing – and asked a man we knew to join them together.

I should explain that the V8 we found was not a 3.5 litre. Richard Hammond has a 3.5 in his stepladder, so we got ourselves a 3.9, which is much better. It's also fitted with carburettors so, if it goes wrong – and it will because it was made by communists – it can be fixed with the only item in my toolkit. A hammer.

Apparently it's very easy to fit a V8 into a Land Rover and even easier to fit a lever on the dash that directs the exhaust gases either down past the catalytic converters and the silencer, or if you pull it, along a length of ventilation tubing. No silencing. No cats. Just 5 mpg and without doubt the best noise in the world.

And because we've fitted all the cool military stuff from the previous model, it looks pretty snazzy as well.

However, despite all the noise and the brouhaha and the 'don't mess with me' combat exterior, it still accelerates with the verve and pizzazz of a coral reef.

Maybe this is an unavoidable problem. Maybe the Land Rover is like a heavy and unwieldy deep-sea diving suit; you can fill it with the world's fittest and strongest man but he's still not going to win any running races.

To find out, I borrowed a new Land Rover. It came with electric windows and heated seats and lots of other creature comforts, and it was finished in a natty silver paint job that made it look very Camden Town.

It also had a relatively modern five-cylinder turbodiesel engine that produces lots and lots of torque. You can feel it when the turbo blows, like a herculean inner strength, an invisible trebuchet that would be capable of freeing you and your suit of armour from the pit of any bog, from the jaws of nature's iciest grip.

But power? No. It still hasn't got any. You have to drive

everywhere with your rear-view mirror full of headlights dancing hither and thither as people behind look desperately for a way past.

It also has a set of gear ratios that may be fine in Swaledale in February but are no good anywhere else. Often fourth isn't enough to get you up a hill, so you drop down to third and it feels as though you've been hit in the back with a wrecking ball. All of a sudden you're doing 35 mph but your eight-ton suit of armour, making a noise that sounds like the birth of the universe, has come to an almost dead stop.

What's·more, there still isn't enough room behind the wheel for anyone with shoulders or legs, there are still sharp edges, it's as bouncy as a small dog at suppertime, and as a result it's about as much fun to drive as a punctured wheelbarrow. And it's not like the misery is short-lived, because each trip to the shops can, and does, take two or three weeks.

So why, in the name of all that's holy, doesn't Land Rover simply stop making the Defender and replace it with something that actually works? Something that's still designed for Swaledale but has space for your shoulders. I'll tell you why. It's because they're suffering from a British disease called Mini Syndrome.

All of us are terrified of change. It's why the Royal Navy's second world war battleships were so crap, because rate of fire was what won the day at Trafalgar, so rate of fire was always going to be more important than size of shell, or indeed accuracy, or armour plating for that matter.

It's why we have a royal family. Of course it's nonsense to hand over the reins of the nation to someone just because they were born in a castle. But hey, we always have done and look what happened when His Toniness replaced the hereditary peers in the House of Lords with a cash for honours system . . .

Then you have the Mini. For years the original version soldiered on because to change it would mean ditching forty years of tradition. And that wouldn't have been on.

As a result the company went bust and along came the Germans, who demonstrated with the new Mini that tradition doesn't necessarily mean driving to work in the automotive equivalent of rickets.

We see exactly the same with the 'proper old Land Rover'. It's rubbish: uncomfortable, slow, impractical and with prices starting at £20,000, not that cheap. But nobody has the courage to pull the plug on a sixty-year tradition, and start again. But somebody should.

Sunday 3 December 2006

Better than a Mini – so just pretend it's British

Suzuki Swift Sport

Nearly everyone is proud of the place where they were born and raised. You see them singing loudly at the last night of the Proms or before a national sporting fixture gets under way, and you think: 'Yes. If I were there, I'd be singing loudly too.'

But in a yawning and fathomless bout of insomnia last night I struggled to think of a single thing that we in Britain could be proud of.

If it was 1875 then yes, we could be proud of our Royal Navy and how Britain was an international byword for fairness, dignity, politeness and only shooting large numbers of unarmed people if they really deserved it.

But now we've had to apologise to the Irish for messing with their potatoes and His Toniness has admitted that our role in the slave trade was a crime against humanity. And that most black people in Barbados or St Lucia would be much better off if they'd still been in Darfur or the Ivory Coast.

Certainly, then, we can't be proud of our prime minister. The man who thanked America for standing beside us in the blitz, even though what they were actually doing was emptying our gold reserves in exchange for some chocolate bars and a couple of rusty first world war destroyers.

Then we have the armed services. Twenty-five years ago we struggled to beat Argentina, but there'd be no struggle these days. We'd lose. And now there are noisy voices calling on the government to ditch the one remaining pillar of our armed superiority – our nuclear submarines.

So what about industry? Well sure, in 1851 visitors to the Great Exhibition might have felt a stirring of pride amid the coal and steam and brass. But now people are saying this was a crime against humanity as well, because it somehow made the sky poorly.

Today all we make is a jolly snazzy vacuum cleaner. Or do we? Its inventor, James Dyson, talks of the time, just thirty years ago, when he needed people and companies to make components for that wheelbarrow that had a ball instead of a wheel.

He remembers going to Birmingham and after just a few minutes finding a plethora of suppliers who could not only provide the metal tubing but cut it, bend it and coat it as well.

Then he started making vacuum cleaners, but almost nothing came from Britain. 'Our British three-pin plugs were made in Malaysia. Our polycarbonate plastics came from Korea. Our electronics came from Taiwan. It was a logistical nightmare,' he said.

But not any more, because now his vacuum cleaners are made in Malaysia and all the components come from factories within ten miles. As a result the people there really do have something to sing about in their Rast Night of the Ploms.

But us? Well, when pushed, we're told by politicians that we can be proud of our tolerance. What tolerance? The tolerance that stops people wearing crosses while reading the news? Or the tolerance that means 13 per cent of those in jail in Britain – more than 9,000 people – hold a foreign passport? A lot of what actually makes a nation proud these days is the sporting success of its national teams. Hmm. As I write, the England rugby team have lost to the South Africans, the Welsh have lost to New Zealand and Scotland were routed by the Aussies who, on the other side of the world, are celebrating going 2–0 up in the Ashes. Meanwhile, members of our football team and David Coulthard continue to be paid very well for reasons I can't quite understand.

Of course, we shall be proud when Britain hosts the 2012

Olympics, but only if the stadiums are built on time and all the athletes aren't blown to smithereens by a Pakistani who came to live here because we're so proud of our tolerance. And even then I bet we only win one bronze for pushing kettles around on some ice.

Today, then, there are only a handful of things in which Britain really does set an example to the world. The BBC. The SAS. The NHS. And our huge and unique choice of national newspapers. Land of Hope, maybe. But Glory? Not any more.

This brings us, naturally, to the Mini. The original was an inspired concept – from a chap with the super-British handle of Issigonis – and it came to represent an embodiment of that whole Paul 'n' Ringo, Carnaby Street, miniskirt thing. But that, like everything else which stirs our jingo soup, was a long time ago. For the last thirty years of its life, you bought one only because it was British. The new one, on the other hand, you buy because it looks great, it goes well and it has a nice personality. For some time it has been the best small car.

But now I'm not so sure because I've just spent a week with the Suzuki Swift Sport.

It looks like the Mini, which means it looks fantastic, and it's practical too. Even though it has deep bucket seats in the front – possibly the best seats fitted to a car since the Renault Fuego turbo went west – there's still enough space in the back for three children. And the boot's quite spacious as well.

Under the bonnet you get a 1.6 litre engine which, if you really grit your teeth, will get you from 0–62 mph in less than 9 seconds and onwards to a top speed of 124. But you really have to be determined to make it go that fast. The last few mph always feel like they've come from the car's heart rather than its engine.

That makes it feel endearing and human, and it's much the same story in the bends. It gives you the fun of a much faster car but at half the speed. They've given it traction control, but I don't know why. The chassis is so good it doesn't really need it.

And it's such a nice place to be. I hate it when Japanese car makers try to give their small cars a sporty feel on the inside by fitting hideous 'sporting' trim. It's a bit like a sixteen-year-old girl trying to look thirty-five with crap jewellery and far too much make-up. But the Swift pulls it off perfectly. Quite apart from the brilliant seats, the steering wheel is thick. And the dash is enlivened by just one piece of aluminium trim. Good stereo, too.

And here's a little bit of parsley to enliven the dish still further. It costs £11,499. Which means it's about £1,500 cheaper than a Mini Cooper.

Yes, if you thump the roof lining of a Mini you get a dull, satisfying thud whereas if you thump the roof lining of a Swift it sort of clangs. This means the Mini is a more relaxing and quiet companion on the motorway. And I must also say at this point that the Mini should do 48.7 mpg, compared with the Swift's 39.2.

But I don't care. The Swift offers you something not used by Foxtons estate agency. I've been toying with giving it five stars but won't, for two reasons. First, it is a bit noisy, and second, it takes ages for the engine to deliver any warm air to the cabin on a cold morning.

Tiny faults in what's a great little car. Sure, it's built in China, Japan, India and Hungary so it's not quite as British as the Mini, but for me that's not such a bad thing.

If it is for you, why not simply buy one and paint a Union Jack on the roof? People do that with their Minis even though some of the engines came from South America and the company is run by a bunch of Germans.

Sunday 10 December 2006

Lost in planet Devon with this big dope

Volkswagen Golf GT TSI

The director was most apologetic. But since we were filming the end of a moving documentary about some soldiers in the second world war it would be best if I was actually on location. Which was in Falmouth, which is in Cornwall, which is as far as you can get from London without being in space.

Choosing what car to take was easy. I'm a huge fan of the Volkswagen Golf GTI and parked outside was its brand new baby brother, the GT TSI. This may only have a 1.4 litre engine but it's boosted with the fitment of a turbocharger and a supercharger. It sounded intriguing. It sounded like fun.

Choosing how to get there was not so simple. The M4, everyone said, is the easiest route. This may be so, but it sure as hell isn't the fastest. These days it's a car park all the way to Maidenhead, and then afterwards, as the traffic begins to ease, you have to slow down even more because they've littered the hard shoulder with cones to make it look like there are some roadworks under way. Pah! It's just a ruse so they can impose a 40 mph speed limit, which they can then police with 'safety' cameras.

By the time you get to Bristol you are either dead from old age or you're on foot because you've amassed so many points they've taken your licence away. I therefore opted for the A303, but this quickly became boring so I started to play with all the buttons. There's one, near the gearlever, which is marked with the letter W. Push it and a small light illuminates, but that's all.

All the way to Salisbury I prodded it, trying to find out what it did, until I became so desperate I actually pulled over and broke the first rule of manliness. I opened the glove box and — take a deep breath — took out the handbook.

You want to know something weird? There was no mention of the W button in there. I think it's just been fitted to keep people occupied on long journeys. So having decided there was no point trying to fathom the wilfully unfathomable, I started to delve into some of the sub-menus on the satellite navigation system.

There's one that baffled me. It's a compass, so you get an arrow that tells you your direction of travel. Fine. But then you also get a dot that shows the direction of your destination. What's the point of that? In a plane it might be useful because you can fly in a straight line. But in a car you sort of have to go where the road goes.

Still, after approximately fourteen weeks I arrived in Exeter, and that, psychologically, is the end of the journey.

It isn't, though, as people down there are only too happy to tell you. For some reason, all petrol-pump attendants in this part of the world ask where you're going and then, when you tell them, they explain with a huge grin exactly how long it will take you to get there. 'Falmouth?' said the man at the till, gleefully. 'That's another five hours!' Why do they do this? Why does my misery make their day that little bit better? Small wonder they all vote for the Liberal Democrats.

To make matters worse, I had one small stop to make in Dartmouth, which — said the petrol man, before I punched him — would mean a three-hour detour.

He wasn't joking. Devon, if it were a nation state, would be the biggest country in the world. If it were a planet, it would dwarf Jupiter. And . . . it . . . has . . . no . . . motorways. You wiggle about in single file, behind a Liberal Democrat in a Rover, until you reach Torquay, which you always thought had a New York post-code. And then you wiggle about some more until the road goes straight into what is undoubtedly the sea.

It turned out that my stupid satellite navigation system had brought me to Kingswear, which is on the way to Dartmouth, but only if you happen to be driving Chitty Chitty Bloody Bang Bang. And I wasn't, so I had to get a ferry.

God, Dartmouth's pretty. And so was the girl in Alf Resco's who made me a great breakfast, for lunch, and then, after I'd stared wistfully out to sea – which is what you have to do when you're making a moving documentary for BBC2 – I hopped back in the Golf for a six-light-year thrash to Falmouth.

Falmouth, it turns out, is the only town in the whole of Cornwall that isn't called Coombe. I don't know how many are listed in the atlas but I went through twenty-six before reaching a place called Coombe, where an old lady reversed into my car.

That livened things up a bit, but not as much as the sign I encountered on one of the endless moorland roads between Coombe and Coombe. It was a red triangle and in the middle was a picture of a bicycle.

What does that mean? That I should look out for bicycles? What, now? Specifically here? At nine at night? And does this mean that in ten miles, if I run over a cyclist, I can sue the council for not warning me that he might be there? It is the stupidest sign in Britain. It's even more silly than one I pass on the M40 most days that says 'Spray possible'. Well yes, in heavy rain, maybe. But in July? In a heatwave? What it should say then is 'Spray not possible'.

It turns out that Cornwall is full of signs, warning of your proximity to all manner of things, none of which is Falmouth. And none of which makes any more sense than the infernal W button in the car.

Ah yes, the car. Well, I was most impressed with the ride, but this, I think, has more to do with the quality of the roads down there in the West Country. Here, in England, we have to spend our money housing Albanian families while their breadwinner is away in a prison that we also paid for. Whereas in Cornwall they think Albania is some kind of skin disease, so they can afford to iron every ripple in every road every morning.

On roads as good as this, the GT handles well too. But that's it, I'm afraid, so far as good news is concerned. The rest of it is rubbish. The headlamps were set too high, so everyone coming the other way flashed me. The handle that you pull to move the passenger seat fell off, and then there was the truly woeful engine. It's all very well having direct petrol injection and a supercharger to fill in the black hole while the turbo girds its loins: this is clever, but my God it's jerky.

I like the power delivery of an engine to be smooth, like a ball bearing rolling down a child's playground slide. In the GT it's delivered with the smoothness of someone in a wheelchair falling down some stairs.

And where's the power? If you're going to stick GT badges on a car and claim it delivers 168 bhp, then kindly give us some oomph to match. Time and again I had to change down on hills, and once, with my foot welded to the floor, I was overtaken by a Mercedes van.

The worst thing, though, is that the GT TSI fails to do any of the things that you might reasonably expect from a car. It doesn't make the journey fun. It doesn't isolate you from the sensation of travel. And it isn't especially cheap. By the time I arrived in Falmouth I was fairly ready to push it into the sea.

The following day, after a seven-hour drive back to London, up the M5 and along the M4, I decided that it was one of the five worst cars I'd ever driven. Yes, the journey, in the middle of the week, in the middle of winter, was horrid. But it's the job of a good car to take a trip like that and make it better.

The Golf made it much, much worse.

Sunday 17 December 2006

Buy one before they ban them

Ferrari 599 GTB Fiorano

In a recent column I suggested that the A44, a lovely road that connects my house with Oxford, should not have a 50 mph speed limit. I argued that most people could see no reason for it and spent most of their time on the wrong side of the road overtaking the Rover-driving minority who will obey any law no matter how stupid and pointless it might be.

Inevitably, my views were reported in the *Oxford Mail*, along with those of Colin Carritt, who's mayor of Woodstock, one of the small towns through which the A44 passes.

Carritt, a former county highways engineer and therefore a man who knows what he's talking about, reckons I'm a big bag of nonsense. But sadly, while making his point, I'm afraid old Col makes a bit of a booboo.

He says: 'The accident record on the A44 is not dissimilar to other roads in the area. It is not an accident blackspot.'

Well, Mr Carritt, if it is not an accident blackspot, could you please explain why there are three fixed speed cameras along its length and one mobile site? Because, you see, the Department for Transport is very specific on this. They say that a road must be an accident blackspot before cameras can be installed.

Actually I don't mind the Gatsos. They're in villages and make sense, but the mobile site, on an open piece of road, has only recently been installed. And now the local mayor is saying there's no reason for it. Good. I expect it to be removed this instant. And if it isn't, I shall pull over and ask the civil servant who operates it why not. If he has no sensible answer, I may have to arrest him and confiscate his van.

I love it when this happens – when authority figures desperately trying to defend the indefensible come a cropper. We see it with climate-change scaremongers who are trying to argue – preposterously – that the only way to prevent the end of the world is to give Gordon Brown five pounds.

Unfortunately, in the big scheme of things, a lone voice discovering that one mobile speed camera is in the wrong place is nothing but a gnat bite on the elephant hide of lunacy that is being used to suffocate Britain's motorists under a blanket of rules and fines.

It's such an all-enveloping blanket in fact that, for the first time ever, last week I actually began to feel that soon there will be nowhere left for people who like cars to have some fun. And that's a shame, because I was driving a Ferrari 599.

There was just the most awful, paralysing sense that if I ever mashed my foot into the carpet I'd go from zero to the local magistrates' court even faster than I'd get from zero to 60 mph. And what's the point of overtaking a Rover when round the next bend you know there's going to be another? And that in the next village a hippie will throw eggs at you because your V12 is making the sky ill.

For the first time ever, I began to feel that the truly fast car might soon become – I hate to say this – pointless.

There are other reasons, too, why you might not want to buy a 599. The first time I climbed aboard it was a dark, swirly sort of night, soggy from the kind of drizzle you can neither see nor feel but which causes you to be soaked in moments.

The 599 was hopeless. Its automatic wipers couldn't cope, either not working at all or scraping themselves noisily over a bone-dry screen. The headlights had the power of candles in jam jars. The heater wouldn't heat and the air-conditioning wouldn't chill. Furthermore, the radio was all in German and the sheer size of the thing made it a nightmare on the tiny lanes round these parts.

Ferrari may have designed the 599 to be a comfortable long-distance cruiser. They may have thought hard about making it a usable everyday car, but as I picked my way along the verge, squeezing past Minis coming the other way, and being dazzled by the 'ambient' interior lighting, it was immediately obvious that they'd failed completely. It'd have been easier to circumnavigate the Arc de Triomphe in a rickshaw.

And then there's the steering wheel. Oh deary me. What were they thinking of? For the most part the interior is a typically beautiful blend of hide and style; as classically Italian as Sophia Loren's sunglasses. But there, right in the middle of everything, is a quartic steering wheel. Yup, quartic, as in square, as in Austin Allegro.

And worse still, it's half carbon fibre and half leather, and it's got all sorts of Formula One-style buttons on the bottom and then, along the top, a series of red lights that come on to tell you when to change gear. Unfortunately they are so bright you think you've been caught in the fearsome glare from a Martian spaceship. So you don't change gear. You crash.

I loathe the way they've shoehorned this Formula One trinketry into such an elegant space nearly as much as I loathe the way that under the bonnet they've fitted a sort of Formula One nose cone over the radiators. This implies that customers will raise the bonnet to show the engine off to friends. And that's like taking your penis out at a party. It's a terrible thing to do.

I wish I could move on to the good stuff at this point. But I'm afraid not. The passenger seat rattled, and a wonky diff meant that in a slow right-angled turn the whole rear end juddered as the inner wheel failed to cope with the outer wheel's higher speed. How can Ferrari fail where even the Belgian army can succeed? Oh, and then there's the flappy-paddle gearbox, something only the poseur will choose. In its normal setting it's only mildly terrible but put it in 'race', which speeds up the change action by a degree no human would notice, and it damn nearly pulls your head off every time it swaps cogs.

So couple all these faults to a car with a pointless turn of speed and you're left with something more useless than a bright green spy. Certainly, you'd have a job explaining to a visitor from outer space why you would spend, with extras, £200,000 on a car that doesn't really work when it's dark, or raining, or if the road's a bit narrow, or even if it isn't. He'd wonder, I'm sure, why you wouldn't buy a Honda Jazz instead.

And yet . . .

You only need crawl along at 20 mph in first and listen to that hollow, plaintive cry from the exhausts. You only need prod the throttle from time to time and feel the surge from that Enzo engine. You only need sweep through a really lovely, well-cambered bend. And you'll know you are driving something so utterly magical that saying no because the lights don't work properly is like saying no to Cindy Crawford because she has a mole.

After just three days the power and the excess that had originally caused me to question this car were now causing me to drool and dribble.

Because, as a piece of automotive engineering, the 599 is biblically, stratospherically, crushingly brilliant. Even at normal speeds on normal roads you know that you're in a thoroughbred. You can feel it straining. You can hear it working. You know that if by some miracle you are presented with a piece of road which is wide and open and free from Rovers and speed cameras, it would deliver a hammer blow big enough to knock down the doors of Fort Knox.

It accelerates with a savagery known only to silly mid-engined supercars or plastic bathtubs from Caterham. It rides on its tall tyres with a composure that's almost diplomatic in its smoothness.

And believe me on this: it looks a trillion times better in the flesh than it does in the pictures. It's not pretty but it has the brooding presence of a mafia hitman.

Yes, Aston Martin can sell you a better looking two-seat GT car for half the price. Yes, Porsche can sell you a wilder ride and yes, in the current climate, a helicopter would be a better long-distance tool. But none of these things feels quite so gratifying, or sorted, or sensational as the 599.

One day cars like this will be outlawed by a combination of laws and dirty looks. But until that day comes, put up with the many, many foibles and irritations. And just get one.

Sunday 24 December 2006

It's damn clever, for a dog

BMW 335i SE Coupé

Last summer, while you were on holiday, I was in the high desert of California tearing around a racetrack in a selection of powerful and exotic cars.

Each night I'd get to the bar in the hotel and relive some of the better moments from my day. The time when the Dodge Viper stuck a wheel on the gravel and made earthquake noises as I wrestled to regain control. The time when I executed a perfect power slide in a Corvette Z06. The time when I hit the ton in Ariel's little Atom.

And then, the next morning, there'd be an all-new selection of cars to drive, and that night an all-new selection of he-man tittle-tattle. Then one day I arrived at the track to find, sitting in the early morning desert sunshine, a BMW Z4-M.

Oh dear. This was a bit like sending a food critic to the best restaurant in the world and presenting him with a Big Mac. It looked all wrong, parked among the Vipers and the Ferraris and the hyper-tuned Mustangs. It looked boring and grey. A Liberal Democrat in a sea of Monster Raving Loonies.

With a limp heart and not much enthusiasm I eased out onto the track and, with my mind in neutral, set off to slither about for the cameras.

The thing is, though, that after a short while it became screamingly obvious that despite the girl-next-door looks and the miserable 3.2 litres of homo-power, this car was head and shoulders above everything else I'd driven out there.

Where a Viper or a 'Vette shouts and waves its arms about, the little Beemer just gets on with the job of going fast and tele-graphing messages to the seat of your pants and your fingertips, instantly and with no ambiguity at all. Out there in the desert, it was a sniper's rifle in a field of howitzers and mortars.

We see this with a lot of BMWs. You may not like the people who drive them. You may not like the styling. You may not like the way they supported the Nazi war machine or what they did to Rover. You may have a million reasons why you would never buy such a thing – I know I have – but the simple truth remains: when it comes to the business of driving, they really are very good indeed.

Lots of cars, for instance, are fitted with antilock brakes, but the system fitted to a BMW is just better. It only cuts in when you are in real trouble, and not – as is usually the case with modern cars – far too prematurely.

And then there are the brakes themselves. We've often wondered on *Top Gear* why BMWs always set such fast lap times round our track. You look at the power. You look at the weight. And you can't really see how it got round so quickly. The Stig always has the same answer. 'It's the brakes,' he says. In Martian.

Because they're so good, and because the ABS doesn't stumble into the equation when it's not wanted, you can hit the middle pedal later than you would in any other car. And when you are against the clock, that makes a huge difference.

I would have to say though that in recent years some of the handling fizz has gone. A modern 3-series, for instance, is nowhere near as electrifying as a 3-series from, say, 1984. But that said it's also less dangerous. You get a small hint of understeer to let you know that maybe you're going a bit too quickly, and then a little yellow light on the dash to say that underneath it all the traction control system is working its magic on the rear end. In an old Beemer you were still grinning from ear to ear, completely oblivious to any danger, when you hit the tree.

And then of course we get to BMW's engines. The V10 in the

M5. The straight six in the M3. And – whisper it – their big diesel. Each has a remarkable knack of blending the need for speed with the peculiar need western man has developed for saving the sky.

Yes, of course, the 1-series is a ghastly little car with very little interior space, a boot the size of a matchbox and bread-van styling, but to drive it's lovely. And it's the same story with the 7-series, and even the Z4 hard top, which beneath that wart of a rear end is a honey. In fact, the only car in the whole BMW range that completely fails to float my boat is the 3-series.

Stung by criticism of the more avant-garde styling seen on other models, BMW took a step back with this car and ended up with 14 ft of automotive wallpaper. It's just a bonnet, a cockpit and a boot. And the last one I drove was more dreary than shopping for bathroom cleaning products.

I really wasn't holding out much hope, therefore, for its coupé sister, the 335i.

As usual BMW claims that it's an all-new car and that every panel is different from the saloon's. But it still looks dull. You'd only really want to get inside it if you were being chased by an armed gang from Shining Path.

And then, when you did get inside, you'd want to get right back out again. In other coupés, from, say, Alfa Romeo and Audi, you get all sorts of fancy bits and bobs, but not in the Beemer. Here you get exactly the same dash that you find in the saloon. It's as dull and as featureless as the inside of a Cheeky Girl's head.

At first glance, then, I could not – and would not – bring myself to buy this car. And certainly not for £33,420, which is a damn sight more than you're asked to pay for a Mazda RX-8.

Yes, the rear seats in the BMW are as big as a sofa, and yes, the days when BMW made you pay extra for windows are gone. But even so, £33,420 for a car that doesn't even look as good as a Hyundai? You'd have to be mad.

And there's more to worry about, because although it says 335 on the back it doesn't have a 3.5 litre engine. What you get instead is a 3 litre straight six, which is force-fed its diet of air by two small turbochargers.

On paper this sounds fine. Because they're small, they don't take an age to reach operating speed, which means there's no turbo lag.

But because each one is feeding only three cylinders, you still have loads of power and loads of torque.

The worry is that BMW may have fallen into the same trap as Volkswagen, which tried a similar two-stage system on the Golf GT I reviewed recently. That didn't work at all. It was horrid and jerky and pointless.

In the BMW, though, there are no problems at all. If you really, really concentrate you still cannot tell it's turbocharged. Put your foot down and immediately there's a meaty, almost diesel-esque shove in the back. But where a diesel would be out of puff after a moment or two, the Beemer just keeps on accelerating in a wall of subdued fury – for about nine and a half weeks.

This engine is little short of a masterpiece. There's so much low-down grunt that even the BMW traction control system – a good one normally – is regularly woken from its electronic slumber by the wave of torque.

And of course it's all fitted to a perfectly balanced chassis with the usual array of excellent steering, fine brakes and a nicely chosen balance between comfort and handling.

As a driver's car, then, this is yet another winner. But I still wouldn't buy one.

You need to think of it as a painting by the world's greatest artist. Yes, the brush strokes are magnificent. Yes, the texture is superb. Yes, the perspective is world class and the detailing is better than you'd get from Leonardo.

But what he's actually painted in this case is a big dog turd.

Sunday 31 December 2006

Worshipping the god of hell fire

Volvo XC90 V8 Sport

The three twentysomething Californians were fairly intelligent so although they'd never been to Europe before, they could take most things in their stride: the smallness of the portions, the warmness of the beer, the lowness of the ceilings, the absence of pick-up trucks and the gunlessness of the policemen.

But then I took them for dinner at a small Italian restaurant in Notting Hill where, shortly after sitting down, all three were struck dumb. 'What,' stammered the first, staring at the ashtray, 'is that?' If you'd asked them to list all the things they'd least expect to find on a table, in a restaurant, in a country that's a member of Nato, an ashtray would line up alongside a child's potty full of sick. They would have been less surprised if they'd been confronted with one of Saddam Hussein's ears.

For all their adult life, these guys have lived in Los Angeles where you can no more smoke in a public place than stick your private parts in a cooked quail and run around shouting 'I am the god of hell fire'.

Now, of course, in America, it's very easy to enforce laws like the smoking ban because this is a nation where people make friends in lifts. So if you light a cigarette on a beach, for instance, you will be shamed into putting it out by a combination of dirty looks and threatening gestures from those in nose shot.

Here, though, we don't like to make a fuss or cause a scene so the job of enforcing our smoking ban will fall to someone in a high visibility jacket.

We saw much the same thing on Boxing Day when 16 million

people climbed onto their horses and spent the day pretending not to chase foxes up hill and down dale. They were forced into the charade because each one was being monitored by someone in a high visibility jacket with a video camera.

Try selling a pound of sausages at a market stall in Britain these days. You'd last a week before the kilogram police descend on you like a ton of bricks. Or should that be a tonne? Since His Toniness was appointed supreme ruler, his government has imposed the equivalent of one new law a day. And with each new law, he's had to employ an army to enforce it. That's why the civil service now employs more people than live in the city of Sheffield.

Strangely, however, the American system of using dirty looks seems to be working already with the large off-road car.

It's not banned, but a constant government-led attack on this type of vehicle, backed by a dollop of fury from the nation's communists and cyclists, seems to be shaming everyone into buying something else. Fiona Bruce, the agonisingly gorgeous newsreader, wants to replace her Volvo with something less enormous. Davina McCall got pangs of guilt over her Range Rover.

The arguments for and against off-road cars are both fairly silly. On the one hand, you have some nitwit from Richmond council appearing on television's *Fifth Gear*, saying that he doesn't like the new Honda CR-V because it's too tall; as though that has anything to do with it.

And on the other, you have Honda arguing that its new CR-V will cause no more damage to the planet than a toaster or a cow. Blah blah blah.

The facts of the matter, however, are irrelevant because if you drive a large SUV round a city centre these days you are almost melted by the hate. You'd get less reaction if you were caught videoing a school playground while wearing a Kiddie Fiddler T-shirt.

Even I've caught the bug. I look at people in Range Rover

Sports, which have the same level of oikishness as Shane Warne's hairdo, and I think: 'My God, you must have a thick skin.'

I've always wanted a proper Range Rover, but today I'm not sure I could actually buy one. It'd become wearisome, I'm sure, tuning in to the BBC news every single night and being told I was personally responsible for every single one of the world's ills. It seems 4×4s kill polar bears, drown Indonesians, bankrupt ski resorts, vote Tory and don't slow down for badgers.

This means the second-hand value is weak. Trying to sell a year-old Land Cruiser is like trying to sell a year-old piece of cheese.

That's why we read recently that sales of off-road cars have fallen by 5.5 per cent in the first ten months of 2006. Without a single piece of legislation, the bubble has been pricked.

Strangely, however, the car makers don't seem to have noticed this. I mean, take Volvo as an example. Instead of launching a new small hybrid to quench the thirst of those who miss the Soviet Union, it has just announced the arrival in Britain of a Volvo XC90 . . . V8 Sport.

Not since Shane MacGowan last picked up a microphone have we heard anything quite so out of tune with the way of the world. But like Shane MacGowan, this thing does have a place.

Like half the school-run families in Britain today, I have an XC90 and it's brilliant. Unlike various other alternatives, it really does seat seven, and even with a full load on board, the boot is still big enough for a couple of dogs.

Apart from all this, it's reliable, good looking, quite well priced and it's served on a big bed of honest to goodness common sense. The buttons, for instance, are designed so that you can operate them while wearing gloves.

The only drawback has been the choice of engines. The V6 was asthmatic and underpowered so I went for the diesel, which is noisy, as powerful as a cap gun and not all that economical either.

The V8 changes everything. I assumed that because Volvo is owned by Ford, which also owns Land Rover and Jaguar, it'd be the Jag V8, or perhaps the pig iron V8 from a Mustang. But no. It's an all-new 4.4 litre unit, designed in conjunction with Yamaha, and it's really rather good.

It makes a nice noise, and because it develops 311 bhp your big old Volvo bus will get from 0–62 mph in 6.9 seconds and reach 130 mph. You really can think of it in the same breath as the BMW X5.

Perhaps because the engine is mounted sideways, the handling is very good. The ride, too, is unchanged from the diesel and, best of all, you should get more than 20 mpg. Not bad for any off-roader, leave alone a V8.

The only drawback is that the turning circle is now rubbish. You'll make people angry by driving such a thing in the first place, but their anger will turn to a murderous blind rage when every mini roundabout requires a five-point turn.

But let's not worry about what other people think. Let's worry only about you and what car best suits the needs of your family.

The only seven-seat cars that are truly comparable to the V8 XC90 are the Audi Q7, which is a woeful thing with no boot and no go, and the Land Rover Discovery, which is a big and spectacularly heavy automotive V sign that chews fuel and breaks your fingernails every time you want to load a child into the back.

The Volvo, as a piece of design, has always been the best school-run car. And now, with that V8 under the bonnet, you can enjoy the run home as well. And if you are glowered at for bumbling round a city in something so seemingly vast and wasteful, simply take a leaf from the book of that great automotive thinker and motoring philosopher, Jack Dee.

Jack says he's particularly fed up with abuse from van drivers who trundle around London in huge Mercedes Sprinters with nothing in the back but a hammer, while his Volvo XC90 is loaded to the rafters with six children. 'By running a big 4×4, I'm keeping three other cars off the school run,' he argues, reasonably.

Have a great 2007, and don't let the nonsense wear you down.

Sunday 7 January 2007

How to overtake everyone without really trying

Mitsubishi Evo IX

Twenty-five miles per hour. On a derestricted national road. That's how fast the little Peugeot was going. Queen Victoria would have called it slow. There were tribes in pre-human Ethiopia that would have called it slow. On the Beaufort scale, 25 mph isn't even classified as a light breeze.

Naturally, there was a huge snake in the Peugeot's wake. Trucks. Vans. Bicycles. Oxen. People going to work. And me, on my way to Birmingham airport. If I'd known I was going to be travelling so slowly I'd have used a horse.

To begin with I was mildly irritated, mostly by my children in the back who wondered out loud and quite often if we were going to miss the plane. 'Miss the plane?' I sneered. 'At this rate we'll probably miss the end of the world.'

But after fifteen minutes the irritation had become rage. 'Why,' I shouted, 'doesn't he just commit suicide?'

After half an hour I was incandescent. If I'd had a knife and fork I'd have forced his car to the side of the road and eaten him.

Finally we reached the motorway, and as I tore past I noted he was a hundred and forty-twelve, a walnut-faced osteoporotic and grey shadow of his former self. I should have felt remorse that I'd harboured such unkind thoughts about a man who'd served his country in the Crimea and in the Spanish war of succession, and probably at Hastings too. But instead I gave serious consideration to ramming his Peugeot into a bridge parapet.

Later I was at the airport check-in desk. 'No. I haven't allowed anyone to put any explosives in my bag.' 'Yes, someone could easily have loaded a pair of scissors when I wasn't looking but I'm buggered if I'm going to admit that to you.'

And then, out of nowhere, another double-centurion shuffled straight past the queue, arrived at the desk and announced in a voice that sounded like the rustling of dried straw that he'd lost his boarding pass.

So we waited twenty minutes while it was found, in the top left pocket of his jerkin, and then began what can only be termed a sprint to security, where a man, who actually remembers the story on which Mel Gibson's new film is based, walked straight past the ticket checker, straight past the queue and straight through that x-ray machine customs men use for looking at women's knickers. It didn't buzz so much as explode.

And again the whole business of catching a plane ground to a halt as he took off his shoes, and his anorak, and his hearing aid, and emptied his bag of knives, Denture Sure, cream, potions and all the other million things Mr Blair thinks could be converted into a bomb.

So then we're on the plane waiting for just two more passengers. And waiting. And eventually on they came, with their combined age of a million. And by the time they'd been bent into the sort of shape that would actually fit in an airline seat we'd missed our slot.

And I began to decide that there must come a time when really old people are not allowed out in public.

Of course they must be looked after and fed, but going out? No, because behind the wheel someone of ninety is as much of a nuisance as someone of nine. And would you let your children loose on their own in an airport? Of course not. So why think for a moment that your parents will fare any better? It's hard enough trying to forge a path through life when we are beset on all sides by Romanian beggars, Bulgarian hitmen and government-sponsored extortion schemes.

But it's doubly difficult when your passage through the Cotswolds is blocked by King Herod doing 25 mph.

Of course chaining old people to their wingbacks will never happen. In fact things will get worse. New drugs will give the elderly a sense that all is working, even though they are going out with their spectacles in the fridge and a pair of onions balanced on their nose.

The only solution, then, is to buy a car with so much power that no matter how small the gap you can always get past. This, of course, brings us to the door of Mitsubishi's new Evo IX FQ-360, which is not to be confused with either the IX FQ-400, or the IX FQ-340, 320 or 300. And though it may look the same as the old VIII MR FQ, it isn't the same as that either.

Like all modern technology, the Evo's nomenclature is deliberately designed to confuse the elderly. Anyone who grew up with the Austin 7 is going to be driven screaming from the showroom by the sheer complexity of all those letters and numbers.

The car, too, is designed to terrify those whose bones are brittle and whose minds have lost the ability to deal with mini-roundabouts or clearly marked signs saying 'Queue Here'.

It doesn't glide or fly, this car. It darts. And it doesn't purr or snarl either. It shouts. Honestly, I'm amazed it doesn't come with an electronic ankle bracelet and a Burberry roof.

The Evo is now in its ninth incarnation. The shuffle from one to the next has been subtle, like the movement in one of Gromit's ears. Only if you compare the ninth to, say, the fourth do you see a perceptible advance.

In essence they're all staggeringly brilliant. Hard and uncompromising and loud, yes. But capable of such immense speed, especially round corners, that anyone who likes driving even just a little bit is always left gasping for breath. My wife, who uses an Aston V8 as her everyday car, says that the Evo is her idea of absolute and utter motoring perfection.

There was one mistake, though. The Evo 400. Instead of

shuffling forward, the engineers tried a giant leap and failed. Yes, they squeezed 400 bhp from the 2 litre engine – an amazing 200 bhp per litre – but the turbo lag was so bad and the speed so great that bits of the body peeled away if you even attempted to go flat out. It was a horrid car.

So for the 360 they've taken the idea of the 400 but reined it all back a bit. Disappointing? Not at all. It'll still get from 0–60 nearly a full second faster than a Porsche 911 Carrera S, but it's all so much more driveable than the car it replaces. Actually, it's much more driveable than pretty much anything.

At first it's scary, but as you get to know it and you start to realise that it won't fly off the road, everything – the grip, the handling and the unbelievable, seamless barrel of torque and power – becomes almost hysterical.

Better still, behind the spoilers and the wheelie bin they use for an exhaust, it has a big boot, four doors and all the luxuries you could reasonably expect. And it only costs £35,539. Or £34,500 if you decide to do without the leather trim.

A car like this, then, is almost never caught out. It works in city centres because yobs love a yob and ecomentalists don't know what it is. It works on the school run. It works on the track. It works, thanks to four-wheel drive, in the gymkhana car park. But it works best of all when you're on the A44 and the bastard in front is doing 25 mph.

Sunday 14 January 2007

Ugly Betty, I want to make babies with you

BMW M6 convertible

What does everyone in Britain do for a living these days? We know that Bulgarians have taken all the jobs picking flowers, we know that London's traffic wardens are all Nigerian, that your cockles were picked by a Chinaman, that your plumber's a Pole and that whenever you ring a call centre it sounds like you've got through to the Kumars at No 42.

So, and I'm struggling here to think of the right terminology, what are the indigenous English doing to fill their days? I pay particular attention to people who appear on gameshows. In the past, people on *Blind Date* would usually claim to be retail managers, i.e., shop assistants, but these days most people buy their groceries and their exercise equipment from the internet.

And we know from recent press stories that people are leaving the army in droves because half are being sent to war by Tony Blair armed with nothing but a twig and the other half are living on bases so squalid you can catch ebola from the light switches.

No one knows how many people are living in Britain at the moment. Some say we're getting a migrant a minute, but that doesn't count the others who are arriving disguised as horses and clinging to the bogey wheels of the Eurostar.

Let's assume that there are roughly 60 million people here and that 30 million are of working age. That's 30 million people getting up in the morning and getting in their cars and going to work. But what are they doing when they get there? Several thousand – and again no one knows quite how many – are on the run from jail, so you might imagine we have a great many police-men trying to round them up. But the police force has mostly been replaced with speed cameras so that's out too.

Also, we know people are not going to factories and making things because all that palaver stopped in the 1980s. We know, too, they're not going up chimneys or down mines, and that all the nurses in the NHS are from Guam. Yes, someone on a recent edition of *Who Wants to Be a Millionaire?* said he was a hypno-therapist, but I can't believe this is a trend.

Obviously several hundred thousand are employed by tele-vision companies to sit in a house, or a jungle, or to slither about a dance floor in sequinned jumpsuits. But that still leaves, what, 29.5 million people. The only conclusion I can draw is that all of them are working in some way for the government.

This makes sense. At present, each of us is governed by a parish council, a borough council, a county council, Westminster, the European Union and whatever regional assembly Blair has deemed necessary for your area.

Each of these elected bodies has to be run by an army of civil servants, who need a team of hit squads to enforce their whims. That's why you have the kilogram police patrolling market stalls, fish Nazis waiting to arrest the country's last six trawlermen and Jonathon Porritt's sustainable development KGB, who can arrest and murder you for having a toaster.

And all this lot have to be paid for by the only non-government employees left in Britain today. That'd be Bruce Forsyth and Jade Goody.

Soon, however, they will be gone too, because as the EU con-tinues its inexorable march towards Kamchatka, more and more people will be needed to monitor the rights, health, safety and sustainable development of each new member state.

I like the idea of the EU. But now it's too big, and too un-manageable, especially as it's trying to make a cohesive and yummy whole from a selection of ingredients that wouldn't fuse even if you put them all in a blender and nuked it. Retsina, bangers, mash, small birds, goulash, dog and bratwurst is not something you'd want to put in your mouth. Ever.

We see the same sort of problems in the car industry. All the players reckon they can shave costs by merging with one another. So you have Daimler and Chrysler, Renault and Nissan, and Ford which has gobbled up Volvo, Aston Martin, Land Rover and Jaguar.

Apparently, however, even this isn't enough so now there's talk of General Motors joining forces with Renault and Nissan, and of Porsche reversing into Volkswagen, which already owns Seat, Audi, Lamborghini, Bentley and Skoda.

Eventually I can see a time when there are only three car companies in the entire world. There will be one in the Far East, one in the West and BMW. Already, I have a sense when I drive a new car that it's really just a mildly altered collection of exactly the same components that I encountered in the new model I drove the previous week. The tyres are from Pirelli, the gearbox from ZF, the brakes from AP, the stereo from Harmon Kardon, the seats from Recaro, the windscreen wipers from Bosch and so on.

Of course, BMW is no different. The bits that make up your 3-series are from the same companies that make the bits for everything else. And yet . . .

BMW is like Switzerland. It's in Europe and the people there have eyes, noses and hair. On the face of it, they're just like us, but they're not.

The Swiss are independent and focused. And BMW's the same. It doesn't make vans or tractors or trucks. The only other places you'll find the blue and white roundel is on a motorbike – which is cool, if you like wearing leather trousers – and on the Gulfstream V, which is cool no matter what strides you prefer. Sure, Bee Em dallied with expansionism in the Nineties, taking on Rover and emerging with Rolls-Royce and Mini, but it is still privately owned, and now has no obvious ties to anyone else.

Theoretically this shouldn't work. BMW should have been crippled by go-it-alone development costs and wiped out by over-production. But last year it sold more cars than ever and predicted pre-tax profits in the region of £2.6 billion.

Perhaps this is because in the one-size-fits-all modern world some of us crave something a little bit different. A Kentucky Fried Partridge. A Big Mac and new potatoes.

Some BMWs don't work. The 335 coupé I tested recently is too expensive and too boring, the X3 is useless on every level and the Z4 coupé appears to have caught elephantiasis of the arse. But when they work, they work very well. And the models that work best of all are the most independent, most focused of the lot. The M cars.

This brings me awfully late to the subject of this morning's column. The M6 convertible. It's ugly, it has a roof from Heath Robinson Ltd and it comes with a frighteningly bad flappy-paddle gearbox. But despite all this I want to marry it, move with it to a croft in the Highlands and spend the rest of my life making M-powered Jezza babies.

There's no real point to the M6 coupé. You're better off buying the better looking, more practical and cheaper M5, which is just as fast.

But an open-air M6? Mmmm.

Of course, a Mercedes SL 55 is better looking and has a much better roof. It makes a better noise, too, and comes with a proper gearbox. But when you delve into the BMW's iDrive system and find the control that unleashes all of the V10's 500 bhp, trust me, the Merc is made to look like it's made from a mixture of wood and wallpaper paste.

The M6 never feels light, agile or sporty. But the speed. Oh my God. The speed. It's hyperspace fast. And that's more addictive than watching *Deal or No Deal* on crack.

I don't know what you do for a living. But if you're the

chap who's paying those Bulgarians 5p a year to pick daffodils, I suspect you're making enough to buy an M6 convertible. You should.

Sunday 21 January 2007

That's enough grief: now we can be kids again

Peugeot 207 GT

Last week the nation was being treated to one of the most eagerly awaited television shows in modern history.

I'm talking, of course, about *24*, the further adventures of Jack Bauer, CTU's shouting whisperer, whose mobile phone never runs out of battery and whose bowels never need emptying.

Meanwhile, on the other side, after intense tabloid scrutiny, and a billion text votes, Davina McCall revealed to the world who had become the best person at living in a house with some other people.

It was a big night for the box, then. But strangely, I'm willing to bet the battle for viewers will have been won by a poky motoring show on BBC2, as half a trillion tuned in to watch a small man have a car crash.

The story of Richard Hammond – or Princess Diana as we now like to call him – has become a national obsession. I am so fed up with people asking how he is that I now smile the smile of a bereavement vicar and say: 'I'm afraid he's died.'

We have seen him photographed in the *Daily Mirror*, drinking a mug of tea. We have seen him in the *Sun*, riding a bicycle. And we have seen him in *OK! Magazine*, wearing a heart-warming pair of trousers available from Marks & Spencer for £49.99. I daren't even look in *Gay Times* in case it's bought some pap pictures of the wee chap playing with himself.

This is a huge problem for *Top Gear*. Before the crash we were a fairly anonymous triumvirate of middle-aged men who went to work every day so we could indulge our fantasy of being nine years old. No one really wrote about us. No one really complained. No one really cared.

We would buy some cars, turn them into boats, go to a reservoir in Derbyshire and sink. And then the next day we'd go on a caravan holiday, when there'd be a fire and everything would be ruined. This was our happy, simple, unassuming life.

But now one of us has become a national treasure, a man who stared death in the face and decided he'd rather go back to his family.

A hero. A god.

I have agonised for months over how the poor bloke should be reintroduced to the show. He thought we could just push him on in a wheelchair, where he'd loll throughout the show, dribbling. James May thought maybe he could come into the studio on a cruise missile to demonstrate his superhuman powers. I reckoned he could enter stage left in a selection of new clothes from Marks & Spencer, to recognise his deal with *OK!*.

But after much soul searching I think the solution – and it's a surprise for him as well as you – is elegant and rather nice. I hope you like it. I hope he likes it, too, because I had to spend a fortune on beer before I thought of it.

What I can tell you is that James and I will present him with a number of lucky charms which we insist he keeps with him at all times, to ensure such a terrible crash never happens again. I've got him a grandfather clock.

Then, after the opening few moments, we're faced with the problem of showing the crash itself. Some of the footage is sickening, so obviously that will be screened in slow motion. But what about the rest? The build-up? The foreplay? The previous runs where all went well? Frankly, I think we should skip it all, go straight to the bone-crunching impact and then invite all the rubber-neckers who've only tuned in to see the little fella get brain damaged to bugger off and watch something more intellectually suitable. *Big Brother – The Final*, for example.

Diana and May are in complete agreement with me on this. So are the producers. We want to get the damn crash out of the way and get back to the business of being nine.

But even here there are problems, because you just know that the hippies and the communists won't turn over or tune out. They'll be watching with their beards peeled, ready to fire off an angry e-mail should we even look like we're going to mention gays, speed, Muslims, gypsies, polar bears, global bloody warming, breasts, disabled people, immigrants, or how jolly nice it is to be middle class.

Happily, this has united May, Diana and me even more than usual. We feel circled, threatened, and can see no way round the problem except to screen the crash immediately and then spend the next fifty-seven minutes talking about gays, speed, Muslims, gypsies, polar bears, global bloody warming, breasts, disabled people, immigrants, and how jolly nice it is to be middle class.

We all want to go back to how it was, because making that show is the most fun a man can have. Apart from being allowed to fire a heat-seeking missile into a helicopter over Hong Kong harbour, obviously.

People think it's all dreamt up by a team of producers and scriptwriters. People think it's all stage managed and that we're just hired hands, paid to fall in water and set fire to stuff. It really isn't. We're not that good at acting. James especially.

The ideas are mostly dreamt up by the one producer and me, usually in a top London restaurant such as E&O or an Angus Steak House. They are then developed with Diana and May in a crap pub where James can drink brown beer and play darts. And then we set off to film our little drama in the real world, among real people. When a policeman comes, he's not an actor out of *The Bill*. He's a policeman. That's why we usually run away.

Scripted? Well, yes, I write the studio stuff pretty tightly. But the films? Not a chance.

In this series, for instance, we attempt to grow our own petrol,

which involves the three of us crashing a lot of tractors and breaking most of Bedfordshire. We build our own road to show how
fast it can be done if the navvies are made to actually work for a
living. We get chased out of Alabama by a stone-throwing mob
who saw James's hair and thought we might be homosexuals.
We drive the usual array of Porsches and Ferraris much too
quickly, while shouting. We play golf, which meant wearing
silly jumpers and crashing our golf carts extensively. We build
stretched limos from entirely unsuitable base products and then,
while using them to ferry celebs to glittering galas in London,
hope they don't – for instance – snap in half.

James and Princess Diana even attempt to get a car into space.

One of the things you won't be seeing, however, is the new
Peugeot 207 GT. Partly because we can't be bothered. And partly
because it's not very good. Oh, at £14,345 it's exceptionally
good value for money compared with rivals from Ford, Vauxhall
and Volkswagen. And yes, it has the same 1.6 litre turbo engine
they put in the new Mini, so that's good too.

What's more, it has a brilliant sat nav system, and thanks to an
unusual rear window with very curved glass it makes every other
car look, in your rear-view mirror, like an elongated gargoyle.
This makes you feel like you have the prettiest car on the road.

However, there are some faults. The driving position is only
really suitable for those whose legs are exactly the same length as
their arms – i.e., no one. There are rattles, the brakes are so sharp
you end up on the bonnet every time you so much as look at
them and, most importantly, it's not as much fun as it should be.

In the fourteenth century, when I was growing up, Peugeot
was master of all it surveyed in the world of the hot hatchback.
Now, though, it's no longer doing what it does best.

This is a bit like Jack Bauer suddenly saying in a normal voice:
'Ooh I need a poo.' Or Richard Hammond coming back on *Top
Gear* to the accompaniment of some kind words, a sensitive
shoulder to cry on and a refreshing cup of tea.

By the way, last weekend a man quoted in this section of your *Sunday Times* claimed that Richard Hammond was to blame for his accident. Not the car. Furthermore, he suggested that a badly positioned onboard camera might have caused Richard's brain damage. Not the car.

Interestingly, these claims come from . . . the owner of the car. He also claimed that vital footage of the crash was 'missing'. You can judge for yourself tonight at 8 p.m. on BBC2.

Sunday 28 January 2007

A case of power corrupting absolutely

Mégane Renaultsport 230 F1 Team R26

A couple of weeks ago Sir David Attenborough went on the BBC – an Establishment double act that's hard to top – and explained exactly what global warming would mean for Britain.

In short, some householders in Worcester will need new carpets every time it rains, the Glasgow sewers will burst and a farmer in Abingdon will be moved to make way for a new reservoir. It was not even slightly terrifying, but nevertheless at the end Attenborough came onto the screen in big nose-hair close-up to explain that we must do something now – now, d'you hear – to prevent this catastrophe.

Doubtless a party political broadcast from such an authority as Attenborough will have had you scampering round the house turning off the lights. And maybe the next day you walked to work instead of taking the car. Though I doubt this, because much to the annoyance of the producers the next day was bitterly cold with snow falling in many parts of the country.

And anyway, even if every nation meets its obligations under the Kyoto agreement, the Earth won't be saved. In fact, the heat expected in 2020 would arrive in 2026. So we ruin our lives to buy just six more years.

The fact is this. Global warming's coming, so you can don your King Canute hat and stand on the beach waving your Toyota Prius at the advancing heatwave, but it won't make a ha'p'orth of difference.

But don't worry, because I have a plan. The biggest threat we face, according to the British Broadcasting Corporation, is rising sea levels. Apparently, seawater expands when it's heated, so the entire population of Britain will have to spend the rest of time perched on top of Ben Nevis.

Plainly, then, there is too much water in the world, so why don't we just call Nasa and ask it to take some of it into space? Technically this is not difficult. Build a fleet of space shuttles. Fill them with seawater. And move it into orbit.

If necessary the water could be stored in a huge balloon so that if the world cools down at some point in the future the shuttles could go up there and bring it back again.

Brilliant, yes? But having given the matter some thought, I think there is room for improvement.

Space is only seventy-five miles from the surface of the Earth, so why not make a giant hosepipe, dip one end in the sea and take the other end out into the void, where, of course, there is a vacuum? That means the water will be sucked up the pipe without the need for any energy-absorbing pumps.

Of course there is a small problem with this idea. Gravity means the hosepipe will keep falling back to the ground again, but I've thought of that.

Initially, I reckoned it could be tethered to the moon, but having studied astrological charts I've realised that in a day or two the pipe would be wrapped round the world. And as any gardener knows, this will cause a kink at some point, which will stop the water being ejected.

There are two ways of addressing this. We could either build a tower seventy-five miles tall to which the hosepipe could be fixed. Or we could fit the space end of the pipe with a watering can sprinkler attachment that is turned to face Earth. This would direct the water downwards and that would invoke Newton's third law. Hey presto: the effects of gravity are overcome and the hosepipe stays up.

Now I'm just a middle-aged bloke with no engineering qualifications whatsoever and yet, in the space of one afternoon, I have devised a simple method that will save the life of everyone in Norfolk, Holland and the Maldives.

Which brings me on to an important question. What, exactly, are those who do have engineering qualifications doing to fill their days in these dark and superheated times?

Are they developing an airborne vacuum cleaner that cruises through the upper atmosphere sucking up the carbon dioxide and turning it into money or cheese or something? Are they working on waterproof carpets for the people of Worcester or pills to reduce the amount of sewage produced by Glaswegians? Sadly not. In fact they're all down at the Dog and Spanner wondering if a front differential might tame the understeer in a powerful front-wheel-drive hatchback.

Here's the problem. To make a hot hatchback appeal these days, it must have more power than all its rivals. But as Vauxhall proved with its insane Astra VXR, you can't just put a million horsepower in a hatchback, because the front wheels cannot be expected to deal with this and the job of steering.

Ford, as I recall, was the first to try to tame big power in a front-drive car by fitting a front differential. It was the RS1600i and I seem to remember it was fairly nasty. But nowhere near as nasty as its second attempt, the Focus RS. Yes, in a tight corner you could shove your right foot through the firewall and the front tyres would still grip. But unfortunately, when you were just driving normally, the car was so twitchy and so prone to even the slightest change in camber that I'd even go so far as to call it dangerous.

This, I felt, answered the question nicely. Yes. A front differential will tame understeer in a powerful front-wheel-drive hatchback. But the price is too high. However, Renault was not paying attention and has now come along with the complicated sounding Mégane Renaultsport 230 F1 Team R26.

It's a very yellow car this, and it comes with all sorts of eye-catching details such as grey wheels, brilliant bucket seats, lots of stickers, including if you want a chequerboard roof and a little plaque between the front seats saying: 'We won the last two Formula One world championships, we did.'

I rather liked it. I liked the engine, too. It's a 2 litre turbo, almost identical to the unit fitted in the old Mégane 225 but tweaked so you get a few less carbon dioxides coming out of the back and a bit more power going to the wheels. The result is 0–60 mph in 6.2 seconds.

Even better, however, is the price – just £19,570 – and even better than that is the ride. Yes, it has stiff springs, but it's got good damper travel, so your teeth stay fastened to your jaw over even the roughest road.

However, if you set off into this absurd name with a magnifying glass and a map, you will note that the car produces 230 bhp. That sounds good in the brochures but you can't put this much power through the front wheels and hope for the best. So they've taken a leaf out of Ford's book and gone, once more, for a front diff.

And sure, on a soaking wet corner, covered with a veneer of leaves, Fairy Liquid and butter, you can stand on the throttle and such is the grip you won't even trouble the traction control system.

But as was the way with Ford's loony tunes Focus, there are drawbacks at all other times. You pull out to overtake a slower car and you feel the wheel tense as you make the move. Then you crest the apex of the road and you feel it twitch again. You have the sense that unless you hold on tight you will be in a tree.

It's nowhere near as bad as it was in the Ford but it's still there, a constant nagging presence, like being in the room with a lion. It means you can never just relax and listen to Terry Wogan.

You are therefore better off with a Golf GTI. And Renault's

engineers would have been better off doing something more constructive with their time. Such as realising my dream of putting a hosepipe into space.

Sunday 4 February 2007

When the beeping stops, you may go

Lexus LS 460 SE-L

There can be no doubt, of course, that the three-letter acronym was created so that people at work could save time while talking. If I, for instance, want something in a medium-sized close-up, I simply ask for an MCU and the cameraman frames up accordingly.

This, presumably, is why TLAs are so prevalent in the army. In the heat of battle you can't very well take up twenty seconds of radio time calling for something when you only need three for the abbreviation. 'Can someone fetch that sort of portable light-machinegun thingy' can be changed to 'Get the LMG' and all is well.

Unfortunately, army people spend so much time with one another talking entirely in TLAs that they can't stop when they're round at your house for a plate of FOC. This means you have no idea what they're on about.

And to make matters worse, half their acronyms take longer to say than the words they've replaced. The late Douglas Adams once joked that the nine-syllable www abbreviation was the only TLA that took longer to say than the words it replaces. But he'd obviously never talked to an army chap about an IED. This means improvised explosive device. Which means bomb.

And then you have ACV, which means armoured combat vehicle. Which means tank. Or ADW, which means air defence warning. Which means siren.

Businessmen are similarly guilty. Instead of talking about work in China (two syllables), they talk about going to the PRC (three). And what's more some even refer to the time it takes to get there as P2P, meaning pillow to pillow, which is just about the most custardish thing I've ever heard.

In other words, people are using three words where one will do, simply so they can use a TLA and therefore exclude you and me from their conversation. One chap even went on the Chris Evans radio show last week and said he was an 'iffer'. It turns out this was an IFA, which is an independent financial adviser, which is a long and complicated way of saying 'thief'.

My least favourite acronym of them all is PLU – people like us. Anyone who uses this has no connection with me, at all, except for the brief moment where my fist is connected to their nose.

I'm bringing all this up because I've just spent a week driving the new Lexus LS, which is so full of acronyms I spent most of my time with it on the verge of a very large crash.

Let me give you an example. There's a feature in this car that monitors your progress down the road. If it senses that you're straying out of lane it alerts you, not with a worryingly pleasant vibration in your seat – as happens in the Citroën C6 – but with an annoying beep.

Of course I knew that it must be possible to turn this feature off, but which button to press? Tricky that, because each time I looked down to identify a likely suspect I'd edge towards the white lines a bit and there'd be another beep.

One button was marked 'TCS off'. Could this be it, I wondered, or might it be some device that detaches the wheels from the car? Hmmm. Beep. So what about this one down by my right knee marked 'AFS off'? Beep. Damn.

I pushed it tentatively and nothing happened. So with a deep breath I hit the TCS button, and again nothing happened. Beep. So I pushed every single one of the car's several hundred buttons, including two that said 'auto', until finally I pushed one of the fifteen on the steering wheel, marked 'LKA', and the beeping stopped.

LKA? I presume the L is for lane and the A for alert. But the K? Khaki? Kind? Kipling? Kuwait? If anyone has any idea do please write and let me know because I've been through the alphabet and nothing seems to make sense.

I even went to the trouble of delving into the car's press pack, but after a page or two I was even more lost. All I can tell you is that the D4S is combined with VVT-iE and the PCS can activate the VGRS, the AVS and the VDIM. You'd need to be a brigadier to have the first idea what the bloody hell all this means.

The boys at Lexus have plainly become so used to speaking in TLAs that they've lost the ability to talk normally. An advert for the Lexus I read recently said: 'If we never came up with an eight-speed automatic transmission would you have asked for it?' That's grammatical nonsense. But I sort of get their drift and the answer is: 'No, because I've tried Merc's seven speeder and that's too many, so why would I want eight?'

There's more. It's also got a device that looks at your head and beeps if you fall asleep. It's got a collision avoidance system like an Airbus. It's got a satellite navigation system that tells you if the road ahead is slippery or blocked, and what it's blocked by. Small wonder there are so many acronyms. This has to be the most advanced piece of consumer electronics ever offered.

And yet, behind the almost impenetrable shield of buttonry beats the heart of a very satisfying car.

What makes it work so well is that unlike Mercedes, Audi or BMW, Lexus has no sporting aspirations for the LS at all. Oh, it shifts, be in no doubt about that, but it is not supposed to be a driver's car. And by taking that out of the mix they have been able to concentrate on making it, above all else, unbelievably comfortable and quiet. Really quiet. It may be a 4.6 litre V8 up there under the bonnet, but at tickover it barely makes a sound. Then there's the suspension. Sadly, it's made from air, which means it doesn't work very well in normal mode, but put it in 'comfort' and the leviathan just glides.

The driver's seat should be singled out for praise too. It's like sitting on a sumo wrestler. Couple that to the gearbox, which changes so smoothly you cannot feel the shifts, and you have a car that can be compared to the Rolls-Royce Phantom. Except for the price, of course. At first the starting price of £57,000 appears to be a lot but a Mercedes S 500 with a similar spec will cost you about £13,000 more.

There are a few drawbacks, though. Its thirst, for a kick-off, but also its looks. It is a very handsome car but the styling means you can't smoke while driving. No, really. If you crack the window open a tad in most cars your ash is sucked outside. In the Lexus, it's blown back in.

This means you spend quite a lot of your time behind the wheel on fire, and that means you swerve about quite a lot as you try to put yourself out. And that means the LKA beeps furiously.

Then there's the boot lid. You press a button on the key fob and it opens automatically, at exactly the same speed America is moving away from Europe. If it's raining this is extremely annoying.

Hopefully this is an optional extra that you don't have to have. But I can't be sure because it's almost certainly referred to in the press pack by a set of initials. LBJ? ACU? DDT? Who knows?

The worst problem, though, is the interior. It's a bit like an executive suite at the Hyatt Regency Birmingham. Very comfortable and graced with lots of features that make your stay more enjoyable. But it's all a bit nasty, if you see what I mean – the half-timbered steering wheel especially.

It sounds as if I don't like this car and that's not right. I do. In the olden days Lexi were bought only by northern businessmen who'd had a row at the lodge with the local Mercedes dealer. They were reliable, quiet and comfortable but utterly soulless. This new one, though, is AFB.

Sunday 11 February 2007

If it ain't broke . . . oh, fix it anyway

Mini Cooper S

A man asked me last week what ringtone I'd selected for my new mobile phone. 'Pah,' I scoffed indignantly. 'The one it came with. Do I look like the sort of person who has either the time or the inclination to change the noise his phone makes?' And then rather more hysterically: 'Do I look like the sort of person who cares what people think when my mobile goes off? Do I? Do I?'

The man was a bit bemused by my ferocity but I was only just getting warmed up. 'Look at my hair,' I thundered. 'That's styled by erosion and time. And have you not seen my clothes? If I haven't changed those since 1978, what makes you think I've changed the ringtone on a phone I bought only yesterday?' Sadly, however, I was protesting too much. In fact I'm a compulsive fiddler, never really happy with anything for more than five minutes. Which means that secretly, and rather embarrassingly, I changed the ringtone on my old phone all the time. It was a twenty-four eeh eeh eehooh, and then it was the first few bars of Bryan Adams's 'Summer of '69', and now it's a sort of soft and unobtrusive pinging noise. So soft and unobtrusive, in fact, that I only know when it's ringing when the dogs start to bark.

There's more. When there's nothing on the television I re-arrange the furniture in my sitting room. And since there's never really anything on television my sofa has covered more miles than the average Boeing 747.

Sometimes I even move the sitting room to another place altogether. I've lived in this house for ten years and so far it's been in four different rooms. Tomorrow morning an architect is coming to talk about changing the shape of the kitchen and whether I can put a bog in the larder.

This fiddling is so bad that I send the children to their bed-rooms at 9 o'clock every night. But it's often gone eleven before they find them. Then there's paint. I've put so many coats on the walls in the spare room that now it's not even big enough to put up a veal for the night.

I bet you have a set route for your journey to work. I don't. And, of course, the utter and absolute joy of this job is that I drive a different car every day. Often I'm relieved to climb out of a Lamborghini and into a Nissan Micra because in my world change is the adrenaline rush. Occasionally I even find myself looking at other people's children . . .

And now it seems I have a kindred spirit high in the manage-ment at BMW, because they've changed the new Mini for absolutely no reason at all.

The last one was still hugely popular, and much loved by everyone except James May, who can't see the appeal, because of his hair probably. So why did someone decide it needed a new engine and an interior rethink? Because he could, I suppose. I like that in a man.

And I especially like the interior lighting he's fitted. Not long ago BMW fitted a pin-prick red bulb on the underside of the rear-view mirror that bathed the interior of the car with the soft red glow of a submarine at Defcon 3. It was without a doubt the greatest single advance in automotive technology since Cadillac introduced the starter motor.

Shortly afterwards Mercedes followed suit, but instead of a red light it went for yellow. And that was good, too. It made you feel all warm fuzzy as you drove home at night.

But the new Mini goes further because you can choose what colour light you'd like to bathe in. And better still there's a slider knob that changes the hue on an infinite scale, from red through scarlet and then purple until it ends up vodka bar blue.

For me this is the greatest piece of in-car entertainment ever. It means I can spend forty miles getting the colour exactly right. And then, after just five seconds, decide it's wrong and start again.

You can also change the perspective of the satellite navigation map. You can change the dynamics of the car itself with the little sport button. And it's very easy to station hop on the radio, which, unsurprisingly, I do a lot.

You're even given a choice of speedometer to look at. One is small and digital. The other is circular and huge. Richard Porter, the man behind the Sniff Petrol website and the chap who writes the only jokes that ever actually work on *Top Gear*, claimed that he'd measured it . . . and it was bigger than his face. That would be true even if he were an elephant.

As you can tell, there is much I like about this new car. Like its predecessor, it pays homage to the original Mini, and has a genuinely classless feel as a result, but it's loaded up with all sorts of gimmickry, too, which gives it a modern, funky feel. The only thing I really didn't like about the look of the Cooper S I tried was the power bulge on the bonnet, which doesn't actually do anything. Though I understand it will in future, suggesting that a more powerful engine is planned.

For now, the most powerful engine you can have is the 1.6 turbo – pretty much the same engine that's fitted to Peugeot's lacklustre 207. But in the Mini it's great. Torquey when you can't be bothered to change gear and zingy when you can. It's surprisingly economical as well. The old Cooper S would do 32 mpg. This manages 40.

The only drawback is that there's so much power the front wheels get all squirmy when you push too hard out of a bend. It's no big deal, but I wish it wasn't there. It means you need two hands on the wheel and that's hard when you've just decided purple's all wrong and Virgin is playing another two hours of back-to-back ads for stuff you don't want.

I also grew rather tired of the traction control, which if it were human would be king of the Health and Safety Executive, a high visibility control freak whose job was to make sure you never tripped over anything. Mostly, I turned it off.

Then on again. I must also say while I'm being negative that the rear legroom is suitable only for amputees and the boot is not even big enough for a mouse's pants. And some of the stuff on the new model is just downright irritating.

You have to put the key fob in a slot before you press the starter button, but the slot is behind the steering wheel where it cannot be seen. And even when you're fully familiar with the whereabouts of all the controls they still cannot be found. Every single time I wanted to lower the window I ended up lowering the temperature by mistake. Although this did mean I could spend the next hour putting it up and down and then up again until it was just wrong.

The biggest drawback with this car, though, is the price. If you want a car of this type, a not very commodious small city car that's fun to behold and zesty to drive, the Suzuki Swift Sport is yours for £11,499. The Mini Cooper S is a whopping £15,995. And if you go a bit mad with the options list you can easily be faced with a bill for more than £20,000. That's way too much.

As a result, I'd probably buy the Suzuki. And then, after five minutes, wish I had the Mini instead.

Sunday 18 February 2007

I saved a little girl's life in this

Bentley Continental GTC

Last year in Britain, slightly more than 5 million people died. Over the course of my lifetime 250 million people have died. And yet it was only last week that I saw my first dead body.

It was lying at the side of a country road near Johannesburg, one of the most dangerous and lawless cities on earth, so initially I thought it had been shot. But then, a few hundred feet down the road, I passed a big Suzuki motorbike, all battered and broken, and just as dead as its owner.

Of course there was no way of knowing the man was dead. He was surrounded by a thousand emergency vehicles and several million paramedics. But there was something about the way they moved, a lack of urgency, that gave the game away. And it was all confirmed two hours later when I drove back down the same stretch of road. Because the big broken bike had gone. The ambulances and police cars had gone. And all bar one of the personnel had gone. But weirdly the body was still there. I haven't been able to get the image out of my head since. Who was he? What had he said to his wife that morning as he'd put on his leathers and gone outside to get on his big bike? What was he planning to do later that day? Or at work the following week? Had he planned a holiday this year? What would his kids do now, without a dad?

One minute he's a human being thundering down a lovely road in an area known, ironically, as the Cradle of Humankind. The next he's meat, a nuisance, a handful of ticks and crosses in a police investigator's report.

Doubtless his wife will have spent the time since wailing and weeping and wondering why the bloody hell he'd gone and got himself a motorbike. And I'm with her. Why indeed?

You get hit by lightning and it's bad luck. You die in a car accident and it's one of those things. You have to drive to get about and people die while driving. You have an accident at work and it's the same story. You get shot by a robber and even then you can still see the logic: 'If I steal your wallet and then kill you, I stand less chance of being caught.' But dying in a motorbike accident seems so completely futile. I know they're a thrill. I know it gives you a buzz to hurtle down a country lane on a sunny day while encased entirely in leather. I know all that. But one tiny mistake, which might have nothing to do with you, and you're a memory, you're a smudge in the hedgerow. You're playing a lottery where the prizes are small and the cost of failure is just gigantic. And I don't get that.

In Britain bikes account for just 1 per cent of all road transport. Yet they account for nearly 20 per cent of all fatalities. Of course, dead bikers do provide a valuable public service in that people with fatal diseases can have new eyes and fresh spleens, but having seen the accident in South Africa last week, I think we could go further. Instead of taking the body away, why not just leave it in place?

All of us fear death, but when you actually see it, you become even more determined to give it a wide berth.

After seeing a body for the first time I have genuinely slowed down a bit. Coming home from London the other night I pulled out to overtake when I was 98 per cent certain the road ahead was clear. But then an image of that poor man's twisted head popped into my head and I abandoned the manoeuvre before it had really begun.

Yesterday, while driving into my local town, a mother was walking down the pavement with a little girl of three or four. Normally I'd have slowed and covered the brake in case the

toddler leapt into the road, but after my South African experience, I damn nearly stopped.

And I can't tell you how that felt when, moments later, the
little girl did indeed run into the road. That dead biker, then,
6,000 miles away in Johannesburg, had unwittingly saved the life
of a little girl in England.

You may think this all a bit too convenient. A bit too editorial.
But it happened. I really was thinking of the dead man, and
braking when the girl ran out. If I'd been doing thirty I'd have
hit her. But I was doing ten, maybe less. So I didn't. Anyway,
onwards and upwards to the car I was driving that day. The
Bentley Continental GTC, which of course is a drop-top version
of a car I don't like very much.

The problem is simple. I know that beneath that two-door
body and those chromed organ-stop ventilation controls the
Continental is a Volkswagen Phacton. And even though the two
cars feel markedly different, I can never really get that thought
out of my head.

It's the same story with my Bang & Olufsen phone. Electronically it's a Samsung, but I paid a billion pounds for all that style and
design, and I'm sorry, every time I use it I feel a bit of a berk.

But the drop-top Continental is different. Because there's no
roof the wind blows away any sense that you're in a Phaeton. It
really does feel completely different, and then there's the noise.
My God. What a wonderful sound. It's a sort of mellow bellow.
I've never heard it in the coupé before, but in the soft top it's
there all the time, sticking its tentacles into your ears and giving
you a nice warm rinse.

Do not, however, imagine that this is some kind of sports
car. It isn't. Bentley, as Ettore Bugatti once observed, makes very
fast lorries. The Continental GTC has more in common with
a Scania than a Ferrari, and that holds true even when you push
the sport button. This just makes everything less comfortable, so
I quickly turned it off again.

You waft in this car. Oh, it'll waft pretty quickly, thanks to that sonorous twin-turbo W12, but there's no satisfaction from taking a nice little left–right switchback and hitting the apexes just right. In fact you feel a bit silly.

Better to kick back and cruise. Select the precise sort of sound you want from the hi-fi, snuggle into the infinitely adjustable seat . . . and relax. It is a very, very nice way of covering miles.

Like falling asleep in the bath and waking up somewhere else. That said, there are a few issues that drove me mad. The boot opens and closes electrically. And extremely slowly. And if it touches the top of your suitcase on its way down, and it will because there's the tonneau cover in there as well, it'll crawl back up to the top again. People have arms, Bentley. And we don't mind using them. Likewise, if you want to let someone in the back, the front seats slide forward as though they're being pulled along by a koala. And while it may have seemed like a good idea when the computer geek said the radio could present drivers with a choice of all the stations in range, it wasn't. Because the other morning it took twenty minutes to find Radio 2.

The worst thing about this car, though, is hard to put my finger on. Maybe it's the lack of sportiness. Maybe it's the size. Maybe it's the footballer ostentation or the pale blue paintwork that had been teamed with a cream leather interior.

I don't know. But I do know this. All the time I was behind the wheel I was slightly terrified other road users might think it was mine.

Sunday 4 March 2007

Mad, bad and utterly wonderful to know

Lamborghini Murciélago LP640

An alarming e-mail has just arrived from the public relations department at Honda. It says I recently test drove the new Legend and wonders when my review might appear in *The Sunday Times*.

This is all frightfully embarrassing because I can't recall a single thing about it. It was a car. It came to my house. I drove it for a week. And then it was taken away. I remember it in the same way that I remember a single childhood sneeze – i.e., I don't remember it at all.

My wife says I came back from one drive in it moaning about the positioning of the headlamp switch, but she can't remember what was wrong with it, or why we'd become so starved of normal conversation that I'd even brought it up.

It must, therefore, be an ideal car for those who've had Vauxhall Corsas all their lives and have now won the pools. You can continue to demonstrate your complete lack of interest in all things motoring with the more expensive and presumably larger Legend – and it will not annoy you in any way, except perhaps for the headlamp switch.

Although we can't be sure about that.

What I can be sure about is that the Legend is not alone. I've just been through my diary and it seems there are hundreds of other cars that have left no stain on my memory banks at all.

Only last week, while preparing a *Top Gear* item on affordable hatchbacks, I had to say to a researcher: 'What is my opinion of the Renault Clio?' Happily, from his point of view, an archive of road tests on Times Online was able to provide an answer.

But now, a week on, I'm afraid it's gone again. I either liked it very much, or I hated it. And I'm damned if I can remember which.

Then you have the Ford Galaxy. Apparently, I drove one two months ago, for seven days, and all I can recall is that it had stupidly hard seats. Engine? Space? Price?

Sorry. It's all a blank.

Strangely, when I first started writing about cars – or carts as they were called back then – I never forgot a thing. What's more, I can still recall the 'feel' of the engine cut-out switch in the Fiat Regata ES, and the exact lilac colour of the front seats in the Renault Fuego turbo.

So why can't I remember modern cars? Well, put simply, they don't have lilac seats or pointless cut-out switches. Many, I'm afraid to say, are nothing more than white goods.

If you go back to a time when buyers could choose between a Golf GTI and a Ford Escort RS2000, the differences between them were huge. Rear-wheel drive versus front-wheel drive. Carburettor versus fuel injection. Hatchback versus saloon. Tennis racket headrest inserts – I even remember that – versus the golf ball gearknob.

Now, though, if you step from the current Golf GTI into, say, a hot Renault Mégane, it's no longer like moving through a wormhole in the space-time continuum. The only way you'll find any differences at all is by burrowing into the brochures and examining the pricing of extras. This is not an interesting way of passing the time. My worry is that if car makers don't start putting a bit of soul and flair and engineering panache back into their cars – and I'm excluding Alfa Romeo and Citroën from this, because they do – pretty soon, motoring will cease to be something that's fun.

And when that happens, you'll not be comparing Volkswagens with Renaults. You'll be comparing 'the car' with 'public transport'. And as often as not, you'll find that 'public transport' is cheaper and more convenient.

I remarked recently in these pages that a VW Golf GT had failed to make the journey from London to Cornwall anything more than a chore. It didn't soothe, or excite, or do any of the things that a car must do if it's to be something more than a personal transportation module.

And now we have the Honda Legend, a car so forgettable I can't remember a single thing about it. Why use that for the drive into London when the train is faster, you don't have to park it, you don't have to pay a congestion charge, and you can while away the journey with your nose in *Private Eye*?

What's more, the train might crash, which is a better foundation on which to build a conversation with your wife that night than the positioning of your Honda's headlamp switch.

This brings us, of course, to the curious scissor door of the Lamborghini Murciélago LP640 – a car some of you may remember was featured on *Top Gear* recently.

Unfortunately, a monstrous pressure on time that week meant the review was rather truncated, so I'd like to fill in the gaps here.

It is an astonishing car, this. Fitted with an enlarged 6.5 litre V12 engine, it develops a massive 495 carbon dioxides and that means the top speed is 211 mph. On the short *Top Gear* runway, I had it up to an indicated 207, which is faster than any other car has managed.

So yes, the power and the noise that goes with it mean you are never likely to forget even the shortest drive. That's good. But the main reason this car is so memorable comes when you get to a corner.

It's fitted with a four-wheel-drive system that feeds the power to whichever axle is best able to use it. Fine, but it's such a dim-witted set-up that you're usually going backwards before it's noticed the rear has lost traction and that it might be a good idea to shove some oomph up front.

Or, it decides that the rear could well lose traction due to the angle of the steering wheel and the speed, and feeds most of the power to the front. And any attempt to unstick the back with a boot full of power just means more and more understeer. I couldn't help wondering what this car might be like if it had a basic, rear-drive set-up. Lighter, for sure, and therefore faster too. Yes, in the rain there might be a smidgeon less grip but, to balance that, it would be a lot more predictable. Better, in other words.

Audi, which has owned Lamborghini for nine years now, has tried to make the cars less wild and mad. You can see that in the styling, and in the headroom, but this handling quirk means it's still far too much of a handful to be taken seriously as a driver's car.

And that's wonderful. Ferrari makes drivers' cars, machines for the terminally earnest. Lambo should be making stuff that puts a smile on your face, even when it's standing still.

Even though I have ordered a Gallardo Spyder, I'm the first to admit it's not quite as good as an F430 round a track. It's less delicate. Less poised. But as a car, a mad, expensive, preposterous waste of money, the sheer force of its personality knocks the techno-Ferrari into a cocked hat.

This is why I still love the LP640. It's flawed. It's silly. It's got a four-wheel-drive system that doesn't really work, a sat nav screen that's been put in place with hammers, and a steering wheel that's coated in what appears to be a black version of *Top Gear* dog. Technically, it's not even as good, I should imagine, as the new Honda Legend. But when it comes to memorable times, do you opt for dinner with a chartered accountant or Lemmy out of Motörhead?

Lamborghini is at the cutting edge of everything that makes cars interesting and exciting and wonderful. And we have to love it for that.

Sunday 11 March 2007

Foot down and mirror, signal, painkiller

Fiat Panda

A little while back I tested a bog-standard Fiat Panda and while it was slower than a real panda, it was also a damn sight cheaper to buy or run. So on balance, I liked it very much.

Since then, though, a couple of things have caused me to look once again at those initial findings. First of all James May, my colleague from *Top Gear*, has bought one, which means there must be something wrong with it, and second, I know what that something is.

Yes, the Panda is very good in town and very good, too, in snow and ice. It is also a great deal of fun on small rural back roads, because even if something does turn out to be coming the other way, there is always room to squeeze between it and the hedgerow.

But the Panda is a very small car, which means it has a very small engine, which means it is absolutely hopeless on the motorway. As hopeless as I would be on the men's downhill course at Klosters.

Driving an underpowered car on the motorway is one of the most dangerous things a man can do. It's up there with sticking your middle finger in the bottom of a sleeping tiger. It's very nearly as dangerous as driving through Alabama with 'Hillary for President' written on the side of your car.

The problem is simple. You come up behind a truck that is doing 50 mph in the middle lane. So you think you will simply pull out and overtake. You therefore indicate, wait for a gap in the stream of traffic to your right and ease out.

Textbook stuff. Worthy of a Mr Tufty safe driving award from PC McGarret No 452. Except you're in for a shock because although you have your foot welded to the floor and you're in third gear and the little engine is screaming itself to death, you are not doing what a scientist would call 'accelerating'.

And now the car in the outside lane that was a speck in your rear-view mirror is leaving thick black lines all over the road as the driver desperately tries to avoid slamming into the back of the 'effing a★★★hole' that pulled into his lane at 50 mph . . . and then failed to go any faster.

You're terrified that at any second it will slam into your tailgate, and this is doubly worrying when you're in a Fiat Panda because the tailgate in question is only 4 in abaft of your most precious and vital organs.

I use this as a general rule of thumb. If a car has less than 100 horsepower, it is never safe to pull into the outside lane if there is a car in sight . . . even if it's three miles away. If a car has less than sixty horsepower, it is never safe to pull into the outside lane at all.

Sixty horsepower was fine in the days when cars had four wheels and a seat but now the average small car has so much safety equipment and so many luxury goods nailed to its dash-board that it weighs more than Bolivia. And to move a country, you need more than sixty horses. A lot more.

As you may know, I'm not well disposed to the idea of governments banning things, except for beards and ginger hair and butter beans and Scotsmen sitting in Westminster and caravans and any talk of global warming by people who don't know what they're on about and the Toyota Prius and books with no plot and costume dramas on ITV and anything with Jade Goody in it and Ken bloody Livingstone, but the only thing that stops me from banning the Fiat Panda from the outside lane of a motorway is that May would become even later for his call times on *Top Gear*.

Actually, there's another reason. Fiat has just brought out a more peppy version of its lovable little car that has – wait for it – a dizzying 100 horsepower. That's about a fifth of what I reckon is necessary to make progress these days, but hey, it's a step in the right direction.

A 100 horsepower Panda should, in theory, be the perfect car. As cheeky and as much fun as its less powerful brothers. But useable on the motorway and not burdened with the ponderous May association.

It looks fab, too, with all sorts of sporty chicken wire grilles and zoomy lights. If it were a dog, it would have patches and cockeyed ears and it would whiz round your mother's ankles whenever she came to stay and make a point of sticking its nose in the vicar's crotch. But nobody else's. If it were a dog, you'd like it a lot.

But it isn't a dog. It's a car and it's good at that, too, easily swallowing two children into the back and, thanks to its boxy body, still having a decent-sized boot. I bet you could get an ironing board in there if you were determined enough.

So snow, ice, the school run, the motorway, town centres, parking, flash dinner parties, the station run of a morning. The little Fiat can take all these things in its stride and still be suitable for the family man who likes to spend his weekends doing extreme ironing. So, as a result, the specialist motoring press has been raving about this car.

Thinking that it might actually be Jesus with alloy wheels, I borrowed one. And I'm sorry but I pretty much hated it.

The problem is that the original, proper, normal Fiat Panda was conceived as a local car for local people. It was designed to be as cheap as possible and it is: £7,000 for a car that has, give or take, just as many parts as a £21,000 VW Golf is little short of remarkable. And it's not like it was made by jungle people who were brought up on *What Ox* magazine either.

The trouble is that by sticking a 1.4 litre engine under the bonnet, you are now paying £10,000 for a £7,000 car. And it shows.

Yes, it's faster. Yes, it corners well. And yes, it rides more smoothly than you might imagine, too, but there is almost no refinement at all. It's like putting a Saturn V rocket in your vacuum cleaner. Sure, you will get the housework done more quickly but there will be some issues with noise, vibration and harshness.

And so it goes in the hot Panda. The engine gave me a headache, and because it's pretty loud I had to turn the stereo up, and that made my headache worse. So then I had to slow down, and then what's the point of all that extra power?

They say it will do 115 mph, and I dare say that's right, but achieving this speed is hard – there aren't enough Nurofen in the world and it's not desirable anyway because the Panda is so small it feels like you're the food and it's the hermetically sealed bag.

The windscreen is right there, in front of your nose. The back window is right there, touching the back of your head, and the deep side windows complete the picture with your peripheral vision. So when you're doing 90 mph it feels like you're doing 90 mph . . . without the benefit of a car around you. That's quite disturbing, especially when you have the headache from hell.

I suppose if I were a well-off youth after a stylish urban runaround, and I never needed to make a long journey, the 100 horsepower Panda might make some kind of sense. But for anyone else, I'm afraid it's time to draw pretty much the same wearisome conclusion that I seem to draw with all small car tests these days. You're better off with the Suzuki Swift Sport.

Sunday 18 March 2007

Unlikely, but it's a ray of sunshine

Ford Focus CC-3

As I write, the Grand National has just been run in a bath of warm sunshine, Chelsea have beaten Blackburn in temperatures better suited to cooking meat, and the newspapers are filled with gloating pictures of people being all wet and soggy in the Costas.

Britain, we're told, is hotter than Athens. Which isn't so much a piece of news as a yah boo sucks to the poor bastards who've shelled out for an Easter holiday in the Med.

I think this is a rather mean trait, especially since I recently spent two weeks in Barbados under a dome of grey skies and light drizzle. 'We've never known anything like it,' said the locals, as though that might make us feel better. The *Daily Telegraph* certainly didn't, with endless shots of pretty young girls frolicking in the daffodils back home. The captions didn't say, 'Hey w****** in the Caribbean. How do you feel now?'. But that was the inference.

We all want a holiday once in a while – I can't see what's wrong with that: it's not paedophilia – and all we want from our holiday is a bit of sunshine. It's not much to ask; a bit of skin cancer to go with your chablis. So why should those at home be encouraged to laugh if it's grey and miserable?

Oh, I'm long past the age when I care two hoots about a tan. In the past I'd stake myself out on a day bed and lie there blinking the sweat out of my eyes and rubbing Mazola into my secret gentleman's areas. This would make me look rich when I got home. But by the age of thirty-seven I'd realised that most of my hard-earned brownness would be left in a series of unpleasant flakes on the homeward-bound aeroplane seat.

So I'd arrive back at Heathrow with one completely see-through layer of skin straining to stop my internal organs sploshing all over the luggage carousel. And I'd be in screaming agony because I always always always forgot to put sun cream on the top of my feet. So they looked like championship salamis.

And it got worse when my hair started to recede, because then my afro was no longer able to protect the top of my head. The result was that every morning my pillow was covered in what can only be described as a *Guardian* reader's lunch.

That's why I gave up sunbathing and decided to spend my time under a hat, a tree and a roof. It shouldn't really matter, therefore, that I had lousy weather in the Caribbean this year. And yet it did. Sunshine, whether I'm in it or indoors looking at it, lifts my world and my spirits. I think more clearly, I write more coherently. I feel better. A while back some American doctor, who wanted some money, came up with the concept of seasonal affective disorder, or Sad. You may think it's idiotic, suggesting that people get depressed if they don't see the sun for long periods. You may argue it's just an excuse for Scottish miserabilism.

But genetically I think I may be 98 per cent bear, with a sprinkling of hedgehog. All I know is that a bougainvillea bush on a grey day is just another plant. In the sunshine it can take my breath away. A well-lit bougainvillea can even make Greece look civilised. Similarly, a ski resort in the cloud is one of the ugliest places on earth. And yet in the sunshine it can be one of the most beautiful.

My office window here at my holiday cottage overlooks the sea, which for most of the year is a big wobbly grey thing from which I pull lobsters. On a sunny day, however, like today, it's a shimmering, glinting, dazzling, inviting navy blue mass of possibilities. It makes me want to run about in the fields singing.

Happily, due to circumstances beyond our control, Britain is becoming warmer and more sunny, but even now you can never bank on it. Just because you go to bed on a Friday under the dying ambers of a vivid scarlet sun doesn't mean it'll be there again in the morning. Red sky at night . . . who knows? That's why I've always argued you should only plan a barbecue when it's raining. This dramatically increases your chances of it being sunny when the charcoal reaches its correct operating temperature. And on the road, what you need is a convertible car. Yes, I know a convertible is always going to be heavier than the saloon or hatchback on which it's based because it needs underfloor beams to replace strength lost when the roof was removed. And yes, I know that because of the weight, and the loss of structural rigidity, a convertible will never handle or accelerate quite as well as a normal car. But who cares when the sunlight is flashing its radioactive Morse code through the overhanging trees, and the morning dew is picked out in the overnight cobwebs and you have an excuse for putting on your Aviators and listening to some Don Henley.

This brings me on to the Ford Focus CC, which like most of the mid-range convertibles these days has a metal roof that folds electrically into the boot. On paper this sounds good. It means that when you're driving with the roof up it's as quiet and as refined as a normal saloon. And when it's parked the roof cannot be slashed by vandals.

There are, however, some drawbacks. In order to fit into the boot a roof that is big enough to shield four adults the rear end must be as big as an aircraft carrier. You only need look at Peugeot's effort to see the ugliness that can result.

What's more, you are bound to end up with very little space for rear passengers, and when the roof is down almost no boot space at all.

At first it looks like the Ford suffers from all these problems and more. The extra weight, thanks to all the ironmongery, means the 1.6 litre version will barely move. Unless you want a diesel, you really have to go for the 2 litre, and even this struggles. And despite the best efforts of Ford's chassis engineers, who are some of the best in the business at the moment, it's not what you'd call a sprightly point-and-squirt car. It feels like you're driving around in Al Gore.

So yes, you get the vandal-proof roof but the price you pay is limited rear space, a small boot, a dramatic loss of performance and some suet in the handling mix. And yet, after a few days I began to like this car very much. Yes, it has the bulbous rear end, but actually when you stop and look at it, as a whole, you have to admit it's a very elegant car. I don't know why but it puts me in mind of a Riva speedboat parked in Portofino with an Agnelli at the wheel. It has a Sixties playboy look somehow.

And while it may not be the best handling car in the world, it rides beautifully, soaking up the worst bumps and potholes without a murmur of complaint. In short, it's tremendously comfortable.

Of course, at this point you may be saying that you don't care, because it's still only a Ford Focus. True enough, but it's built in Italy by the people who styled it – Pininfarina – and it's available with a range of colours both inside and out that are bound to appeal.

Will it go wrong? Well, I've had one of the old Focuses for six years and it's still as tight and reliable as the day I bought it. So no, I don't think so.

It isn't what I was expecting, the Focus CC. I thought it'd be an updated version of the old Escort cabrio, a molten banana with an Essex girl at the wheel. But it isn't. It's a refined, elegant, comfortable and remarkably well priced tool that's ideal for those of us who are 98 per cent motorist and 2 per cent hedgehog.

Sunday 22 April 2007

Trying sooo hard not to be a hatchback

Nissan Qashqai 2.0 Tekna (4x4)

As you may know, I do not like stretched limousines very much. And nor do I care much about the wellbeing of the planet. It's big and old enough to be able to look after itself. So I was not best pleased last week when the BBC announced that I was to be picked up at Los Angeles airport in something called an eco limo.

Horrible visions kept me awake and sweating on the flight. It'd be an elongated Prius with a nasal George Monbiot at the wheel. Or a G-Wiz with a trailer full of wheat juice. Or a tandem with Bill Oddie at the front and a disturbingly empty saddle at the back.

I needn't have worried, though, because while California is embracing all aspects of the green revolution, it seems it really hasn't got the hang of a nuclear-free fairtrade peace limo.

It was a Ford Excursion, the largest SUV made by Ford. It was so big, in fact, that it was parked outside terminals one, two and three. And the back was picking up someone else . . . in San Francisco.

This is a car that weighs more than most people's houses, and the eco version weighs even more because they've taken out the petrol engine and replaced it with the same diesel motor that's used to move the space shuttle to its launch pad. When it chugged into life you could see people at the airport diving for the earthquake shelters.

No matter, emblazoned down the side was a green sign saying it was an eco limo, and in the back were certificates from the state of California, commending the vehicle's owners for their responsible attitude towards Mother Earth.

The driver, a chap we shall call Swampy Bin Laden, was very proud of his car; so proud that he launched immediately into a not very scientific lecture about the benefits and origins of the fuel he was using. 'It's from a bio-plant,' he beamed. To hammer the point home, he'd placed some stickers in the back window that said: 'This vehicle runs on foreign oil.' Only the word 'foreign' had been crossed out and replaced with the word 'vegetable'.

I asked him if he would mind using British oil, expecting that this might have him stumped. 'Yessir, I would,' he replied. 'But,' I said, 'you don't mind leaving all the world's normal oil in the ground and running your car on what could be an African's lunch?' Bzzz went his head. Then he twitched a bit. For a while he looked a bit like a sci-fi robot that had been given conflicting orders.

Other motorists, however, thought he might be the second coming. At every set of lights they'd pull up alongside and wave their arms about, frantically pointing to the back of the car as though it might be on fire. But no. They simply wanted to know as much as possible about bio-plants before the lights turned as green as they hoped to be.

'It runs real good,' said Swampy, which was a lie. It had the smoothness of a Bulgarian road drill and the volume of a swimming pool full of kids. And every time he wanted to make it move he had to plant his foot deep into the carpet. 'Yeah. And I'm getting sixteen to the gallon,' he'd add. I seriously doubt that. Not with the air-conditioning on full blast and his shoe in the engine bay.

Swampy may have thought he was doing his bit for the world, sticking a lentil into the side of George Bush. But the truth was that every time he started that engine half the bougainvillea bushes in LA County withered and died.

An eco limo cannot be. It's like a torpedo that's built to be harmless or an alcohol-free beer. It has no point. It is as useless as a Jamaican pathologist. One element of the name will always cancel out the other. If you want to be green, you can't tool around town in a limo. And if you want a limo, you are on a hen night in Bradford and the only green element of that is what comes out of your stomach at four in the morning when you're on your hands and knees in a shop doorway.

Now, though, I'm back from the land of the free and the home of the confused and am behind the wheel of a Nissan Kumquat, which offers another solution to the problem of making an eco-friendly four-wheel-drive car. Cleverly, it doesn't have four-wheel drive.

Oh, it looks like a four-wheel drive, which means other road users will think you've just come back from a kayaking expedition up the Zambezi. And yes, it's named after an Iranian tribe and means, literally, 'Your marines are rubbish'. But don't be fooled because the base models at least are just run-of-the-mill, two-wheel-drive five-seater hatchbacks with plastic kneepads.

Brilliant. You can't drive it across a field or through a puddle but it looks like an SUV, which means you must bathe in a sea of hate from the world's liberal democrats every time you go anywhere. That sounds like lose lose.

It'd be like walking into a crowd with a false beard and a back-pack full of alarm clocks and then shouting: 'Only kidding.' That's why I chose to test the top-of-the-range model, which does have four-wheel drive. This is like walking into a crowd with a backpack full of explosives and then actually exploding.

Of course you might say at this point that you don't need a four-wheel-drive car, and that you'd rather just have a normal Nissan hatch. Tough, I'm afraid, since Nissan doesn't actually make a normal hatchback any more. The Kumquat, it says, is the future. And it's not a warped Japanese idea of the future either. It was designed in Paddington and engineered in

Bedfordshire. It really is as British as a plate of Chinese chicken, except of course Nissan these days is French.

Anyway, the problem with making a family hatch butch is that it becomes bigger and therefore harder to park. And heavier, too, which means less oomph and more frequent trips to the pumps. The downsides seem big on paper but in reality all is surprisingly good.

The Kumquat rides smoothly, thanks to independent suspension, and if a sensor detects that you may have been too exuberant with the throttle, some of the power is sent to the back wheels. Engine-wise, I tried both the turbodiesel, which was fine, and the 2 litre petrol, which was perfectly all right.

To drive, then, it's good. And it's a nice place to be as well. Sure, you don't get three rows of seats or a back bench that swivels or revolves or turns into an ice breaker, and at first that's disappointing. But then you don't get these things in a Ford Focus either and that's what the Kumquat – despite appearances – is up against.

The Ford, of course, is nicer to drive – with a lower centre of gravity it has to be, and it's easier to park as well. And cheaper. And more roomy in the back. And is the one I'd buy.

But I sort of get the Kumquat. For all its abilities, and there are many, the Focus is a bit boring. The Nissan isn't. It gives you a sense of wellbeing, a sense that while you may live in a normal house with two normal children, at least the car you use makes you look a little bit interesting.

What's more, if anyone does come up at the lights and ask what on earth you're driving, and what kind of gas mileage you get you can just take a leaf out of Swampy Bin Laden's book. And lie.

Sunday 29 April 2007

A bad attack of the Melvyn Braggs

Audi S3

Last week I was in Isachsen, a remote settlement high in the Arctic. It's so far north that anyone who lives there would be well within their rights to call the Inuit of Greenland a bunch of southern poofs.

Except no one lives there. It was created in 1948 as a US cold war 'weather station', a place where 'meteorologists' could keep their eye on any unpleasantness coming over the pole from the Soviet bloc. But then, one day twenty-nine years ago, the scientists just upped sticks and left.

Today it is easily the most godforsaken place on earth. Already listed as having the worst weather in Canada, the motley collection of buildings stands alone and deserted. Doors bang forlornly in the wind. Vast tundra buggies – caravans on wheels taken from monster trucks – stand in snow up to the midriff. And scattered around are the vehicles we saw in *Ice Station Zebra*, a movie that was made here.

Inside, newspapers from the Seventies are left open, indicating precisely what day the men left. Manuals and charts remain pinned to the walls. The larder is stacked with food, all of which was 'best before Gorbachev'. Spooky is the word for it. But bleak would do as well, because it's all coated in a foot-thick veneer of snow. You walk into the dining room and everything, the tables, the chairs, the cutlery and cookers, is discernible only from its outline in the untouched smooth white blanket.

Sadly, however, the station's runway was not as the scientists had left it. Wind and time had taken their toll on the surface. And the potholes that had resulted had become clamping points for the sheet of industrial-strength weather that this place has endured over the years. Get out of the wind, in May, and it'll be about minus seventeen.

Plainly I needed to get out of this place, but unless that runway could be cleared I wasn't going anywhere.

In one of the sheds I found a selection of diggers and pickup trucks from the 1970s, which like the chairs and the beds were entombed in what appeared to be an impregnable fortress of snow and ice. You would have bet your eyes and your liver that none could ever be started.

But happily, because I'm a lucky sort of soul, I happened to be travelling with an Icelandic mechanic called Halli. And Halli wasn't so sure. So, armed only with a tin of start gas and the news that the keys were still in the ignition, he set about a sorry-looking Komatsu WA180 while I trudged off to look for Ernest Borgnine's frozen corpse.

Fifteen minutes later I could scarcely believe my ears, because what I was hearing, 400 miles from anything that could even laughably be called a road, on a lifeless island a spit from the North Pole, was the sound of a diesel engine.

Now Halli was not the sharpest knife in the cutlery drawer. I can't see that he'd ever be invited on *In Our Time*. I feel sure that if you asked him to define human thought from a left-bank perspective he'd be a bit stuck. In short, you probably wouldn't have him round for dinner.

And yet he has been blessed with a gift. Halli can mend stuff. He can get your iPod to work when it's minus twenty-five. He can weld up a fuel tank using nothing but a lightning conductor and three car batteries. You can lie him in the snow and get him to fix the air locker on a leaking differential and he'll find it no more difficult than turning on a light switch.

I saw those iced-up diggers and thought 'not a chance'. He saw them and saw only an opportunity.

And what worries me here is that he's part of a dying breed. When the chain comes off my son's bicycle he can no more put it on again than he could perform a heart transplant on a wasp. What's the point? Such skills mean he'll either wind up in Kwik-Fit or working as an engineer for £2.50 a year.

Best he brushes up on his Voltaire and then there's a chance he'll end up with Melvyn on the radio talking about the Poincaré Conjecture. That will earn him much respect and lots of dizzy socialist women will want to sleep with him.

But the fact of the matter is this. Melvyn Bragg could not start a Komatsu digger that had sat in an ice coffin for twenty-nine years. And Halli the Icelander could. So who's the daddy now?

I read last week that children must be taught in schools how to be black. And that if this isn't possible they must be made to go on school sharing exercises to other educational establishments, where everyone is a Muslim. That's all well and good, but wouldn't it be better if the teachers showed them how to mend a bicycle and how to refit the belt on a front-loading washing machine?

I've just realised that my twelve-year-old daughter cannot wire a plug. So how's she going to get by if she ever finds herself at a remote Arctic weather station with a blocked runway and she doesn't have an all purpose Halli-tool with her? She'll be up a gum tree.

Strangely, this brings me neatly on to the Audi S3, which is an Audi A3 that's been to the tanning salon and, like Melvyn, the hairdresser.

What you have, then, is an A3 with huge 18 in wheels, a chin spoiler with stubble, and a luxuriant hairpiece on the roof. Inside they've really gone to town, giving the pedals and the gearlever an aluminium effect.

Of course this new look only works if the car has also been to the gym, and it has. So under the bonnet there's the 2 litre turbo engine from a Golf GTI. Only instead of the 197 bhp you get from the VW, the S3 churns out a simply staggering 261 bhp. Good job you're given four-wheel drive.

On paper, then, this looks like a pretty good car. Lots of power, 0–60 in 5.7 seconds, a price tag of £27,000. And because Audi makes its cars, in my opinion, more beautifully than any other automobile firm in the western world, there's very little chance that the children of Melvyn will be left at the side of the road, unwilling and unable even to open the bonnet.

Unfortunately, though, all is not sweetness and light. The biggest problem for me is the engine. It's not very nice. It's harsh when you rev it, and there's far too much turbo lag when you don't.

And it's not like they were stuck for something thrusty and powerful to give this sporty car some extra oomph. Why didn't they go for the V6 currently used in the Golf R32? And even more strangely, why not the exquisite, light and compact V8 from the RS4?

So the engine's wrong, along with the feel of the thing when you're driving it.

Unusually for an Audi it rides quite well most of the time and is therefore a comfortable companion, but when you push it, and that's surely the point of a car with stiffened springs and fat wheels, it feels woolly and cumbersome.

I'd like, at this point, to advise you all to hold off until the much talked about RS3 comes onto the market. But I'm reliably informed that despite much speculation in the motoring press, and even a handful of spy pictures, no such thing will be launched until after the all-new A3 is introduced, two years from now.

So if you want a sporty, reliable, well-made car for around £27,000 what are your choices? There's the hideous Mercedes C-class coupé or the bread van BMW calls a 1-series. Or, in the true tradition of multiple choice, c) none of the above.

What I'd do is save nearly £3,000 and buy the Golf R32,

which has the same four-wheel-drive system as the Audi but comes with a much better V6 engine.

It's also a Volkswagen, and as Woody Allen showed us in his 1973 film *Sleeper*, they also start on the button having been abandoned for years.

Sunday 13 May 2007

Max power, mid cred

Vauxhall Corsa VXR

When you first spend a bit of face time with the new Corsa VXR you can't help thinking, 'God Almighty. Can Vauxhall never get anything right?'

It appears to have crashed into an out-of-town motorist accessory superstore and emerged on the other side with every single part attached to every single bit of its bodywork. There are spoilers, extra lamps, fat wheels, Philishave, Just For Men bits of aluminium-look plastic here and there, and sills like an American footballer's work garb.

This might have worked ten years ago when every super-market car park echoed on a Saturday night to the pulsating bass beat of the customising culture and *Max Power* was one of Britain's bestselling magazines. But today *Max Power*'s circulation is in freefall – down from 240,000 in 2003 to just 71,000 last year.

The trend for young people to fit exhausts like Kazakhstan pipelines and illuminate the underside of their cars with neon is over. Just as Vauxhall gets round to milking it. This is not the first time the British arm of General Motors has missed the boat. You remember the first Vectra. Designed in a rush by a man who was plainly going through a messy divorce, it had a bonnet, a place where people sat, a boot and an engine.

It would have been fine for the Terry and June company car rep who had no choice in the matter. But it came along just as the rep scene was dying, and Terry and June was affording us nothing more than a glimpse into the nation's 'ooh look, there's a black man' past. In fact we were in a coffee bar, experimenting with zinc-topped work surfaces and skinny lattes. And Vauxhall was still trying to sell us British Rail tea with wheels.

And now, just as everyone is going green, they're trying to sell us a Saturday night supermarket car park special. G force? Who cares. All the youth want today is a G-Wiz.

The thing is, though, and you can call me old-fashioned if you like but – ahem – I rather like the look of the new Corsa. Think of it as a council house at Christmas time.

Utterly vulgarised by a million plastic Santas and two zillion fairy lights. But it puts a smile on your face and what more could you ask than that?

I also like the interior. The seats are of a type I thought had gone west with the old Escort RS2000. They're big Recaros with lots of side bolster. Not easy to get in and out of, for sure, but once you're in place you aren't going anywhere. Even if you attempt a hairpin at 600 mph.

The rest of the interior is as insane as the exterior. Take the steering wheel. They've fitted a flat bit at the bottom and coated that in plastic, which is supposed to look like aluminium. At the top you get a marker to show you where straight ahead is. Then, at ten to two, you have knobbly bits, which is fine – it reminds you of the correct place to have your hands while driving. But you get similar knobbly bits at twenty to four.

The upshot is something that's no more circular than the trunk of a baobab tree. Let it slide through your hands after making a turn and you'll end up with a fistful of broken knuckles.

The idea is that you feel like Colin McRae before you've even turned the key. But what you're actually doing is trying to suppress a giggle. Because while all these race'n'rally add-on parts give the car a purposeful – if dated – appearance, you just know that the badge on the back says Vauxhall, which is bad, and Corsa, which is to motoring what Nicholas Witchell is to wrestling.

Every single Corsa I've ever driven has been terrible, with

wooden controls, asthmatic engines and nothing in either the price list or in the styling that made me want to sign on the dotted line. In a spoof advert for the Corsa, shown on the Sniff Petrol website, there was a picture of the little Vauxhall and underneath a line that said: 'Show the world you know nothing about cars.' Bang on.

It did, just, as a device for driving schools, but if I'd learnt to drive in a Corsa I'd have done one lesson and given up on the whole business of cars. The bus would have seemed a better option. Also, it was a cheap-to-insure starting point for the Max Power boys. But even they've moved on these days.

And let's be honest, Vauxhall hasn't. So the chances of the new Corsa's undersides being able to cash the cheques its body and steering wheel are writing are, frankly, zero.

Wrong. With a turbocharged 1.6 litre engine it will hit sixty from rest, without too much torque steer, in less than seven seconds. Keep churning away at the manly six-speed box and in fairly short order the needle will be nudging 140. That's fast for any hot hatch. For a small Vauxhall it's amazing.

Better still is the way it corners. The lifelessness of old is gone and in its place is a chassis that lets the tail drift when the limit is reached. It puts me in mind of an old Peugeot 205 GTi, and that's about the highest praise you can lavish on any car. Oh, and then there's the hill-hold device. When you arrive at a T junction on an incline and you take your foot off the clutch in a normal car you roll backwards. Not in the VXR you don't. It's held in place until you prod the throttle and then it sets off. In a town like Chipping Norton or Malvern or Harrogate this alone makes the Corsa worth a look.

Add reasonable rear seat space, a usable boot, and a ride that works well as long as you avoid the optional 18 in wheels, and things are looking good. In fact there's only one issue. While it may appear to be well priced – it's £15,625 – almost everything you might need is an option. Realistically, it's an £18,000 car, and that sounds like a lot until you remember that the Mini Cooper S, which is less practical, costs even more when it's fully loaded.

My conclusion then is simple. The Corsa is great. A bit vulgar perhaps – the steering wheel itself is right up there with Del Boy in his pina colada phase. But this aside, it's an enjoyable, charismatic car that's fun to drive, reasonably priced . . . and why am I bothering?

You don't want one, do you? I could have told you it cost 8p, ran on water and was made from solid gold. I could have said each car came with sixteen free Angelina Jolies and that the floor mats had been made from the pubic hair of Thai virgins. And you would still be yawning and wondering what restaurant AA Gill has savaged this week.

The fact of the matter is that Vauxhall has had it, really. And it's the same story with Ford. For the past seven years they've been trying to sell you a V6 Mondeo but you wouldn't pay any attention. You wanted an Audi, or a Lexus, or a BMW. Not a Mondeo, even though, pound for pound, the Ford was demonstrably and obviously better than whatever you ended up buying.

We're going to see the same sort of thing with this Corsa. It's really good and although it's too early to say whether it will be reliable, I bet you'll not even consider it and buy the Mini instead.

Vauxhall and Ford were part of the fabric of British life in the 1960s and 1970s. They were as entrenched in our psyche as British Rail, the National Union of Mineworkers and Terry Scott, each an institution that seemed to be immortal. It turned out not to be.

And unless someone can come up with a way of making the Ford and Vauxhall badges acceptable once more, they'll end up on the scrapheap as well.

Sunday 20 May 2007

Yes, it's a radical new concept . . . the boneshaker

Honda Civic Type R

You might fondly imagine that the drive outside my house is full to overflowing with all the latest cars, their tanks brimmed with fuel and the insurance paid. And you'd be right.

This week it looks like the long-term car park at Heathrow out there. Under the pergola is an Audi R8 that I'd very much like to drive, but I can't get it round my Lambo without driving over the herb garden. And I can't move the Lambo because it's blocked in by my Mercedes, which hasn't been used for two months and now won't start.

Round the back there's a Golf GTI which arrived for no reason that I can fathom, a Vauxhall Corsa, a spare Volvo XC90, an Aston Martin Vantage – in white, so that won't be going anywhere – and a perfectly hideous Mitsubishi people carrier of some kind.

But then the last Mitsubishi people carrier that came here turned out to be rather good so I'd like to take this new one for a spin, but I can't because it's blocked in by a Ford Ka that doesn't seem to belong to anyone.

In fact the only car I've been able to use these past few days has been the new Honda Civic Type R, and if you're a young man you're probably salivating with envy at this point.

The old Civic Type R was the car of choice for those who listen to their stereos with the bass on ten and the treble turned off altogether, people whose idea of facial hair is a faint earwig on their top lip.

Older people were surprised by its sudden popularity, but not me, simply because it is impossible to be surprised by anything the earwig faces do these days, from wearing their trousers in the manner of a Los Angeles inmate, to the Bacardi bruisers they buy for their girlfriends. Who say 'like' after every other word.

My daughter, who's a bona fide young person, has taken to wearing her school summer dress as though it's some kind of bushel, with the waistline around her chest and a belt around her bottom. And anyone who chooses to do this is plainly going to make an unusual choice when it comes to saying which car's cool and which car's not.

The old Civic Type R won favour not because it was the best hot hatchback but precisely because everyone's parents – me – were still harping on about the brilliance of the Golf GTI and how sad it was that Peugeot had gone off the boil.

But once the youth moved into Honda-land they found that, actually, the Civic had a number of things going for it. It was relatively cheap to insure – and thanks to a big Honda scene in Japan there were many performance and styling parts available over the internet.

There was something else, too. It was actually very good fun to drive. It wasn't the fastest car in the world but for the money there was very little else that could put such a huge smile on your face. The way its little engine revved, and revved willingly, to 8,250 was always a rare treat.

Even today there are global websites for owners of this pocket rocket. Every night young men are rushing back from the call centres where they work to offer and discover tasty titbits about their beloved Hondas. 'Kind of like, you know like' say the forums. Over and over again.

So that's why your kids are going to be interested this morning in what the new Civic Type R is like. You should maybe read this out to them. They may even grunt, or if you're really lucky, shrug.

Here goes then, and first of all it looks fantastic. When Honda first showed off the basic Civic a couple of years ago we were all stunned by the detailing. The triangular exhaust pipes, the door handles that appeared to have come from a 1950s fridge and of course the *Space: 1999* dashboard.

But then they put their new car on the road and oh dear. To save £1.50 they'd all been fitted with the wheels from a baby buggy. So you had this huge, super high-tech body with its art deco detailing sitting on the foundations of a Silver Cross pram. And there's nothing that says 'Hey, I'm not a serious player' in the car world more than a set of inappropriately small wheels. See the old Vauxhall Nova for details.

The Type R gets round this because its wheels fill the arches properly. That simple thing, all on its own, transforms the Civic into a properly exciting-looking car. The sort of thing you'd buy for your son, and then keep.

Don't, though. Because almost everything else about it is rubbish.

First of all there's the driver's seat, which is adjusted with a ratchet rather than a wheel. This means you can't fine-tune the angle of the backrest. You either sit bolt upright, like you're at the kitchen table, or you lounge, like Sylvia Kristel in those early Emmanuelle films.

Next there's the rear spoiler. From the outside it looks great, arching across the rear window like that, but from the inside it means you cannot see the car behind. You may as well use the rear-view mirror as a handy place to stick Post-it notes for all the good it does.

And now we move into the realms of what you get for the money. I'll save you the bother of looking it up. It's diddly squat. Not even sat nav, which is a nuisance when you're on that big roundabout in Rugby and all the signposts are pointing to places you've never heard of. Leamington or Southam? How about neither.

Engine? Well what they've done is taken the 198 bhp unit

from the old Civic and popped it, pretty much unchanged, into the new one. That, of course, would be fine if the new one weighed the same as the old one, but it doesn't. It weighs a whole lot more.

This then is like saying, 'Hmmm. We need a new engine to power the Queen Mary. I know. Let's get one out of that jet ski over there.'

Yes, it is still a fine engine. I really do love the revviness of all those VTEC units. But the new Civic is bound to be slightly slower and slightly less economical than the old one. And where's the progress in that, Honda, with your Earth Car and your Power of Dreams ad campaign? The fact of the matter is that Ford, Renault, Vauxhall and Volkswagen can all sell you a hatchback with much more get up and go.

Cunningly, Honda has tried to mask this lack of oomph by fitting the new Type R with a suspension system that, plainly, is made out of bricks. Even my wife, who likes hard-riding cars and thinks the Subaru Impreza is 'a bit soft', was alarmed by the way the Honda leapt and crashed down the road.

Me? I think it's a disgrace. I don't care what it's like on a track, or when it's doing handbrake turns in a supermarket car park: on a normal road, on a normal day, the ride quality is completely unacceptable. Anyone whose body is held together with a skeleton is going to come home every night in several agonising pieces.

And on top of all this the car I drove could not find Radio 2. It just locked on to Radio 1, which completed my discomfort as surely as if I'd slammed my head in the door.

All things considered, then, I pretty much hated it. It is nowhere near as good as a Golf GTI because, to be honest, it's nowhere near as good as walking. This, I feel sure, will guarantee its success among the earwig boys.

Sunday 27 May 2007

It's so comfortable you can run over anything up to a medium-sized fox and not even notice

Audi R8

We all know what businessmen's hotels are like. There's a priority check-in section where you wait behind some rope, on a bit of carpet. There are staff in shiny suits who say things like 'If there's anything else at all for yourself at all'. And you are given a credit card key that makes lots of whirring noises when you put it in the lock but will not, no matter what you do, open the door.

After you've kicked it down, you have the room. There's no obvious button to turn off the fan, which sounds like a Foxbat jet. The light switch by the bed turns all the lights off, except one. Which can only be extinguished by hitting the bulb with your shoe. The plug you need to charge your mobile is always behind the mini bar, and the 'tea and coffee making facilities' are designed to ensure you can't make either.

No, really: the kettle lead is never more than a foot long and the brown powder they put in the sachets is way closer on the periodic table to radium F than it is to coffee.

The restaurant, furnished in beige, is overseen by a woman who says: 'Can I get any bread items for yourself at all, sir?' and then hands you over to a fourteen-year-old Latvian girl who arrived in Britain that morning on the underside of a Eurostar train. Beer is not a word she's familiar with, which is annoying because it's what you want most of all in the world.

Your fellow diners are chomping their way through their suppers, some reading books, some newspapers, and there's always one who's reading the hotel's smoking policy leaflet over and over again. Just killing time till they can go to their room and watch pornography.

Businessmen's hotels, I think, are the most miserable, soul destroying, soulless, energy sapping, embarrassing, badly run and badly organised edifices in the entire world. I'd rather stay in an igloo. And that's before we get to the food.

The menus are always written in a massively squiggly, curly-whirly typeface. And there's much talk of *jus* and things being drizzled onto other things. But you know the chef is not from Paris or Rome. He's from Darlington and he hasn't a clue what he's doing.

As a general rule, I order items that even I couldn't mess up, which is why, at a businessmen's hotel next to Manchester airport last week, I went for a lamb chump with mashed potato and cabbage. 'No, lamb. Lamb,' I said to the Latvian teenager. 'A baby baa baa black sheep . . .'

I was expecting something irradiated, something the colour of a camel's dingleberry and with the texture of a cedar tree. But you know what? It was absolutely brilliant. Historic, as Michael Winner would bark.

I thought it would be impossible to be so pleasantly surprised ever again. But then, as the next day dawned, I found I had to drive back to London in a new Range Rover . . . wait for it . . . diesel.

The Range Rover is a car so ideally suited to a V8 that putting a diesel in the mix completely spoils the point. It'd be like putting diesel on your supper instead of gravy. The worst thing about a diesel is the noise it makes when you start it up. A Range Rover is elegant, dignified, luxurious. And a diesel's rattle and clatter just don't go with the look at all. It's like ringing a sex chat line and being put through to the Duke of Marlborough.

Strangely, however, the Range Rover made almost no noise when I started it, and even less on the move. What's more, the fuel gauge stayed pretty much where it was on the entire three-hour schlep back to England. That was an even bigger surprise than the hotel's chump.

But it was nothing to the car that was waiting for me in London. The Audi R8. I had seen pictures of this mid-engined supercar and they left me underwhelmed. I thought it looked a bit boring, like a slightly bigger version of the TT. And it wasn't going to be a real supercar, was it? Not when you remember Audi owns Lamborghini. I mean, why make a car to compete with your own brand? That'd be stupid.

This view is reinforced when you climb inside. There are very few supercar extravagances. There's no panic handle. No stitching made from yellowhammer feathers. No titanium machinegun triggers. It's very grey, very Audi, very normal. And that's fine, actually, because there are very few traditional supercar drawbacks either.

You can see out, there's room for your head, even if you have truly enormous hair, and there's space for briefcases and whatnot on a shelf behind the seats. It's big in there; much bigger than you'd believe.

Then you set off and there are no histrionics. The exhaust makes a deep, meaningful rumble, but as is the way in Jaguar's XK you can't really hear it when you're inside. So it's spookily quiet, and that's just the start of it. Because it is also spectacularly comfortable. I don't mean comfortable . . . for a sports car. I mean it's so comfortable you can run over anything up to a medium-sized fox and not even notice. Couple this to the usual array of Audi in-car entertainment – sat nav, a hi-fi from Bang & Olufsen no less – and you have a car that, like the Porsche 911, you really could live with every day.

You needn't even worry about the engine. It's not a W16 with eight turbos and plugs that foul themselves at every set of lights. It doesn't run on fertiliser and grated tiger chippings. Instead, it's the 414 bhp 4.2 V8 from the RS4. I've described this as one of the best engines made today and a drive in the R8 has not changed my mind. It does everything, brilliantly.

Of course, you cannot really expect a quiet, comfortable car with the engine from a saloon to perform well on a track. The suspension would be too soft. The power not quite grunty enough. The track is Lambo land. The Audi belongs in a city, soothing the fevered brow of the man with the midlife crisis, while massaging his ego, all at the same time. Wrong. Very, very wrong. In fact the Audi is outstanding when there's nothing coming the other way. It's not blisteringly fast. From rest to 120, it goes at almost exactly the same rate as the Porsche 911 Carrera S. And flat out it'll be out of steam before it gets to 190. But to dismiss it for this is to miss the point.

The four-wheel-drive system affords a huge level of grip, but because it's been tuned so no more than 30 per cent of the power is ever sent to the front wheels you don't get the dreary understeer that's plagued all quattro cars in the past.

You turn in, feel the grip, add power, the rear starts to slide, you apply some opposite lock, balance the throttle and then ... and then ... you start to realise you are driving one of the all-time greats. It's not a hefty car. You don't manhandle it through the bends. It flows, delicately and precisely.

I don't think I've ever driven a car that works so well on both the road and the track. Even if you remove my natural prejudice against the Porsche 911, I believe the Audi has it licked on all counts. Except perhaps one ...

The Audi is listed at just under £77,000 and that looks good, but if you want any equipment at all, that shoots up fast. The car I drove, which had a manual gearbox rather than flappy paddles, and normal brakes rather than ceramic discs, still cost a whopping £92,000. Even the leather interior was an optional extra.

But look at it this way. The R8 shares some parts and infra-structure with the Lamborghini Gallardo. And that's £125,000. Anyone who's just bought a baby Lambo – me – must be feeling as sick as a dog right now. Because in so many ways the R8 is better. Yes, the Lambo is more exciting, louder and harder. But on the other 363 days of the year, when you just want a nice car . . .

The only problem is that Audi cannot build the R8 fast enough. There are difficulties with making the carbon-fibre panels, and as a result it can manage just twenty a day. That's nowhere near enough to satisfy demand, especially when a more powerful V10 comes on stream next year.

In the meantime I can safely say the R8 is one of the best surprises of my motoring life. It is one of the truly great cars and the only hesitation I have in giving it five stars is that, ideally, I'd like to give it six.

Sunday 3 June 2007

You're going nowhere, sunshine

Mitsubishi Outlander Elegance

Are you in the north? And are you thinking of maybe moving down south for a better job and a better way of life? Well don't bother, because it's full. Last night I left the *Top Gear* test track in Surrey for the journey home. Simple. Go to Guildford, up the A3, round the M25, along the M40 to Oxford and then up the A44 to Chipping Norton. Do it all the time. Takes ninety minutes; less if I have some horsepowers.

Unfortunately, as I left the track a woman came on the radio to announce that some imbecile had crashed near Heathrow and that the M25 was all snarled up.

No big deal, I thought. It's a lovely evening, the sun is shining, I'm in no desperate hurry and I'm in a Lamborghini Gallardo. I shall get the roof down and go home on the nation's A roads. It'll be like the olden days. I'll feel like Christopher Plummer in his Battle of Britain MG. It'll be fun.

It wasn't. First of all, Guildford is a smallish town but evidently it has a population greater than that of Tokyo. And unlike London, where people work till six, seven, even ten at night and the rush hour is prolonged, this is the provinces, where people leave the office at 5.30 on the dot. The result is as dramatic as a summer thunderstorm.

I arrived at Guildford at 5.31, at the precise moment 8 million IT consultants climbed into their BMWs and hit the road. It was a staggering, choking, infuriating, miserable crawl all the way to the A3 and I knew, as I joined it, heading south, that the M25, no matter how bad, would have been quicker.

Then I missed the A31 turn-off. Which meant I had to take the B3001 to Farnham. This is a nice road, snaking through some reasonable views and a couple of Ma Larkin villages. You might imagine, if you lived there, that you were in the countryside. But you bloody well aren't because the road was chockablock. More crammed than a public bog in Algiers the day after Ramadan.

And because it was a lovely evening, some of the local cycling Nazis had slipped into a pair of Lycra shorts and, to get rid of the stresses of consulting an IT all day, gone out onto the road to get in everyone's way.

It's all very well thinking that your bicycle is only a foot wide and that there's plenty of road for people to pass. But if we give you only a foot, you bang on our boot as we drive by and call us names. So we have to give you 3 ft and we can't because there's a constant stream of traffic coming the other way, which means we're forced to stumble along at 6 mph with nothing to look at except your wizened, walnut hard, shiny black bottom jiggling about in front of us.

Then it was Farnham, which has a level crossing right next to a set of lights . . . that went red as I straddled the railway lines. I was therefore stuck, right in the path of the jammed-up commuter trains that rattle about at this time of day disgorging red-faced businessmen into their cars for the crawl home.

So I was forced to drive on the wrong side of the road – in a Lamborghini, which is not inconspicuous – and take shelter in a garage forecourt. So here we are, in 2007. I'm trying to get from Guildford to Chipping Norton, and I'm stuck on a forecourt, in the wrong town, sheltering from a train.

Eventually I arrived at the biggest roundabout in the world looking for signs to the next town on my list. Basingstoke.

There aren't any. The council and the Highways Agency have decided instead to list a number of villages no one's ever heard of. So, using the sun, I took a stab and miraculously ended up on the right road. Which, with no warning whatsoever, became the wrong road.

So then I was in a housing estate, stuck behind a school bus that was attempting to turn right. This might have been possible in the 1940s when there was a war on and no one had any petrol. But it isn't possible now; not in the southeast of England – which, I learnt last week, would be the eleventh richest country in the world if it were a state.

And no one got that rich by stopping to let a school bus past. So I sat there, with the metronomic dashboard clock ticking away my life, knowing that if I had set out on foot I'd have been home by now.

Eventually the bus oxidised and I was able to drive over it and back, through an industrial estate, on to the A287 to Basingstoke. Which I decided to miss by going along the A303 and then turning north onto the A34.

Now the A34 is a big road, a fast dual carriageway mostly and scene of those protests over the Newbury bypass. In essence, the town needed to divert traffic away from the town centre so there'd be fewer outbreaks of cancer, less smell, less noise, and fewer children being run over. But a chap with long hair, called Swampy, decided the bypass was a bad idea because it would mean having to rehouse some snails he'd found. So he made a lot of noise and lived in a tree.

Common sense, however, prevailed and the road was opened. But no one has thought to put up a signpost advertising its presence, which meant I was now on my way to Wiltshire. I like Wiltshire very much. The rolling chalk hills are beautiful at this time of year and there's a chance you might catch a glimpse of Peter Gabriel.

But then again, I also like the south of France, northern California and the Italian lakes. I like lots of places but where I wanted to be was at home. So I pulled off the A303, only to discover that it was one of those junctions where you can't get back on again, going the other way. This wasn't signposted. It never is.

I wonder sometimes how much of the traffic on our roads today is made up of people in strange towns trying to make some kind of sense of the signs.

There's one, in Olympia, in west London, that says the right turn ahead will take you to Clapham. Yes it will, but it will also take you to Earls Court, Fulham, Chelsea, Putney, Brixton, Brighton, France and the Kamchatka peninsula in eastern Russia. Why single out Clapham?

Then there are one-way systems. The day before my four-hour trip across the southeast I was in Lyndhurst, down there in the New Forest. You arrive at a set of lights and want to go straight on, but instead you're forced to go left, into a one-way system of such mind-boggling complexity and such length that halfway round most people pull over and try to will themselves to die. Well I did.

And have you been to Stroud? You arrive from the west and no matter what you do you end up in the railway station car park. And Basingstoke, where you are sucked off a dual carriageway, whether you like it or not, and wind up in a multi-storey car park.

And you have to pay to get out again. How fair's that?

And now this idiotic government is trying to build another God knows how many million houses in this part of the world to accommodate people from Albania and Huddersfield who think life in the southeast is a bath of ass's milk. It isn't. It's a seething mass of superheated metal, tarmac, frayed tempers and decking. It's a manicured pressure cooker, a forest of carriage lamps, up-and-over garage doors, and ego. It was full years ago, and they keep on cramming more and more people into it so that now it doesn't work any more.

Yes, there are tiny pockets of peace and tranquillity. There are roads, too, where you might have fun with a car. But the only reason they are empty is because they serve no useful purpose any more. They were created by sheep but the sheep have gone, replaced now by – well, more sheep actually, with suits and ties and tennis lessons.

There is, if you live in this vast suburban sprawl, no point having a nice car. It'd be like living in Niger with a Gordon Ramsay recipe book. The ingredients just don't exist, not on the roads you actually use to get about.

What you want, then, is something reliable and practical but so unutterably boring that you never feel inclined to open it up anyway. The Mitsubishi Outlander fits the bill perfectly.

Enough said.

Sunday 17 June 2007

Good news and bad news for Mondeo man

Ford Mondeo Titanium X

We all tend to have a sense that if something is complicated and difficult, it is bound to be better than something that is simple and straightforward. Tchaikovsky's '1812' overture, for instance, is considered by almost everyone to be a better piece of music than 'Baa Baa Black Sheep'.

This is certainly the case with acting. The purists with their mad hair and illuminated ballpoint pens will tell us that performing in a soap opera is nothing more than reading out words and slamming doors. For real acting, we are directed towards Olivier in *Richard III*, Brando in *On the Waterfront*, and Gielgud in *Hamlet*. These are the colossuses, the giants. The men who bestride oceans with their talent.

Yes, I'm sure. But actually the best piece of acting I've ever seen came from Paul Whitehouse in *The Fast Show*. Olivier, I'm sure, was jolly good at strutting about on a stage, slamming important documents into the palm of his hand and making himself heard at the back. But as Rowley Birkin QC, Paul was in a different league.

Each week he simply sat in a chair, by a fire, with a drink, and cheerily mumbled his way through an anecdote in which only one word in fifty was even halfway audible.

And yet you always got the gist. And you always laughed . . . right up to the very last episode, when he told how his wife had died. For a comedian to make you cry, in a comedy show, without really saying anything . . . well, I doubt you will see genius to match it in your lifetime.

And now we shall move on to food. Of course, when it's sculptured and drizzled with *jus*, and it arrives on your plate with everything balanced on top of everything else, you know you are in the presence of greatness. Particularly if the waiter has revealed it to you from under a cloche with an unspoken 'Ta Daaa!'.

Best food ever? Ooh, that'd be a boned pigeon at Pic, near Valence in France, or the ortolan I had in Gascony, or maybe the crab and rabbit pasta that came from the two-star kitchens of Louie's Backyard in Key West. Oh no, hang on a minute. I've just remembered the absolute best thing I've ever eaten was in fact the poached egg on toast I had for lunch.

In fact, come to think of it, the five best things I've ever eaten were not boned sparrows or potatoes cooked in myrrh. They were simple things: bacon and egg. Lobster from my pots with samphire from my garden.

And the watercress you get from the beck just outside Appletreewick in Yorkshire. It's so peppery that you eat it not by the sprig, but by the acre.

Ooh, and then there are the radishes I grow. The agony of waiting for them to ripen is so intense that when I do finally pull one up, stinging my hands gently on its leaves, I can never be bothered to wash all the mud off before I pop it into my mouth. And then I just stand there, savouring it, pulling a face normally only seen in a pornographic movie when the lead is being warmed up by half a dozen naked Californian teenagers.

I like my art work simple as well. Yes, you can be dazzled by Turner's brushwork and by Constable's attention to detail. But the best piece of art I ever saw? It had been done by Tracey Emin and it was a couple of pencil squiggles. Was it a girl? Or a dog? I don't know but I'd be happy to stand there, with a radish in my mouth, looking at it until the end of time.

And this of course brings us nicely on to the Ford Mondeo. The previous model was a masterpiece. Every single time I drove one I emerged from the experience thinking, 'Why doesn't everyone own one of these?' It was just so simple. A perfect poached egg, on a perfect piece of toast.

It handled beautifully, it was surprisingly fast, it was roomy and practical, and if you actually took away the familiarity it was also extremely good looking. Much better than a BMW 3-series, or a Mercedes C-class. Better too than the Jaguar X-type that it spawned.

Sadly, though, the old Mondeo is no more. There's a new version in town that you may have seen in the Bond film *Casino Royale*. It comes from a very different Ford than that which created the old one. Back then, the blue oval was in rude health. It was buying up Aston Martin, Jaguar, Land Rover, Volvo . . . it would have bought your old bathroom furniture if you'd thought to put it on eBay.

Today, though, Ford is in what economists call 'a right old pickle'. As an investment opportunity it's up there with a semi on the Gaza Strip. Its shares are listed as junk, biscuits are banned in board meetings to save money, it has sold Aston Martin, it is shutting fourteen plants, shedding 30,000 jobs and business articles speak of there being no obvious solution. One analyst I spoke to said: 'If it were a corner shop, it would have gone bankrupt years ago.'

So how does it find the cash needed these days to design an all-new car and tool up the factories to make it? Realistically that costs a billion and a billion is one thing Ford does not have. In fact, a billion is what Ford is losing every four or five months. The last I heard it was trying to borrow £10 billion just to stay afloat. You have more money than Ford, even if you are a postman.

That's why the new Mondeo contains, as far as I can tell, no new technology at all. The Focus, designed in a bath of cash, had expensive independent rear suspension. A big advance for that part of the market. The Mondeo has no similar technological leaps.

That said, what you do get is tried and tested. Largely the parts come from the Ford S-Max and the forthcoming Volvo V70. And all Ford has done is screw them together properly. You'd be amazed how solid it all feels.

And big. It's much wider than the old car and a full five inches longer. Perhaps that's why it's 175 kg heavier – and that's like adding the weight of a medium sized motorcycle. The upside of this swelling, however, is that it's truly huge on the inside. The back in particular is roomier than a concert hall and the boot is big enough for a game of football.

I must also say that it's exceptionally good looking. Colleagues in the motoring press have called it pretentious but I disagree. I think it's balanced, handsome and that all the trinketry is well chosen. On looks alone, and interior space, it leaves all of its rivals trailing.

And that's before we get to the price. Whatever model you choose is going to be thousands and thousands cheaper than anything from Audi or BMW. And about a million less than any-thing from Stuttgart. What's more, the Ford should be cheap to insure as it has special deformable panels on the back that boing back into shape after a bump.

And the news gets better still when you go for a drive. Because of the size and weight, it feels a very different car from the old model. The fun, the joie de vivre, has gone. Even the 2.5 turbo I drove doesn't encourage you to stick it into a bend and revel in the electric responses. Now, it feels refined and comfortable. It feels, unsurprisingly I suppose, like a Volvo. And for that reason you should avoid the optional sports suspension. It'd be like teaming a well cut tweed suit with a pair of training shoes.

Ford has done a good job with this car – an outstanding job when you realise how strapped for cash it is. The only real problem is that downmarket badge.

Or is it downmarket? It was, for sure, when Mr Blair came to power. But since then Mondeo man has jumped ship, which is why in Britain today the BMW 3-series is by far the bigger seller. No one wants a poached egg any more. Everyone wants drizzle and *jus* and Ian McKellen in *King Lear*.

It's a pity, really, because as a result Ford is teetering on the brink. It may well go and if it does we shall be waving goodbye to the company that gave us the Model T, the GT40, the Mustang, the Sierra Cosworth, the Escort RS2000 and the Cortina 1600E. The company that powered *Minder* and *The Sweeney* and *The Professionals* and *Bullitt*. The company that made mass production work. In historical terms, Ford is like a combination of Ferrari, Nasa, ICI and the National Trust.

I won't urge you to buy a Mondeo just to save an institution. It's your money and your choice. But I'll be sad if you have the wherewithal and you don't.

Sunday 24 June 2007

Me, Grace Kelly, and an Italian love affair

Ferrari 275 GTS (1964)

When you drive into a village these days there is often an electronic sign that flashes on to tell you how fast you're going. That's very useful ... but not half as useful as a sign to tell you how much of a berk you look.

I even have a name for such a device: a cock-o-meter. The idea being that it would process an image of your face, your hair and your clothes, and marry this information to the sort of car you're driving. You'd then be given a score out of ten.

BMW M3s driven by people with shaved heads would get ten. Saabs driven by people in linen jackets would get maybe one or two.

And anyone in a Ferrari 275 GTS – even if they were a curious mixture of Bill Gates and Kim Jong-il – would get zero. In this car it is impossible to look like a cock.

Even if you are one.

This is not one of the great Ferraris. It is not a 250 GTO or a Daytona. It's not a shark-nose racer or an F40.

Many car enthusiasts have never heard of it. Even among the Ferrari cognoscenti it's a little known oxbow lake, Tim Henman with wire wheels.

If you liken Ferrari to the Who, it's not 'Baba O'Riley' or 'My Generation'. It's more like 'Happy Jack'.

Part of the problem is that even by the contemporary standards of 1964 it really wasn't very good.

The best thing is that it had an unusual fixed propshaft which, because the engine moved around on its rubber mountings, would wear out in moments. This meant owners never really had a chance to discover that the braking system was made out of what appeared to be veal. For stopping a GTS you'd have been better off opening the door and running your shoe along the road.

For reasons lost in the mists of time, the 275 was fitted with 14 in wheels, which meant the discs had to be smaller than the engineers would have liked. They were fine for popping to the shops for milk, and at speed they'd work once or maybe twice. But after that I'm afraid you were going to meet your maker with a rather surprised and annoyed look on your face.

There was another interesting issue, too. Ferrari decided to fit a small two-man sofa instead of a passenger seat, saying they'd made a 2+1. And indeed they had, but woe betide the man who put a girl in a skirt in the middle. Because every time he went for fifth he'd get a slap.

None of this matters though, because, and I'm afraid I can't take any argument on the matter, this is the prettiest Ferrari ever made. And that would make it the prettiest thing ever made, including Raquel Welch, who owned one.

I worry about modern Ferraris. They are deeply, deeply impressive and my respect for the technological abilities is boundless. They really do feel very far ahead of all other cars on the road. But emotionally they leave me unaffected: cold.

The 430, the 599 and to a lesser extent the 612 are as brilliant as laptop computers. But what I want from a Ferrari is not science and maths. I want heart and soul. I want love and affection. I want them to be less like a laptop and more like a book or a painting.

Perhaps this has something to do with the company's current, and misguided, obsession with putting as much Formula One trinketry into the road cars as is humanly possible. Square steering wheels with gearchange advisory lights. Flappy-paddle gearboxes. Five-way traction control. Look under the bonnet of a 599 and you'll find the plastic sheet fitted to shroud the radiators has been sculptured to resemble the nose of an F1 car. That's not clever. It's naff. Drive past a cock-o-meter in a car like this and it will explode.

In the early days Ferrari road cars were not designed or marketed to exploit the company's track stars. When the 275 came along in 1964 it had nothing in common with the V8 F1 car that John Surtees used to win the championship that year. And there was no attempt to pretend it did, as there is now with the grand prix tinsel and traction control malarkey.

Back then, yes, Ferrari's racers kept the name in the headlines, but the road cars were made for playboys. People like Porfirio Rubirosa, who at 3 a.m. in a Montparnasse nightclub called New Jimmy's suddenly remembered he was due to take part the following morning in a tennis tournament in Monte Carlo. Giddy, shall we say, after an evening in Paris he roared off in his Ferrari and did well, making it as far as the Bois de Boulogne before he veered off the road and into a tree, dying instantly. The 275 came from the days when Ferraris were bought by the white knights, the people who invented the jet set, not a bunch of IT consultants who want a flappy-paddle gearbox so their stupid friends might think they're Michael Schumacher. See a 599 and who comes to mind? Gary Neville? Philip Green? See a 275 and it's a different picture that fills your head. It's Grace Kelly in a headscarf cruising down the Promenade des Anglais. It's Gianni Agnelli stepping off a Riva speedboat in St Tropez and screaming down the Riviera for a dinner date in Portofino. That's why the 275 is a cock mask.

When I saw one in the flesh for the first time last week I didn't really want to get in it and go for a drive. And not only because I knew the brakes wouldn't work and I'd end up all dead. No. I didn't want to get inside because then I couldn't look at that gasp-inducing Pininfarina styling any more.

In some ways, I suppose, it's a bit like the old Fiat 124. But because of the 72-spoke wire wheels and the four exhausts you just know it's a bit more special than that. And it is. Under the bonnet there's a 3.3 litre V12 engine. We forget these days that to the Ferrari purist the V8 is a coarse aberration, an American import which has no place providing the propulsion and the soundtrack in a real car. A Ferrari must have a V12 in the same way that a real guitarist must have a Fender Stratocaster.

Of course by the standards of the twenty-first century it's a woeful engine, drinking enormous quantities of petrol through its six carburettors and only handing 260 bhp back in return. You get nearly as much as that from a Vauxhall Astra these days, and the same sort of performance. Zero to sixty in around seven seconds and a top speed of 149.

The handling is similarly out of date. This may have been the first car in the world to be fitted with independent rear suspension – not a lot of people know that. Not a lot of people care. But you need to be a brave man to find what it feels like at the limit. I wasn't. Not with the owner watching.

All I know is that at surprisingly moderate speeds the wheels feel like they're not really connected to the car at all, flopping over in the arches as the suspension fails to keep the tyres in flat contact with the road. At fifty, in a gentle bend, the rubber was howling in protest.

This was fine by me because the slower you drive this car the more time it takes to get somewhere and the longer, therefore, you are in it. If it had had a stereo, rather than a medium-wave radio, I'd have slotted Matt Monro into the CD, and with the strains of 'On Days Like These' filling the cabin I'd have set off at thirty and spent a month driving to the south of France.

Sadly it's very difficult to buy one. Just 200 were made and only fourteen had right-hand drive. They come onto the market from time to time and go for around £200,000 – roughly what it would cost to buy a new 599.

I'd go for the old car in a heartbeat. It's not big and it's not clever and it's certainly not fast. But possibly, just possibly, this is the most exquisite car I've ever driven.

Because here, wrapped up in 14 ft of steel and glass and wire, we find everything – everything – it was that made me fall in love with cars in the first place. A ton and a half of style, heart, and soul.

Sunday 1 July 2007

Darling, I'd forgive you anything

Aston V8 Vantage Roadster

Recently I wrote about Britain's badly signposted towns and I have been inundated with absolutely no correspondence on the matter at all. I can only presume this is because everyone who has an opinion on the matter is busy doing a three-point turn in Stroud railway station car park, unable to find any road that actually leaves the town. I have some new evidence to back this up. Apparently two-thirds of Britain's motorists get lost up to ten times a year, and while trying to find where they are clock up an astonishing 325 million wasteful and pointless miles.

Naturally, like everything else these days, including chickens and vacuum bags, this causes unnecessary global warming.

But if we skip over the report's eco-babble, we find some interesting observations. In London, drivers do 26 million miles each year while lost, and that's the same as driving from New York to Los Angeles 9,200 times. Needlessly.

Even in Scotland, where there are only three roads, motorists can't get from A to B without ending up in a haggis. Apparently 54 per cent say they get lost the noo up to twenty times a year.

So plainly the problem is even worse than I thought, and there can only be one culprit. Satellite navigation.

Ironically, this is bad news for the people who paid for the survey because they work for a company called Becker, which makes sat navs.

The trouble is that sat navs lull us into a false sense of security by working without fault for a month and then suddenly deciding that the A40 doesn't exist.

And when you rely on a sat nav, you don't notice that the sun is in the wrong place in the sky. You stop using your inbuilt compass, your innate sense of which way is up. And don't argue with any of this. Everyone can navigate by instinct, and if you can't there's something wrong with you and you should be in prison.

The only people who can't navigate instinctively are women and anyone trying to find Malpensa airport in Milan.

I tried to do this last week and it is impossible. The map quite plainly said we would cross a motorway that we needed to ignore. But this motorway does not exist, so when I crossed the motorway I definitely didn't need to ignore I thought it was the first one. Quickly, because of the position of the sun and my innate sense of distance and time, I realised my mistake and asked Richard Hammond, who was driving, to turn round and go back the other way.

Almost immediately we happened upon a green autostrada sign which pointed us to Venice and Bologna. Both lovely places. But both in the wrong direction. The sign going the other way wasn't there.

So then we were in a housing estate, with just ninety minutes to go before our plane was due to leave. Both of us were regretting stopping on the shores of Lake Como earlier that afternoon for a beer. I, especially, was regretting the second and third. And fourth, because it made reading the map so very difficult.

James May was especially regretting my extra beers, partly because he can't read maps and partly because he was due to host a charity day for sick children the next day. So he had to catch that plane.

Soon, however, thanks to my brilliance, we found the autostrada and joined it. Only to find it was the missing autostrada, which had now miraculously reappeared. So we turned off, and in a temper James broke out his hand-held sat nav system.

This took us to the city centre, which even I, in my semi-sozzled state, knew was wrong. I've seen many things in the middle of Milan over the years, including lots of pretty women, many pavement cafes, La Scala, the Duomo and the Leonardo da Vinci museum of science and technology. But I have never seen a large international airport.

This is the problem with sat navs. James and Richard are bright blokes – well, James is – but give them an electronic master and they lose all sense of reason. If the sat nav had ushered them into a river, they'd have gone in. And if it had then said, 'You have arrived at your destination', they'd have got out and tried to check in.

We did finally arrive at Malpensa, by following signs to Como, just seventeen minutes before our flight was due to leave. And using smiles instead of boarding passes we caught the plane.

None of this has anything to do with the new Aston Martin V8 Vantage convertible.

I've been nervous about the arrival of this car because I didn't think it would be any good. When they removed the roof from the DB9 – a car I love – they ended up with something that didn't look quite right. And if you take away the looks from an Aston Martin, you take away just about everything.

If the beheading of a V8 caused the styling to go wonky then what would you have? A not very fast two-seater that wouldn't be quite as reliable as a Porsche 911, or quite as beautiful as the much cheaper Jaguar XKR. The V8 convertible had to look not just good but so bone-quiveringly brilliant that men and women would fall to their knees and whimper whenever they saw even a small part of it.

And I'm delighted to say, it does. Aston sent a green one round, with a matching green roof and a green interior. And even this failed to take away the sheer beauty of the thing. Every time I walked out of my house and saw it, I had to bite the back of my hand to stop crying out.

To drive, things are slightly less rosy. The coupé version, with its dry-sumped and slightly enlarged version of Jag's Welsh-made

V8, is not slow. But it's not that fast either. Certainly it isn't as fast as the exhaust bark would have you believe.

In the convertible you can hear that wonderful noise even more clearly. So you expect to be going faster. But the new car is heavier than the coupé so it's even slower. The gap between aural expectation and reality is therefore even wider, but it doesn't matter because it's so pretty.

The reason why it's heavier is simple. Not only is there the added weight of the roof motor, but they've had to strengthen the chassis. They claim, however, that because of the way Astons are made not much beefing up was necessary.

I'm not sure about that. On fairly normal roads, especially when the roof's down, you can feel the car flexing slightly. Look at the rear-view mirror and you'll find it moves out of synch with your head. Most convertibles do this, of course, and it's always annoying. But less so in the V8 because, of course, it's just so pretty.

Inside, we find the same irritations that blight the hard top, a Volvo sat nav system glued to a flap and buttons that cannot be read when the sun is shining. But none of this really matters because, of course, it is very pretty.

I did enjoy driving the drophead, though. Despite that noise, which is intoxicating, and the man-sized gearchange action, it is a refined and comfortable place to sit. This is a car that glides, rather than scrabbles. I'd even call it relaxing. Reliability? Well, my wife's V8, which was one of the first ever made, has not been bad at all. The boot filled with water on one trip to London, which was odd since it wasn't raining, the petrol filler cap fell apart once, the handbrake gets stuck on from time to time and the tyre pressure sensors have a mind of their own.

Tiny things, in other words, and worrying about any of them in a pretty car like the Vantage is like climbing into bed with a supermodel and noticing she has slightly unruly pubes.

Yes, you can buy cars for less. You can buy cars that are faster and nicer to drive and more practical. But the first time you see one of these things, roof down, on a sunny day, you'll know what I'm on about. This is not a car you need to buy. It is not even a car you want to buy. It's a car you simply have to buy.

Just so you can look at it.

Sunday 15 July 2007

Drive this and the road zealots will have you

Mercedes C 280 Sport

While I was away last week, someone came in the night and erected a couple of handmade road signs on the grass verge outside my house.

They advertise a new website that encourages road users to report fellow citizens for dangerous or antisocial driving. I think it may be called www.interferingzealot.com. The idea is simple. If you are annoyed by someone's driving you simply post their numberplate, and a brief description of their crime, in the hope that they'll log on too and be so ashamed they'll turn over a new leaf and become a vicar.

Let me give you some examples. A chap with the username of StephenHarrison, who has made 157 posts so far, quotes the numberplate of a car that, he says, on 9 July in Birmingham city centre 'positioned itself in the left/straight-on lane, then turned right at the roundabout'.

It gets worse. Another chap, called Kev627, tells us that in Perham, Hampshire, a chap driving a Ford Fiesta 'indicated 100 yards before the exit prior to the one it used to leave the A342'.

I'm surprised to find that someone in Glasgow didn't tell the members he'd seen two Muslim men 'drive right over the pavement and into the terminal at the city's airport in a burning Jeep Cherokee'.

Sadly, I'm afraid I don't know whether I appear because I don't know what my numberplate is.

But I do know this. We are talking here about the dullest

website in the whole of human history. And also the most terrifying . . .

The problem is that we now have so many laws in the UK and so few policemen to enforce them all that the slack is being taken up by an army of bitter and twisted fiftysomething busybodies with beige clothes and upper lips puckered so badly by rage that they look like one of Mr Kipling's cakes.

Think about it. When we were growing up it was illegal to murder someone, and er . . . that's it. Now it is illegal to eat an apple while driving, or use a mobile phone. It is illegal to smoke a cigarette in a bus shelter or use more than two dogs to kill a fox. It is very illegal to smack your children and if you try being a Brazilian in a Tube station you're in real trouble.

To enforce all these new laws we have a police force of 140,000, most of whom do four days a week of ladder training and one day a week arresting doctors for attempting to explode.

To try to get round the problem the government has introduced new tiers of policing such as speed cameras and those Highways Agency teams you see on motorways in chequerboard 4×4s. They look like policemen and they have the legend 'traffic officer' emblazoned in the back window. But their main job is to clear up the mess after an accident. Which means, technically, they are Wombles.

Then you have the community support officers, who have fewer powers than Luxembourg and are really nothing more than neighbourhood watch wardens in hi-viz jackets.

If they see a Brazilian fox eating an apple in a bus shelter they have to call for a proper policeman, who can't come because it's night time and the station is shut, or because he hasn't had any fox training or because he's otherwise engaged on the top deck of the No 42, arresting a doctor for having a backpack full of baking powder and hair gel.

The fact is this. The government is churning out the laws, and the only way they can be enforced is if ordinary people start to shop their fellow citizens. That brings us neatly to two places at the same time. Moscow, in 1967, and www.interferingzealot .com. Which, actually, are the same thing.

No, really. How long will it be before you will only confide in your oldest friends, and then only in a whisper, in case an agent of the state is listening? You think I'm joking but trust me on this. Today you are being reported for indicating a bit too early in your Ford Fiesta. Tomorrow, when they get round to making climate change scepticism a crime – and they will – the equivalent of StephenHarrison and Kev627 will shop you for leaving your TV on stand-by.

It all flies in the face of everything I learnt at school. That you never, ever shop anyone to the teachers.

And it's all the wrong way round. Instead of setting up websites where people are exposed for breaking laws that shouldn't exist, I suggest we set one up that reveals the names and addresses of those who call for such laws to be imposed in the first place. I even have a name for such a thing: www.shop-a-dingleberry .com.

In the meantime, though, I must thank the people who put up the signs outside my house. On these chilly summer evenings they came in very handy. As firewood. And now it is time to move on to the subject of this morning's column. The new Mercedes C-class.

Aaaaaaaaaaaaaaaaaaaaaaaaaaaaaaaaaaaaaaaaaaaaaaaaaaaaaaaaaaaaaaa-aaaaaaaaaaaaaaaaaaaaaaaaaaaaaaaaaaaaaaaaaaaaaaaaaaaaaaaaaaaaaaaa-aaaaaaaaaaaaaaaaaaaaaaaaaaaaaaaaaaaaaargh.

I haven't finished yet.

Aaaaaaaaaaaaaaaaaaaaaaaaaaaaaaaaaaaaaaaaaaaaaaaaaaaaaaaaaaaaaaaa-aaaaaaaaaaaaaaaaaaaaaaaaaaaaaaaaaaaaaaaaaaaaaaaaaaaaaaaaaaaaaaaa-argh.

I've owned a couple of Mercs in the past four or five years and have grown accustomed to the way the on-board computer works. I know how long you hold the mute button down to

make the traffic announcement system go away. I know that
you have to push the second button up on the right twice to
make the sat nav map bigger. I know how to use the phone. It's
all intuitive.

And now they've changed it, which means I spent most of my
time in this car fiddling with what looks suspiciously like a rip-off
of the BMW iDrive system. I'm sure that in time you could get
used to it. I'm sure it's all very German. But so was the old
system. So why change it, you clodhopping imbeciles?

Occasionally I was able to ignore the hulking presence of the
new computer system and concentrate on the car itself, and I
must say it wasn't too bad in a straightforward, Mercedesy sort of
way. It's bigger than the old model, a little bit heavier and it rides
around on suspension that can trace its roots back to the 190 from
the early Eighties. That said, the 280 I tried came with the seven-
speed gearbox – that's two more than it needs – but the changes
were so smooth you never really noticed that it was doing them
more than is actually necessary.

Other things? Well, it was quiet, extremely smooth riding and
quite fast. Although the diesel version you'll buy won't be.

I liked it more than the dreary BMW 3-series, but is it, I
wondered, significantly better than the much cheaper Ford
Mondeo?

The Ford is more spacious and better looking – the C-class,
with all its fancy styling details, looks like a Kia Magentis. But
there's a sense in the Merc that you are driving something that's
been hewn from the solid rather than assembled.

There's some evidence to suggest this might be the case.

When Daimler-Benz merged with Chrysler, the American
engineers realised after a short while that the Germans at Mercedes
were paying five times more for their seats than they were.

So they sent some Chrysler seats to Stuttgart saying, 'Hey, guys.
We think you're being overcharged.'

Having spent a few weeks examining the Chrysler seats, the

Germans replied, '*Nein*. Ve zink it is you who are being over-charged.'

There was a time, I agree, when Mercedes stopped taking such care, but they're back in business now. You can't quite put your finger on why, especially when a woman from Radio Nether Wallop has just interrupted Terry Wogan to say the pelican crossing on Acacia Avenue has stopped working and you can't find a way to shut her up.

And as you fumble about with all the buttons on the centre console you won't be looking where you're going. Which means that when you do finally get home you will turn on your internet to find that Kev627 and StephenHarrison have put you on www.interferingzealot.com.

Sunday 22 July 2007

Sorry, this drop top is stuck in Normal

BMW 335i SE Convertible

When it was opened in 1881, pretty much everyone hated the Natural History Museum.

That ornate gothic style was just slightly out of date. In the same way that going to the Wolseley in a pair of Joan Collins *Dynasty* shoulder pads would be slightly out of date today. And just as risible.

The thing is, though, that now absolutely everyone loves the place and the person who loves it most of all is me.

I know it's more gaudy than Paris Hilton's knicker drawer and I know it's full of ecologist schoolteachers telling groups of un-interested children that unless they stab their gas-guzzling parents all animals will end up as bones in glass boxes in there.

But my oh my ... what a temple, what ambition, what detailing!

Paid for with money generated from the Great Exhibition, the Natural History Museum is like all the world's best cathedrals. It's much more interesting to look at than anything that's going on inside it. It is brilliant, and every time I come into London on the M4 I fervently wish for a traffic jam on the Cromwell Road just so that I can spend a little more time drinking it all in.

And naturally this brings me on to the boot lid of the 7-series BMW.

There was a problem with it from the start. You see, BMW had employed an American stylist by the name of Chris Bangle, who had a beard and a not-bad CV from Fiat, where he'd done the 1990s Fiat Coupé. Not a bad looking car in many ways, except that Chris had given it four eyebrows.

Anyway, Johnny Yank had arrived at BMW determined to breathe some new life into the brand, which – until that point – had stuck very rigidly to the principle that all cars should be styled with nothing more than a sturdy 2HB pencil and a ruler. His first attempt was the 7-series, and it was a complete disaster, chiefly because he'd fitted a boot lid and then left it in the oven for too long. So it had melted and sort of dribbled down over the rear valance.

Horrified by slow sales of this unlovely monster, BMW quickly ordered a redesign. But Chris mucked this one up as well. And the one that followed shortly thereafter. And by this stage he'd set to work ruining the 6-series too – a job he completed spectacularly well. This one had an even bigger, even more melted boot lid, which, if you squinted, looked like a forgotten soufflé. In the meantime he was starting work on a sports car called the Z4. It was imperative that this car should look good, because good looks are the raison d'être for cars of this type. But I'm afraid he made a complete hash of it.

And then, to make matters worse, he came up with a trendy designer handle for what he was doing, calling it 'flame surfacing'.

Others called it 'bollocks'. The designer J Mays at Ford laughed openly, while Marc Newson, an industrial designer, said the Z4 appeared to have been designed with a machete. Meanwhile, Renault's stylist, Patrick Le Quement, politely described it as 'hollow'.

And as for me? Well, I'm sorry, but Bangle said that his influence for the Z4 was the Guggenheim museum in Bilbao.

I see. So you modelled a car on what looks like an aircraft carrier that has crashed into a city. Wouldn't it have been better to maybe use a shark, or perhaps a tiger as your starting point? Just a thought.

Sadly, Chris wasn't listening. He was busy working on the new 5-series – his absolute worst effort so far, with headlamps like Dame Edna Everage's spectacles and lines that make no sense at all.

Then, after the 1-series came out looking like a severely kicked-in bread van, BMW had plainly had enough, so it booted its American whiz-kid upstairs, where he could do less harm.

And that's a pity, because it was at this exact moment that I realised that the 'flame-surfaced' Z4 is just as striking and wonderful as the building that inspired it; and that the 6-series is in fact perfectly balanced and gorgeous; and that the 5-series – when it has the right wheels on – makes the rival models from Audi and Mercedes-Benz look as dumpy and lumpy as phlebitis.

And that brings us on to the BMW 3-series. Frightened that any more mad Banglism might scare away buyers of the cash cow, the company high-ups insisted that this model should be a fairly normal looking affair.

And so it turned out to be. Fairly normal. And as boring as a bucket of wallpaper paste.

This is a car you would buy like you would curtain material – by the foot.

'Yes, I'd like 15 ft of car, please.' 'Certainly, sir. How about a 3-series?' It is a magnolia bathroom suite. It is beige paint. It is biscuit carpeting. And worst of all, from the back it looks like a Kia.

In a BMW showroom full of Bangle's brilliant early works, it sticks out like an art school doodle in the Tate Modern's engine room.

And the convertible is worse. As is the norm these days, the convertible roof is made from metal, and that's just fine. But to stow such a large lump of ironmongery, and the rear window, the boot has to be as big – and as stylish – as a Korean grain carrier. To make matters worse the model I tested was the big-engined 335i, which is all yours – fitted with a few necessary extras – for a whopping £46,000 (though a basic model costs £38,035).

Make no mistake, this is not a bad car. No, the manual gearbox is not completely precise, and yes, there is a whisper of wind noise from the point where the roof meets the windscreen, but this is only audible on the M26 motorway at 7 p.m., when you have a 7.50 p.m. flight to catch from Gatwick . . .

Of more interest is the twin-turbo motor. This is a straight-six and any engineer will tell you that this is the smoothest cylinder configuration you can have for an engine. He will also tell you – if you don't punch him in time – why that is.

But in this BMW it isn't smooth. In fact on tickover it rumbles and judders like a big American V8, and I think they may have done this on purpose by messing with the crankshaft or the firing order. Maybe they wanted to give it some character, and if that's the case it's worked – I liked it a lot.

As you'd expect, it's a dream to drive on really good roads. When the going is empty, all BMWs feel balanced and neutral, and while they may not all be as fast as the 'ultimate driving machine' tag would have you believe, the 335i Convertible . . . er . . . is. Especially when you're really, really late for a plane.

In sixth gear it will accelerate even faster than the old M3 would, but it won't shake your head off in the process. Yes, the ride is firm, but it's bearable.

And while we're on the subject of comfort, full marks – plus a star – for all the oddment stowage space they've provided in the cabin. It's especially useful in a convertible, and doubly especially useful when the boot, despite outward appearances, really isn't that big at all.

But I'm sorry, we have to go back to that price tag. At £46,000 it is dangerously close to the Audi RS4 Cabriolet, and probably not that far behind what one of the new soft-top M3s will cost.

And I'm sorry again, but anyone with a 335i is going to spend his entire life explaining to colleagues why he didn't go the extra mile and get the big boy instead. It will be particularly painful when the time comes to sell. M3s on the secondhand market are always fairly cheap, so to make your 335i look attractive you'll have to sell it on for mere pennies.

And even that might not do the trick, because of the way it looks. I stand corrected with other BMW models. But with the 3-series, I'm sorry.

It's not the Natural History Museum or the Trellick Tower, and it never will be. It is, I'm afraid, Coventry Cathedral. A turd that even time cannot succeed in polishing.

Sunday 29 July 2007

Kiss your knees goodbye, green people

Reva G-Wiz DC

At school I used to adore physics lessons. The laboratory was full of things that could be accelerated at great speed either into the teacher, when his back was turned, or more usually through the window.

In fact the only thing I loved more than physics was chemistry, because we could put acid in one another's pockets and make bombs.

No, really. Put a tiny piece of sodium in a bit of water and you had a fizz that could blow up another boy's homework. Put a lump of the stuff into a filled sink and you could take half of Derbyshire off the map. I used to sprinkle it in the teacher's hair and hope for rain.

And as a result of chemistry, I was never caught smoking. 'No sir. They're not nicotine stains. My fingers are yellow because I spilt some potassium permanganate on them this morning.'

Unfortunately this sort of thing is no longer allowed in school laboratories. All the dangerous liquids are kept under lock and key and no child is ever allowed to sprinkle polonium onto another boy's lunch.

And the result is plain for all to see. Since 1996 entries for A-level physics are down by 5,000 and there have been seventy-nine university science department closures. What's more, in the next few years half of the nation's physics teachers will retire, leaving a gap that cannot be filled.

What makes all this doubly alarming is that we are living in an increasingly technological world. The demand for phones that can play tunes, jet engines that run on manure and game consoles that mince pigeons is increasing at an exponential rate. And as it increases the number of people in Britain able to design and develop these new ideas is dwindling.

That's why it is critical the Science Museum wins a forthcoming competition to get its hands on £50 million from the Big Lottery. They're up against, I should imagine, a collective of fair-trade vegetarians who want to build a nuclear-free peace windmill in Scotland. And because of the way of the world these days, the wimmin will beat the blokes in cornish-pastie shoes who want to reignite Britain's love affair with machines, technology and stuff that explodes.

Pity, because at the moment only 8 per cent of the museum's exhibits are on display. The rest is held in seven giant aircraft hangars on a bleak hillside just outside Swindon.

I went there last week and it's a truly jaw-dropping experience. Just to the left of the creaking, rusted door, tucked away in an unlit corner, is the Blue Steel missile, Britain's first nuke. And parked behind it is a two-stage Polaris rocket.

Then you've got the world's first hovercraft, the mini submarine used in *For Your Eyes Only* and an early Hawk jet trainer, lost under the wings of a Comet airliner. Elsewhere there's a huge 1930s hot metal printing press, several seriously important cars, and lots of early PCs: blue cabinets the size of small vans, some of which have the computing power of a modern-day wristwatch.

In another hangar there are miles of racks, stacked from floor to ceiling and stuffed with everything that was ever important. Honestly, I half expected to find the lost ark of the covenant in there.

It is properly spooky; like being in a 3-D reach out and touch pop-up book on all the stuff that changed our lives. And what made it even more eerie is this: I was the only person there.

The plan is to change that. The men in cornish-pastie shoes want the lottery cash so they can build an architectural wonder

where all the quarter of a million exhibits can be displayed properly. A place that should help Britain's schoolchildren understand
that it won't be environmentalists or politicians that'll save the
world from global warming. It'll be a scientist.

If you want to ensure the Science Museum gets its cash and the
windmill fails, go to www.voteinspired.org.uk and vote. I have.

And now let us move on to what happens when you let a bunch
of nitwits take charge of the greenhouse gas debate. The G-Wiz. I
have often mocked this little car for being slow, ugly, unsafe and
hypocritical. But I have never driven one . . . until now.

First things first. It is very small. And it is even smaller than that
when you're inside. It is so small in fact that anyone over the age
of four will find their left knee is jammed behind the windscreen
washer switch, causing to it spray the windscreen constantly as
you drive along.

Actually, that's not true. You will only spray the windscreen
until you get to a right-hand bend which, no matter how slowly
you go, and believe me the G-Wiz goes very slowly indeed, will
cause you to slide right across the car until you are sitting in the
passenger seat.

In many ways this is better. Because while you can still easily
reach and operate all the controls, other road users will assume
you're the passenger, and therefore that the stupid little car is not
yours.

Sadly, however, the moment only lasts until you turn left.
Because then you'll slide back behind the wheel and the windscreen washing will start all over again.

Until you brake. Then your knee will shoot forwards into the
radio release button, which will pop the fascia on to the floor.

Still, at least it has a radio, because otherwise luxuries are few
and to be found only in the shape of two crummy cupholders
and some leather-look fabric that is glued haphazardly to the door
linings. Imagine a coal cellar and you have some idea of how well
appointed this car is.

And so what about life in the back? Well, there are two seats back there but God has not yet designed a creature that could fit in them, and it's pretty much the same story in the boot, which is the size of a mouse.

Speed. Well 0–60 mph is impossible because it won't do 60 mph. In fact, this is the first car I've driven that seems to have no top speed at all. It's like walking, only less comfortable.

Small wonder this is not classified as a car by the European Union. They call it a quadracycle, which means it can be sold without having to pass the usual safety tests. Pity, because a recent test by *Top Gear* magazine found that it was unsafe at pretty much any of its speeds. All two of them.

Actually, I should be serious because boffins using the much respected Euro NCAP test procedures found a number of design flaws that could kill or maim. You may save the planet with this car. But you could well lose a leg in the process.

You will certainly lose all your friends because to justify your significant £7,000 purchase (£8,299 for the newer AC version), you will need to explain, loudly and often, that it uses no fuel, that you simply charge it up at night – using power from a power station incidentally – and you're good to go forty miles. Unless you use the lights. Or the radio. Or the washer jets. Which you will, a lot. In which case it's only thirty miles, or maybe twenty, before you coast to a halt . . . in the rain you caused by not buying a Range Rover.

There's another thing, too. Children playing in the street can hear a Range Rover coming and know to get out of the way. The G-Wiz, on the other hand, is near silent, which means they may run in front of you to retrieve a lost ball. You may then hit them . . . causing your car to disintegrate and your legs to come off.

Even if I were a committed environmentalist I would not buy this car. It is too small, too dangerous and I'm sorry but it runs on juice from a power station, hardly a flower in the big green scheme of things.

What's more, a few luvvies in London are not going to make the slightest bit of difference, even if it's correct that cars are buggering up the ice pack. We will not be saved by going backwards. We will be saved by someone using technology to go forwards. We will be saved, in other words, by science, maths and the lost British art of invention.

Sunday 5 August 2007

Silence, please, for a new king of the road

Mercedes-Benz CL 600

When you go to buy a new car, you will be greeted by a salesman who has a ghastly suit and an unusual haircut. He will begin by indulging in a spot of reflexive-pronoun abuse and then he will offer yourself a list of juicy options that will enhance your motoring pleasure.

It's delicious agony, running down the possibilities, wondering what sort of satellite navigation you will need, whether the extra expense of 20 in wheels is worth it, and exactly what sort of cow you'd like to have killed to make the seats.

Eventually you will have balanced your natural instinct to splash out with the needs of your family to eat, and you'll present the salesman with the completed form. But frankly, you may as well give him a box of frogs for all the good it does.

'Yes,' he'll say, 'it is possible to make the car you want, in the colour you've chosen, with seats covered in the skin of a cow called Brian. But not this year. Or next.

'However, if your good self can't wait that long, myself happens to have a car in stock, which is similar to the one you've ordered ... except for the size of the engine, the sort of fuel it runs on, the fact that it has no sat nav, has an automatic gearbox and it's pink.'

Naturally, you will leap at the chance because you are all excited, which means you will spend the next three years driving round in something close to what you wanted.

Which is another way of saying 'something you didn't want at all'.

No, really. Buying a blue diesel estate when you wanted a grey petrol saloon is the same as booking a holiday in the Dominican Republic. And then going to Haiti because the flight leaves ten minutes earlier. It's like falling in love with a house and then buying the one next door.

I'd love, at this point, to lay into car makers, telling them to buck up their ideas, but sadly there's no point. Let's take Mercedes as an example. Currently they can offer you a massive range of cars, each of which is available with a choice of trim levels and engine sizes. I've done a quick head count and, amazingly, your local Mercedes dealer is able to offer around 300 different models.

And now it gets tricky because, on average, each of those models is available in a choice of ten colours. So now it's 3,000 models, and that's before you get to the colour of the interior trim.

Mercedes is famously mean-spirited in this respect, and once you've chosen a colour for the body you only get about five choices for the colour of the seats and carpets.

Even so, that means we're now up to 15,000 different models, each of which is available as a manual or an automatic. So that's 30,000 then, and each of those is available with probably fifty different options. The result is that Mercedes-Benz is able to offer you 1.5 million different permutations of one car.

Not that long ago Mercedes announced they were going to extend their range of saloons and estates to 'make something for everyone'. I didn't realise at the time that they were being Germanically literal. They could make 1.5 million cars and no two would be the same. Which is why, I'm afraid, it takes an age for you to choose the right model. And even longer to get it trimmed, painted and specced to your precise requirements.

I can't speed up the Stuttgart production lines, but happily I can at least steer you through the maze that is the brochure. So here goes. What you do is buy a gunmetal-grey Mercedes-Benz CL with a black interior.

The CL is a coupé version of the S-class and must not be confused with the CLK, which is a two-door version of the old C-class, or the CLS, which is a cut-down amalgamation of the E-class and the S-class.

Because it is a two-door coupé version of the S-class, the CL is meant to be quiet and comfortable. It is also fitted with a Rolls-Royce-style column-operated gearshifter, which gives you the relaxing options of backwards, forwards or parked. And because of all this pillowy smoothness and mattress simplicity, it wouldn't really suit Merc's magnificent but shouty 6.2 litre V8 engine.

And nor should you go for the entry-level V8, because nothing says a man has failed in life quite so well as a 500 badge on the back of his Mercedes. Apart, perhaps, from a Porsche Boxster. This is Premium Economy spec; it signifies you are clinging to respectability at the golf club by a mere thread.

So, you cannot have a V8, which means it must be a V12. It'd be tempting, I'm sure, to go for the 65, the most powerful engine in the world until Bugatti came along with the Veyron. It has so many torques you can light up the rear tyres so violently, they will actually dig holes in the road. I know this because I've done it. The power is stratospheric, atomic, and if I'm honest a bit idiotic.

That leaves you with the normal 600, a 5.5 litre, twin-turbo 12-pot that makes exactly the same amount of noise as the crowd at a five-day cricket match – i.e., none at all. Well, actually, not none exactly. If you listen very, very hard you can sometimes hear it snoring. And that means it's ideally suited to the smooth suspension and the waftmatic gearshifter. Driving it is like lying in a vat of baby oil, dreaming that you can fly.

Until you put your foot down. There's still no noise, and that's spooky because suddenly the view out of the window has gone all bonkers and you are overtaking light aircraft. It is properly fast, the CL 600. Even though it weighs 2.1 tons it will get you from 0–60 mph, silently, in just 4.5 seconds.

Being overtaken in this is like being overtaken by a ghost. You sense a blur and you feel the air move. But that's it.

I absolutely adored driving this car. It was a new experience – power without sound – but the thing I loved most of all was the way it looked.

They've tried to ape the shape of the old model's sublime rear window – and failed badly – but the rest ... oh my God, it's gorgeous. The balance, the flared wheelarches and the nose. Holy cow. This has the best nose on any car ever made.

It does not, however, have the best ride. Naturally, it has air suspension, not because air suspension works better than coils and springs and dampers but because it allows the computer geeks in Merc's underground design bunkers to fiddle about with their laptops, making it move the car about as the speed and driving style change.

In theory it's brilliant. In practice, it doesn't work. And it really didn't work in the CL I drove. It felt, sometimes, like I was on a water bed and I simply don't believe it's supposed to be that way. I honestly think there was a small fault in the system. And that's good, because it means I can ring Mercedes-Benz with a perfect excuse to borrow another 600 CL for a week. Or two, just to be sure.

Price? Well, the 600 CL costs £107,097, which is known in banking circles as a very great deal of money. It puts the CL in the same 2+2 marketplace as the Bentley Continental, as well as offerings from Porsche, Aston Martin and Maserati.

As a badge, the three-pointed star sits among this lot like a branch of Marks & Spencer on Bond Street. But the simple fact of the matter is this. As a car, it beats all of them. By a country mile.

Sunday 12 August 2007

Clarkson went on holiday to Ottawa, hired a dodgy Dodge and 'hosed the Garden of Eden down with 600 gallons of adrenaline'

Dodge Grand Caravan

Whenever there's a global survey to find the best places in the world to live, Canada always does well.

We're told that no one in Canada is ever robbed, butchered, stabbed, murdered or blown up by a doctor. And I don't doubt that all of this is true.

But by the same token no one in Canada ever wins on the horses, or escapes from a knife fight with their life, or has an orgasm. It is Switzerland with wheat.

They try to tell us that it's a wilderness full of bears who'll kill you if you run away or stand still – I can never remember which. But do you know how many people in the whole of the vastness of Canada have been killed by bears in the past two years?

It's one. Honestly, more people than that are killed in Britain by their trousers.

Anyway, Ottawa is the capital and it's really lovely. Lovely, lovely, lovely. More lovely than a pressed wild flower in a copy of *Jane Eyre*. If it were a person, it would be Jenny Agutter in *The Railway Children*. If it were an animal it would be a fluffy rabbit. And no one would ever eat it and it would never catch myxomatosis.

Strangely, however, despite the complete lack of pressure, and the plentiful supply of cheap parking, what the people of Ottawa do come the weekend is drive half an hour to their cabins by the lake. The lake is (gravelly voice here) really lovely. Take your breath away, roll your eyes, God-I-have-got-to-dive-in-that-right-now gorgeous.

I spent some of my holiday there this summer, and it was like lying in a nest of cotton wool, being hypnotised by a tin of treacle. I liked to swim in the morning, when the mist was rising, and in the afternoon I'd go kayaking for hours round all the islands and through the forests, soundlessly, apart from the paddles making eddies in the water. And the occasional satisfying crack as the beavers gnawed their way through another pine.

At night I'd lie in bed listening to the loons, those beautiful diving birds, and the gentle slop of the calm waters lapping against the untouched shoreline. And I couldn't help thinking: what I need to make this the best place on earth is a speedboat ...

Happily, my host had such a thing tucked away in his boathouse, and so for the next few days I never heard a loon, or a beaver, or the gentle slop of the wavelets. Instead it was wall to wall grrrrrrrrrrrr from a 70 horsepower Johnson outboard, and the excited shrieks from all the children who were being towed behind on big inflatable rubber rings.

I don't think the locals liked it very much. Canadians reckon the speedboat sits on the scale of antisocial behaviour between heroin and rape, and they plainly thought that we might have been emissaries from Satan. Certainly, they watched us in the same way that an Amish village would watch a performance by Babyshambles.

But the fact of the matter is this. God had done well with his side of the deal. The sky was blue, the sun was warm and the views were postcard-plus exceptional. But we had completed the picture with two cubic feet of internal combustion. We had hosed the Garden of Eden down with 600 gallons of adrenaline and turned it into paradise. It's lovely, as I said, to drift aimlessly through the forests on a canoe. But it's so much better to be hurled through them at 40 mph on a big, bouncy and almost completely uncontrollable inner tube.

What's more. Falling off a canoe is a bloody nuisance, chiefly because you cannot get back on again. Whereas falling from a hurtling piece of plastic is just about the biggest laugh a man can have. Especially if you go in upside down and your shorts come off.

I would recommend a holiday on a Canadian lake to anyone. But I'm afraid the recommendation comes with a bit of a proviso. To get from where the aeroplane lands to where the lake is you will need to drive. And that means you will need to borrow a car from a manufacturer's press fleet.

But since you can't do that, I didn't either. I hired one from a company called Thrifty. I looked for one called Extravagant. Or Expensive. But no such thing existed, so Thrifty it was.

The girl on the desk took my details, and as is the way with all hire-car companies, began to enter the full name of every single company on the Footsie 100 into her computer. Finally, after about a year, she looked up and cheerily announced that no cars were available.

I explained that we had made a reservation and that we had three small children who had just emerged from seven hours in the care of Air Canada – which is a bit like spending seven hours in a sensory deprivation tank – and that we needed some wheels.

This made her smile: a big, toothy, well-there's-nothing-I-can-do-about-it smile. Big mistake. My children saw what was coming and ran for their lives. My wife went the colour of a tomato and shrank into her own handbag.

When I'm faced with intransigence at a car-rental desk, what I like to do is summon up some little nugget of military history. It's never difficult. In Germany I tell them about Dresden, in France it's Agincourt, in Spain I wax lyrical about Drake, in Italy I'm spoilt for choice, and in Argentina, where I'm going next year, I shall be mentioning Goose Green.

In Canada I told the smiling girl at the Thrifty desk all about the massive superiority of General Wolfe over the pitiable

Marquis de Montcalm and explained that if she didn't come up with a car – right now – I'd visit the Plains of Abraham on her desk. It worked, and ten minutes later I was driving through Canada . . . in a Dodge Grand Caravan . . . from a company called Thrifty. As recipes go, this is right up there with a plate of pork sausages and strawberry ice cream served in a puddle of tepid Greek urine.

According to the bumf, this year's Grand Caravan comes with the Swivel-N-Go system, which means the two middle seats rotate to face backwards, as well as the Stow-N-Go setup, which means you can stow the back seats away . . . and then, er, go somewhere else.

On top of this, it comes with a stowable table, a MyGIG infotainment radio with AM/FM/CD/DVD/MP3 as well as a 20GB HDD, touchscreen, a USB input, GPS navigation, second- and third-row 8 in video screens, Sirius Satellite Backseat TV offering Cartoon Network Mobile, Nickelodeon and the Disney Channel, LED interior lighting, a ParkView reversing camera, a nine-speaker Infinity sound system with a 506 watt amplifier, thirteen cupholders, and sunshades for the second- and third-row windows.

Sadly, my car appeared to have none of these things.

What it did have was a nasty scrape along its flanks and a steering wheel that was not on straight. I think. It's hard to be sure, because where I pointed it seemed to have little or no bearing on my direction of travel. Small wonder that the Caravan's sister car, the Chrysler Grand Voyager, did so badly in the Euro NCAP safety tests.

Happily, however, if you do crash you won't be going very fast. Apparently this car is available with a choice of three engines – a 3.3 V6, a 3.8 V6 and a 4.0 V6. I think mine, in the best traditions of multiple choice, had d) none of the above.

I don't want to be stupid and say it was powered by something you might find in a cement mixer, but that's how it felt. Really.

It had no power at all, and if you dared to floor it to, say, get up a small hill, the gearbox would swap cogs with a force capable of beheading everyone inside.

I think I'd been given this car because the girl at the desk had tried to outwit me, in the same way that Montcalm tried to out-wit Wolfe. Happily, however, we won – again – because just five minutes before we handed it back my youngest daughter did the decent thing. And vomited in it.

Before I went away, I wrote a review of the glorious Mercedes-Benz CL 600 in which I said the suspension was not quite right. Well, Mercedes has sent another one round and I'm delighted to say it feels fine.

But I'm not sure about the shape of the speedometer. So I might hang on to it for a few more weeks, just to be sure . . .

Sunday 2 September 2007

Don't call it ugly, call it quite brilliant

Skoda Roomster

I daresay we all remember the bad old days when you came back from the shops with a new and exciting electrical appliance. And found it had been sold without a plug. Nowadays, though, thanks to the exciting Plugs and Sockets (Safety) Regulations 1994 (No 1768) any domestic appliance with a flexible cable must be fitted with a plug and the plug must be fitted with a fuse link that conforms to BS 1362.

As a result, you now come back from the shops to find that your shiny new toy has a plug. But that, unfortunately, the product itself hasn't actually been built. Last weekend I bought some outdoor lights for the garden. Except I didn't. What I actually bought was a box full of pieces that could be turned into some outdoor lights for the garden. By anyone with a simple degree in mechanical and electrical engineering.

Of course, there were some poor-quality instructions which explained that all you needed to assemble your quality product were fingers like cocktail sticks and six and a half thousand tools that you do not own.

It was truly and genuinely extraordinary to find how little had been done at the factory. And this is not a one off. These days we see exactly the same thing with furniture and all children's toys. The outdoor garden heater I bought back in May, to annoy George Monbiot, is still in its box in six bits because I simply cannot fathom how they all go together.

Of course I commend any company that can maximise its profits and quench the thirst of its shareholders. This is all excellent and makes the world go round, but implying on the box that the customer is buying a garden heater when in fact he's buying a box of pieces: that's flirting with fraud.

How long will it be before the box contains nothing but some iron ore, a piece of the Russian gas fields and 6,000 miles of pipeline? How long before Ikea sells you a tree in Finland and a saw? And as we edge slowly towards the meat of this morning's missive, how long before car makers catch on to the idea that people are idiots?

At present it costs the car makers a fortune to assemble a car. The parts are made elsewhere and then nailed together by billion-dollar robots at the plant. So how long will it be before Ford notices what's going on in the garden lamp industry and simply ships the components directly to your home? Along with a scrappy instruction book, saying, in French, that all you need to put everything together is some oxyacetylene, basic arc welding skills, and a robot.

This isn't as far fetched as you might imagine, because already almost all the cars we buy are made in kit form. The Aston Martin DB9 is a case in point. It was specifically designed so that the basic structure could be clothed in a different body and sold as something else. The V8 Vantage, for example.

Then there's the Rolls-Royce Phantom. It is built in the British factory like an Airfix kit, using parts that come in boxes from the BMW plant in Germany. Great. But think how much cheaper it would be to deliver those boxes straight to your door. Along, perhaps, with some walnut and fourteen cows that you'll need to skin and turn into seats. All you need is a large potato peeler and a sewing machine.

The ultimate kit car, though, is the Volkswagen Golf. Its underpinnings are used to make lots of other Volkswagens, like the Beetle, as well as by Audi, Seat and Skoda. Sometimes I wonder why anyone actually buys the daddy because it's possible to buy what's essentially an identical car. Usually for a lot less.

But then when I look at those identical cars I stop wondering. I mean, it's all very well imagining that your new Seat is made from Golf parts but it was assembled by Spaniards. And that's like buying a garden lamp that has been assembled by me. Yes, it's cheap, but every time you turn it on you will be electrocuted.

Skoda, however, is different. As we know from all the excellent new houses that are being built in Britain these days, the eastern Europeans are fine engineers. It is in their culture, somehow.

So a collection of German parts made by Petr Cech: that should be pretty good. The only problem is that Skoda has never actually made something brilliant enough to overcome the Primark badge on the back. Until now . . . Ladies and gentlemen, please be upstanding for the Roomster.

Ordinarily, there is nothing on God's earth quite as depressing as a mini-MPV. Whether it's a Renault Scénic or a Citroën Picasso or that truly terrible Toyota Yaris van, we know that you are biding your time until you are unlocked from the shackles of life by the blissful relief of death.

We know that your life has turned out to be nowhere near as successful or as happy as you'd hoped. We know that you have no imagination. And we know that you have no sense either, because a mini-MPV offers exactly the same number of seats as a normal car.

We can deduce from this that you've spent more money on something which comes with a bit more headroom. And what's the point of that, unless your children are actually giraffes? And if they are giraffes, then you are plainly way too interesting to waste your life in a bloody MPV.

The only exceptions to this rule, thus far, have been the Ford S-Max and the Citroën Berlingo: two genuinely clever and appealing cars. But the Roomster is better still. First of all there's the price. It's just £13,500. And for that you get – yes – a Skoda badge. But you also get alloy wheels, antilock brakes, a full-length glass roof, rear parking sensors, an alarm, cruise control, curtain and side airbags, electric windows and door mirrors, a front arm rest, an immobiliser, a stereo capable of handling an MP3 player, a delightful leather steering wheel, a trip computer and an astonishing array of potential seating positions in the back.

The rear seats, in fact, are so flexible that I managed to get three kids on them. And a full-sized trampoline in the boot.

Eventually, of course, we arrive at the styling. In the same way that you can discuss the merits of Gérard Depardieu for hours but at some point you have to discuss his nose.

Yes. It's odd. I'll grant you that. It looks like a cut and shut car. A mangled-up blend of Postman Pat's van, a Wendy house and a Lancia Stratos. But here's the thing. I loved it. I thought it was unusual without being sweet. Striking without being daft.

I should also explain at this point that while most car makers offer only four colours – silver, silvery grey, greyish silver and grey – the Skoda brochure looks like it comes from Dulux. There's a choice of five blues, two reds and two greens. Mine was olive metallic and it was great.

I'm procrastinating. And that's because the Roomster (was it named after Marc Bolan's lounge?) has a bit of an Achilles' heel. It's, um, not very nice to drive.

It should be fine. The front end is essentially from a VW Polo and the back from a Mark 4 Golf. But the steering is far too quick. You ease the wheel a tad and whoa, the whole thing darts left in a scuffle of tyre squeal and body roll. I liked the car so much I wanted to get used to it. But I never did.

And then there's the engine. It's a 1.6 litre VW unit but not one of their best. It's rough, unwilling to rev and not that powerful. Perhaps the diesel would be better. I hope so because mechanically the only really good bit in my test car was the automatic Tiptronic gearbox.

Ordinarily this would be enough to render the whole car

worthless. But sometimes the driving experience must play second fiddle to the whole ownership package.

That's certainly the case with the Volvo XC90 diesel. It's a dreadful car to drive, really, but it's so clever and so well thought out we're on our second. And about to buy a third.

The Roomster falls into this category. Yes, it's wobbly and rough, but it's extremely clever, well equipped and best of all it brought a great deal more light into my life than my new garden lamps. Which, incidentally, are now on eBay.

Sunday 9 September 2007

The sausage dog with rottweiler bite

Ascari A10

If the motor car were invented today, there is absolutely no way that any government in the world would let normal members of the public drive one. They'd argue it'd be too dangerous, too complicated and suitable only for presidents and members of the armed forces.

Happily, however, it was born at a time when the world hadn't got round to muddling up liberty with freedom. And as a result, it's become jolly popular. Today the world is groaning under the weight of 600 million vehicles. And Japan alone is adding to that number at the rate of 22,000 a day. That is unsustainable growth.

It's always hard to predict the future, but in our lifetime – unless you are shot prematurely – there will be only four motor manufacturers. One in America, one in Europe, and a couple in the Far East. And none will be making anything we would recognise as 'a car'.

The notion of travelling with the wind in your hair down a country road at 100 mph, with petrol providing the firepower and four big exhausts producing the soundtrack, will be an image every bit as outdated as diphtheria.

I have no doubt, for instance, that the speed-kills lobby will eventually win its argument. Dead babies trump 400 bhp every time. So all cars will be fitted with a satellite-monitored electronic overlord that will physically prevent you from ever breaking the limit. I'm also confident that the steering wheel will be removed.

Already Mercedes has technology that will apply the brakes whenever it's necessary. The only thing that's stopping them from fitting it is legislation; the same legislation that insists on two pilots in the cockpit on many commercial flights where only one is needed to actually fly the plane. Even though 80 per cent of all plane crashes are caused by pilot error.

The upshot, then, is that you won't actually drive your car. You will merely climb in, tell it where you want to go and sit back as it takes you there. Think Will Smith in *I, Robot*.

All this is certain. And anyone who begs to differ may as well sit on the beach in a robe telling the sea to go away.

Another thing that's beyond doubt is that you won't be driving round in a hybrid, such as the Toyota Prius. These use just as much fuel as normal cars and are designed only to assuage the guilt of people whose opinions come from a man so hopeless he couldn't even beat George Bush to the White House.

You will not have an electric car either. As the G-Wiz proves, They. Do. Not. Work. They run out of juice whenever it's raining, or dry, or windy. And to charge them up again you have to plug them into a socket that is fed by . . . a power station. Yippee.

No. According to the eggheads, your car will almost certainly be powered by hydrogen. The most abundant gas in the universe. And something that, when burnt, produces nothing but water.

This raises an interesting question. If we're so worried about melting ice caps and rising sea levels, what's the world going to look like when 600 million motor vehicles start to chuck water out of their tail-pipes? A point only I seem to have spotted thus far. Which means it's probably irrelevant.

It is possible to use hydrogen in an engine instead of petrol or diesel. Using current technology, you lose about a fifth of the power, and that sounds bad. But come on. To be just 20 per cent behind petrol, which has been fuelling engines for more than a hundred years . . . that's not a bad starting point.

Except I don't think it will be the starting point. I think that, soon, the holy grail will be cracked: the hydrogen fuel cell.

Think of it as a battery that is constantly charged by feeding it with hydrogen and oxygen. No, really. You mix them together and all you get in return is pure drinking water, and electricity. Which is then used to power your car, soundlessly, and for ever.

It all sounds like some kind of Monbiotic wet dream but the big players are close now. Close to making the dream of a world without oil a reality.

And please don't imagine that you'll have to tootle about in a road-going version of the Hindenburg, exploding in a Nagasaki-style fireball every time you drive under a pylon. The fact is that the best way of storing hydrogen is between the atoms in metal. Already some scientists reckon they have gone one better and have worked out a way of putting thirty litres in a single gram of graphite. And thirty litres would be enough to take a family saloon of the future 5,000 miles. So there we are. Problem solved. Personal transportation will survive. What will die, however, is the notion that 'the car' symbolises personal freedom. As you sit there, being 'driven' home, at a speed preordained by the government and on a route chosen by Nasa, you will have no control.

The device, the tool, the machine will be no more an extension of your hands and feet than a tumble dryer. It'll be no more exhilarating than a vacuum cleaner. So yes, while the world will be cleaner and quieter, it'll be like drowning in ditchwater.

So let's cheer ourselves up this morning with the fearsome Ascari A10. Normally I avoid road testing cars made by small British companies because no one's going to buy one anyway. So all I'm doing by saying it's rubbish is giving the owner someone to blame when the bailiffs come round.

And they are, always, rubbish; hideous carbon-fibre and magnesium reminders of what cars used to be like before we got robots to build them.

That's the thing, you see. The man who started the company

can't afford a robot or a proper factory. So he makes the cars on a soulless out-of-town industrial estate, by hand. And saying a car is a handmade is just another way of saying the door will fall off.

A car made by a small British company won't have been hot-weather tested in Arizona or subjected to trial by ice in Finland. Chances are, it won't have been tested at all. And so it goes with the Ascari. I bet that if you bought one it'd be a constant trial.

However, some things are worth a bit of extra effort. And this is one of them. With a tweaked version of BMW's old M5 engine sitting in the middle of the carbon-fibre tub, you have the power of 600 horses in a car that weighs about the same as a sausage dog.

The result is epic. You put your foot on the accelerator and then you become somewhere else. This is hypercar fast. Koenigsegg fast. It really is a tankbuster.

Naturally the sequential gearbox needed to transfer all this power to the rear wheels is substantial. Even the lever is huge, like something from the bridge of a 1960s cargo ship. It's noisy, too, so noisy that you can hear it whining and clunking above the sound of the four Alpine tunnels masquerading as exhausts. This is a car that makes you just fizz with excitement.

Sitting in the cockpit, hemmed in by strengthening beams and assaulted by the noise, gives you a sense of what it might have been like to be in the engine room of a second world war submarine that was being depth-charged.

But it isn't all brute-force barnyard technology. It has quite the best steering of any car I've ever driven. Perfectly weighted. Perfectly linear in its response. All car makers should be forced, by law, to drive an A10 so they can see what they're aiming for.

My favourite part, though, is the way it looks. It manages to be pretty and muscular at the same time. Combining the appeal of Kate Moss and the Terminator is a trick no other supercar designer has managed before. Of course, it's not very cheap. It costs £350,000 and for that you don't even get a radio. Not that you could hear it anyway.

The A10 is daft, for sure, and not at all relevant in the modern world. It consumes oil and smashes up its environment. But elephants do that as well; they destroy their habitat and drive themselves to extinction. And I bet you'll be sad when they die out.

Sunday 16 September 2007

Oh yes, it's the great pretender

Volvo XC70 SE Sport

There's a very good reason why *Top Gear* never allows its tame racing driver to speak. It's because he might express an opinion, and the opinions of all racing drivers are completely worthless.

You could put one in a Bugatti Veyron and while he might have a few kind words to say about the power, he'd dismiss the steering, the brakes and the grip as rubbish. To a racing driver, a BMW M3 is crap, an Audi RS4 is terrible, a Lamborghini Gallardo is gutless, and as for the Aston Martin Vanquish . . . oh dear. Damon Hill drove one once and wondered every time he put his foot on any of the pedals if perhaps something had broken.

Michael Schumacher is no better. Many years ago he hurled me around some sinewy ribbon of a track in a Ferrari 575, and in every corner the V12 wail was drowned out by a series of guttural Germanic expletives. He moaned about the understeer, the lack of grunt, the gearbox and every other feature of what I thought was a pretty good car. Then when he got out, he declared it to be s★★★, and went to the bar for an orange juice.

This has always annoyed me . . . until earlier this month when, for the first time, I drove a proper racing car, in a proper race. And now I know exactly what racing drivers mean. All road cars – every single one of them – are useless.

My racing car was a BMW 3-series with a diesel engine. It had covered about a million miles, ferrying PowerPoint equipment, I should imagine, to and from various out-of-town business hotel conference suites. So as a result, I was able to get it for just shy of £11,000.

It was then taken to a workshop where all of the interior was replaced with a roll cage and one seat and a fire extinguisher. Underneath, we simply fitted better brakes, lowered suspension and slick tyres. As racing cars go, then, it was far removed from a McLaren-Mercedes. Think of it as a worn-out fat man in a tracksuit and running shoes.

But oh my God. The tiny changes we made transformed this humdrum little rep-mobile into a car that was more exciting and more fun to drive than any supercar. No really. Give me the choice of driving around Silverstone in this, the world's worst racer, or a Zonda, one of the world's best road cars, and I'd take the diesel in a heartbeat.

At the track, I started out braking for the bends where I would brake in a road car. But this caused the BMW to just stop. Immediately. So then I'd have to engage first and accelerate up to the bend I had been trying to slow for. It was not a good look and many spectators laughed.

Quickly, I realised I could brake about 6 in before the turning-in point and even then I wound up going too slowly. On slicks, a car will go round any corner at any speed that takes your fancy. No really. Through Stowe corner, a Lexus road car is right on the raggedy edge of controllability at 70 mph. In our diesel you could take it at 100 mph . . . while doing a crossword.

After a weekend spent revelling in the incredible grip and the braking, I climbed into my Gallardo for the trip home and it was like I'd inadvertently got into a time machine and gone back 200 years. It would go all right but it wouldn't stop and it wouldn't grip.

Finally, then, after twenty years in the business, I began to see why racing drivers don't like road cars. It's simple. It's because any car designed to cope with speed humps and potholes, any car fitted with tyres that last more than an hour is bound to be less capable than any car designed purely to go round corners as fast as possible.

I therefore find myself this morning hooting with derision at the current crop of so-called track-focused road cars. The Porsche GT3 RS is a classic case in point. Yes, it has a roll cage and, yes, it's jolly light. But will it corner as fast as a diesel BMW on slicks? No. Will it brake more abruptly? No.

All Porsche has done by lowering it and firming it up and removing the soundproofing is make it noisy and uncomfortable on the road. Does it work on the track? No. In the big scheme of things, not even slightly.

The only way you could do that is by fitting slicks. But if you do that and try to drive home afterwards, the constabulary will want a word.

Then there's the bothersome business of cost. A full exhaust system for an M3 costs BMW £76. That is cheap. And cheap doesn't work on a racetrack. After our twenty-four hours, for instance, we got a bill for tyres that amounted to £6,000.

I'm sad to announce, then, that road cars and track cars are two separate entities and that neither will work, no matter what you do, in the other's domain. A racing car on the road will be brutal, unforgiving and noisy. A road car on the track will go into a barrier and kill you.

Imagining, then, that your GT3 RS or your Gallardo Superleggera or your M3 CSL gives you a feel of the racetrack is as mad, I'm afraid, as imagining that if you eat a rasher of bacon, you'll have an idea what sausages taste like.

It is very difficult to build a car that can do two things, a point demonstrated this morning by the meat of the missive – the Volvo XC70.

What we have here is a normal five-seater Volvo estate car, converted with some stilts so that it can get down your rutted driveway without losing its sump to a stone.

Sure, it can't climb the north face of the Eiger, and it would come unstuck if it were pressed into service with the Highland mountain rescue service but because of the extra ground clearance and four-wheel drive it'll be fine when you go to those parties where you're made to park in a muddy field.

In theory this is excellent. Because it isn't a proper off-roader, environmentalists won't throw eggs at it and leave insulting messages under the windscreen wipers whenever you leave it alone for a moment. And nor will you have a typical off-roader's fuel bill to foot.

What's more, the car on which it's based is much underrated. The new version of the V70 is nowhere near as pretty as its predecessor – no, don't laugh: it was a good looking car – but it is hugely spacious with a boot big enough to stage a medium-sized air display. It's nice to drive as well, in a quiet, softly softly sort of way.

Sadly, many of these attributes have been lost in the XC version. You can fiddle around with the suspension settings but no matter which button you press, the ride is never anything other than soft, with a hard and chewy centre. I didn't like it at all.

I'm not sure either about the tough looking body cladding, principally because I'm not sure it's tough at all. I suspect it's just something else to mend after a crash. And I wasn't all that fussed about the engine. It was a 3.2 litre six, and while it wasn't very bad, it wasn't very good either. If it were a person, I suspect you wouldn't invite it round for drinks because it would bore your friends.

The most worrying thing about this car, though, is who you're buying it from. Ford, as we know, is thinking of selling Volvo, and I don't know about you, but I wouldn't pay nearly £36,000 to a car company if I didn't know who was going to be running it next week.

In many ways the XC70 is a good car. It's light and airy, well equipped and fitted with every safety feature known to man. It also meets a genuine demand – for a non off-road car that can do a bit of off-roading if asked.

But it doesn't quite work. As a result, unless I really needed the Volvo's vast boot, I'd save myself £14,000 and buy a Subaru Legacy Outback.

Sunday 23 September 2007

It doesn't have to do anything but arrive

Rolls-Royce Phantom Drophead Coupé

Someone with a cruel mouth and a spiteful demeanour announced the other day that all car advertisements should carry a government health warning. 'Driving while pregnant harms your baby.' 'Cars lower your sperm count.' That sort of thing. This would be a pity because apart from Griff Rhys Jones in his underpants and Mazda's international zoom-zoom efforts, almost all car advertisements are better than almost all the programmes they help to fund.

It was always thus. Back in the early Sixties television commercials were rammed with smiley people cramming as much information as was humanly possible into the thirty-second slot. Prices, ingredients, comparisons. The lot.

Then in 1963 along came an advertisement for the VW Beetle. Written by Bill Bernbach at Dingleberry, Dunkirk and Bedhopper, it showed a pair of headlights picking their way through a blizzard and arriving at a big wooden hut. The doors opened and out came a snowplough. 'Have you ever wondered,' asked the voiceover, 'how the man who drives the snowplough drives to the snowplough?' And we were left with a picture of the little Bug by the big hut.

It changed advertising for ever because here was a commercial that apparently contained no information at all. But which actually told you more about the Beetle than a million Colgate rings of confidence.

We see this now all the time. Honda has that man with the Mr Kipling gravel in his larynx telling us that it's nice when things just work. We have Audi telling us something in German that we don't understand and we have Saabs leaving vapour trails through deserted city streets. 'It's based on a jet fighter,' they tell us. Even though the truth of the matter is that it's actually based on a Vauxhall Vectra. But never mind.

Lamborghini has a brilliant campaign. Set in the company's home town, one shows a cautious woman waiting by a crossing and the other locals protecting their hearing from passing super-cars.

But the best, by a mile, has never been shown. Not even in the furthest reaches of the internet. It shows a pair of headlights in a blizzard. But they're not like the candles in jam jars you found on a Beetle. They are funky, halogenesque with a Daz blue white feel to them. Other than this, it's pretty much the same as the original Beetle ad. The lights forge a path through the blizzard to a big wooden hut, from which a snowplough emerges.

'Have you ever wondered,' asks the voiceover, 'how the man who owns the snowplough gets to the snowplough?' And as the plough breaks frame, we're left with a shot of the Rolls-Royce Phantom.

It'd be a shame, I think, to clutter up this simple parody with a lot of guff about carbon dioxide and baby seals and how many children in Birmingham have small brains.

Whatever, I don't know why the ad never made it, even as a viral e-mail. Maybe it's because Rolls-Royce doesn't need to advertise. Not when you have Alan Sugar whizzing hither and thither in his Phantom every week on *The Apprentice*. And on the other side, Simon Cowell doing much the same thing on *The X Factor*.

Or maybe it's because there is simply no alternative. The Phantom has the pluto-matic market all to itself. And puh-lease do not introduce the Maybach at this point because while it's a good and noble thing, it is a first cousin of the Wakefield hen night stretched limo. The Phantom is a first cousin only to the

God of silence, and manners, and breeding. It is an exquisite car and I would have one tomorrow if it weren't so bloody expensive. That and the fact my wife has said she would divorce me. And then kill me with a knife.

And now comes the convertible and, oh deary me. When I came home to find it sitting in my drive, all huge and brilliant, I'm afraid I started to dribble.

Like its hard top brother, this also has no rivals. Well, unless you count the Bentley Azure, which is of course excellent. If you like to waft around in something that can trace its roots back to 1959. Which means you'd be wafting around in something that's older than me.

The Rolls doesn't look or feel old-fashioned at all. Everything, from the unpainted bonnet to the backwards-opening suicide doors to the rattan carpets and, yes, even the teak Sunseeker-style decking on the back, makes it look as fresh and as futuristic as tomorrow morning's papers.

Maybe its back end is a bit wonky, but other than this the styling, roof up or down, is just the most inspired piece of automotive design since ever.

And then my wife came home. 'Jesus H Christ,' she said. 'What is that monstrosity doing here?' An argument ensued. She said it was vulgar. I said she was from the Isle of Man so she'd know. Some doors slammed. And I went for a drive.

Oooh it's big. Sumo-wrestler big. Eighteen feet long and six feet wide big. But you ignore this and assume that because it's a V12 convertible it must have some sportiness in its complexion. I did. But it doesn't. In fact it is hard to think of anything in the world that is less sporty. Mount Fuji, perhaps. But that's about it.

Part of the problem is that you sit so high. You really can go eye to eye with people in Range Rovers. And that gives you the impression that actually you're behind the wheel of a drophead truck.

Add to this steering, suspension and a gearbox, all of which feel decidedly American and you very quickly learn to back off and waft. I must say I came home that night a bit disappointed.

The next day we took it to a party in Marlow, me in the driver's seat and my wife curled up in the passenger footwell in case she was seen. But it didn't matter, because we weren't speaking anyway.

This is mainly because we had comprehensively failed to find a way of opening the boot, so she'd put her bags on the back seat and her favourite scarf had blown away.

And also, the satellite navigation system – one of the few bits on the car obviously to have been lifted from a BMW – steadfastly refused to acknowledge Marlow existed.

If I'm honest, I was finding it difficult to defend the Drophead. It wouldn't fit on even the widest high street. It does fewer than ten miles to the gallon. It has the get up and go of a potato, and a boot, when you do finally get the lid up, that is smaller than the fridge in a caravan. Oh, and it costs £307,000, which means it's £80,000 more than the Bentley.

I must also say I disliked the wooden dashboard, which appeared to be a bit half hearted. There was a sense that it had been put there because of tradition, rather than because it looked good. It certainly didn't match the backlit blue dials.

And I have to say that while the seven-layer roof is good when up, the buffeting when travelling with it down is intolerable at anything more than eighty. But then we arrived at our party in Marlow and everyone went berserk. I've never seen a car cause such a stir, and suddenly the point of the Roller became crystal clear.

It is not built for speed or grip. It is not built to excite with its handling or the roar from its exhaust. It is not built to be safe, or frugal, or cheap. It is not built to do any of the things we have come to expect of cars in recent years. It is not built to go places. It is built to arrive.

This car, then, is not a car at all. It is a fanfare. A blast of trumpeteering to silence the crowds when someone special is about to enter the room. The reason why there's no advertising for this car is simple. It's built to advertise you.

Sure, I will admit that in England it is a bit ostentatious, a sunflower in a field of weeds. Arriving anywhere here in such a thing is the same as arriving with a Rolex at an NUM reunion. But arriving in a Drophead at the Oscars or at the casino in Monte Carlo would be more impressive, I suspect, than arriving in Keira Knightley.

And because of this I shall ignore the pleas of my wife. And give it five stars.

Sunday 30 September 2007

Let's go tombstoning in carpet slippers

Maserati Quattroporte Executive GT

So, tombstoning. It's the latest craze and what you do is simple. You go to the seaside, climb the tallest cliff and, without bothering to check the depth of the water, hurl yourself into the unknown. Then you go home in an ambulance and spend the rest of your life in a wheelchair, dribbling.

I suppose one reason why people do this is because they have been brought up in a world with no danger. They have not been allowed to play conkers or climb trees, so everything they have ever experienced is safe and comfy. It stands to reason, then, that jumping off Beachy Head into 2 ft of water will be safe and comfy too.

The other reason is that the participants are young. And young people like discomfort, speed and adrenaline so much they are prepared to risk a lifetime of head wands and mashed food to get it.

Older people are the exact opposite. They like wingback chairs and being warm. What I crave in my middle age is an empty diary. Page after page of nothing. Sometimes these days I get up and spend all day counting the minutes until I can go back to bed again. Sleeping is now my absolute favourite hobby.

I still like going quickly, of course, but only if I can sit down. It's why I have no interest in making a parachute jump. You have to get off your seat and hurl yourself out of the door. That's too much effort, especially as you could achieve much the same sensation by driving to work with your head out of the sunshine roof.

Then there's white-water rafting. Why would I want to do that? All that huffing and puffing. I'd rather eat a bar of Cadbury's Fruit & Nut chocolate.

And what really annoys me is that car makers just don't seem to have cottoned on, which means that just about every single expensive and desirable car on the market today is aimed at people who go tombstoning. And not people who sit in chairs all day dreaming of sleep and eating chocolate.

When a rich person – someone who could afford a Ferrari or Lamborghini – is asked by an airline where he'd like to sit, he will say 'in first class where the seats are sumptuous and the wine is fine'. He will not say, 'Ooh, is there any chance that you could spread-eagle me across the jet intake?'

I should make it plain at this point that I still like fast cars. I like them to telegraph their intentions through the fabric of my underpants. I like them to be crisp and responsive and loud and powerful. But I am unusual.

Most people are typified by my elderly friend Brian. He rarely exceeds 30 mph. He is baffled by gearboxes. He often forgets what the steering wheel does. And as a result there is no pillar, post, pylon, hedge or low wall in all of southeast England that he hasn't scraped, hit or backed into.

If Brian were a benefit cheat or a shelf stacker all would be well. He could buy an automatic Kia Rio and trundle about at 6 mph, delirious with joy. But unfortunately Brian runs a successful business and is therefore in a position to spend a lot on his cars. Which he does. And he hates every single one of them.

Since I've known him he's had two Aston Martins, two supercharged Jaguars, a Porsche 911, a Ferrari 360 (which he really, really hated), and a Maserati. As I write he's waiting for the new Maserati coupé and I feel fairly sure he'll dislike this as well. There's a good reason for this. All these cars ride harshly and make a lot of noise.

They are designed for speed and handling and thrustiness.

Things that Brian doesn't want. Things that few people want once they're past fifty. And let's be honest, you have to be past fifty, really, to insure cars like this.

Of course, there are exceptions. The Rolls-Royce Phantom, for example, but it costs £250,000 and by the time you have that kind of money to spend on a car you'd be 7,000 years old.

Then there's the Bentley Continental. It is fast. It is expensive. And, unusually, it is comfortable as well. But that's because, underneath, it's a Volkswagen Phaeton.

The Lamborghini Gallardo – not a lot of people know this – is available from the factory with a choice of three suspension settings. Sport. Normal. And Comfort. But I bet it isn't comfortable at all. I bet it's a relative thing: like having your head put in a vice is 'more comfortable' than being shot in the back of the knee.

So if you want to spend a lot of money on a comfortable car that isn't a Volkswagen Phaeton in a Bento-frock, what about the new Maserati Quattroporte automatic?

Its lovely V8 engine is not squeezed to hand over as much power as possible. Without really trying it serves up 400 bhp and that's plenty.

And inside there's no carbon fibre creaking noisily against magnesium struts. It's leather and wood and opulence. It's exactly the sort of place an older chap might want to sit after a hard day in a chair.

Unfortunately, when it first came along the Quattroporte was only available with a stupid flappy-paddle gearbox. The worst, most dim-witted paddle shifter ever made. And as a result the older generation, the people with the money to buy such a thing, said 'no thanks' and bought a Mercedes instead.

You might think it'd be easy, replacing the manual with an auto. But no. The manual was fitted at the back of the car for better weight distribution but the auto is up at the front, bolted to the back of the engine. That meant redesigning the whole floor, the rear suspension, and even the engine itself. It now has a wet sump.

But it was worth the effort, because now you sink into your Quattroporte, fire up the lazy V8 with a key – you're not expected to push a stupid starter button like you do in most expensive cars these days. And then you go home. Quietly and with no need to change gear. It all sounds too wonderful for words.

And it gets better, because this car has such dignity. There's a very real sense that no footballer would buy a Quattroporte. It is a dashing car for people who think the only thing in the world that's worse than a fake Rolex is a real one. It really does have a sky-high want-one factor. And now it comes in a package that's no harder to operate than a toaster.

And oh, how I wish I could stop there. But I'm afraid there are some problems. Some, like the unfathomable sat nav, the broken air-conditioning and the scattergun switch arrangement are small, and you could get used to them. One, however, is big. The way it drives.

It is absolutely horrible. It fidgets whenever the road surface is anything other than millpond smooth, it crashes over bumps and it hunts camber so violently that once it flicked onto the wrong side of the road.

Weirdly, I did not notice this when I drove a manual Quattroporte and I can only presume that by removing the tube that connected the gearbox to the engine they've removed some of the car's rigidity. Either that or the tyres are made from plywood.

Whatever. They have removed one big problem and created another, even bigger one.

I wanted desperately to like this car. I even hung on to it for an extra day to see if my mind would change. But I could not live with the problems. Not in a car that sheds value like it's sitting in a bath of acid. And so if you are an old man who likes being comfortable, there is still no expensive car that fits the bill.

The only solution, then, is to buy a Ford Mondeo and fit mink seats.

Sunday 7 October 2007

Call me stupid, but I like it

Fiat Bravo

The new Highway Code is full of many worthy and ethnically balanced tips for making the world a greener and safer place. You can't smoke. You can't leave your engine running unnecessarily. You can't apply make-up if it's been tested on cats.

And if you must eat at the wheel, make it a biodegradable pot of fairtrade hummus and not some corporate ghastliness like a Big Mac. There are also many rules for the elderly. Motorised wheelchairs, it says, should be driven on the pavement wherever possible, at no more than 4 mph. And if the driver does have to venture on to the road, he or she should think about wearing a high-visibility jacket, especially when negotiating roundabouts.

Strangely, however, the vegetarian lunatic who wrote all this guff has no specific advice for older people who have not yet got themselves a Stannah stairlift on wheels. The three score and tenners who still have a car. I do, though. And here it is. Get a bloody move on.

I want to make it absolutely plain at this point that I have no beef against the older generation. They fought Hitler. They invented coal. They made a quarter of the world pink while eating nothing but cabbage. And I'm grateful for all that. But if we delivered your meals on wheels at the speed you drive, you'd end up with botulism. There are no depths to which my shoulders will not sink when I happen upon a spotlessly clean Peugeot – and it is almost always a Peugeot – that is being coaxed along the highways and byways by someone whose ears are so big he can use them to pick up the shopping channels.

Of course, the poor old chap is in no rush. He has spent his life relentlessly dodging Nazis and diphtheria. He has worked his fingers to the bone for forty years. And now he's retired, he can slow right down. Potter to the potting shed. Take his time. Relax.

Hmmm. If you are Japanese or French, then this is undoubtedly the case, because you will live until you are a hundred and forty-twelve. But here in Britain, the average life expectancy for a man is seventy-seven. So, if you are seventy now, there is no time to lose.

No really. If you only have seven years left, that means the Reaper will be dropping round for tea and buns in about 61,000 hours from now. You therefore shouldn't be wasting time by pootling to the garden centre at walking pace. So come on, grandad. The clock's ticking. Pedal to the metal. Or you'll be in your flowerbed before the plants you bought.

I was particularly distressed by a piece of geriatric driving last weekend since it was my eldest daughter's first leave-out from boarding school and I wanted to be there on time. Unfortunately, she has made it crystal clear that I am never – never, d'you hear – to pick her up in any car that is even slightly flamboyant or flash. Nothing with four-wheel drive. Nothing with only two seats. Nothing with a big snarling engine. Nothing yellow. And as a result, I was tootling up the Fosse Way in a placenta red Fiat Bravo.

It was the sporty version, I'm afraid, but even so, it simply didn't have enough oomph to get past the inevitable Peugeot. Which meant I arrived at the school late. Thanks, Mr Mole-husband. I hope you have a big-end failure very soon. And because you chose a Peugeot, you probably will.

And speaking of unreliability . . . I honestly cannot work out how Fiat is still in business. British Leyland failed because it made rubbish cars, essentially for the home market. And yet – somehow – Fiat has been doing exactly the same thing for years but is still with us.

Yes, it survived in Italy because its market was protected from imports. But it isn't now. And anyway, because it costs a billion to develop a new car, Fiat has to sell its products all over the world. Which means someone in Britain has to think: 'Yes. There are many great cars out there, all of which suit my needs perfectly. But I'm not interested in speed, style, reliability, fuel economy, performance or value. So I shall buy a Punto.' Every single time you read a customer satisfaction survey, all the Fiats sit down at the bottom. Above Peugeot for sure, but often below Citroën and even Renault. And for Fiat to survive it has to reckon these disgruntled customers will say: 'My Punto is terrible. I hate it. It is always going wrong. So I shall buy another.' The thing is, however, that somehow Fiat does survive, and I'm extremely glad because I like what it makes very much.

You get in a Fiat and even though the headlining has fallen off, and is draped round your head like a nun's hat, and the engine sounds as if it's being fuelled with gravel and there's a smell of melting glue, you always think: 'This is fun.'

It's much the same story with the new Bravo. It's available with a wide range of engines but, inevitably, I asked for the most powerful. It's a turbocharged 1.4 that chucks out 150 bhp. That's a lot from a small amount of space. But it doesn't feel like half enough when you're on the Fosse and you can't see what's coming the other way because your view is blocked by the ridiculous ears of the man in front.

Maybe because it's quite a porker, it really isn't a fast car. So in desperation, you press a little button on the dash that says 'sport'.

Fiat says this changes the shape of the engine's torque curve. Instead of getting a dribble, low down in the rev range, you get a torrent coming on stream at 3000 rpm. Hmmm. Having experimented with this button on a number of occasions, I've decided that what it actually does is illuminate a little light on the dash. And that's it. I don't care, though, because it is a fun car to drive. There's a looseness to the controls that you may interpret as poor build quality or a slackness in the system, and I'd be the first to agree that the steering's not that great and the handling isn't especially noteworthy. However, somehow, it puts a smile on your face. Maybe it's because it feels so very, very different to a taut and muscular Volkswagen.

It looks different, too. I was going to wax lyrical about how the Italians, even when they're asked to come up with a practical five-door hatchback, somehow manage to give it a bit of flair, a bit of panache. But then I noticed it was designed by a man called Frank Stephenson. Who sounds about as Italian as a Fray Bentos steak and kidney pie. Whatever. It's a lovely looking little thing with a stylish nose and tapering windows. I think you would feel fairly pleased to have one sitting on your drive.

Inside, it's pretty much the same as all the other cars in the world, except for one thing. I could never quite get comfortable. Italian cars always used to be designed for creatures that are only found under rocks in the sea, and while they've got better, they still refuse to accept that a human being's legs are usually longer than his arms.

Other things. Well, you can have it with a voice-activated sat nav system, which won't work, and will then break. And my test car came with a USB connection port for an MP3 player. Lovely, except it appeared to have been put in place by an ape.

There's no point going on. There are many issues in a Bravo that you just won't find in a Volkswagen. So we're back to square one. To buy this car you must decide that what you really want is something that's not quite as good as a Golf.

Except for a couple of things. The way it feels and the way it looks. If these are important to you, try one. You might like it. I did.

I also liked the huge ashtray. It was easily big enough to hold the ashes of a freshly burnt copy of our ridiculous new Highway Code.

Sunday 14 October 2007

The gun in Queen Victoria's knicker drawer

Jaguar XJR 4.2 V8 Supercharged

Hyde Park Corner was its usual jammed-up self yesterday morning. But as I gazed upon the scene of overheating metal, missed appointments and frayed nerves, I noticed something a little bit odd. Every single car on the entire roundabout was a big Mercedes–Benz.

Now I know Uncle Ken's congestion charge keeps the poor out of central London and I know, too, that this is the time of year when celebrities come out of the closet to promote their latest book. So the demand for chauffeur-driven Mercs sky-rockets.

I therefore peered from the back of my chauffeur-driven S-class into the others, hoping to catch a glimpse of Helen Mirren on her way from GMTV to a chat with Steve Wright. Or Kerry Katona perhaps, on her way from Fern and Phillip to Radio 5 Live to plug her new fitness video 'Fart Yourself Thin'. Maybe I might even see Richard E Grant.

But no. Apart from James May on his way from Teachers TV to a shopping channel to talk about his new scratch'n'sniff book on armpits, most of the people in most of the Mercs looked fairly normal. Some were fat, some were thin, some were men and some were women. But they all had one thing in common. They'd been driven into a Mercedes because there's absolutely nothing else on the market that will do.

I touched on this a couple of weeks ago while reviewing the new automatic version of Maserati's Quattroporte. The amazing lack of choice for the fortysomething chap or chapess who just wants four wheels, iPod connectivity and a sepulchral silence from the engine.

The Maserati didn't cut it at all. It was rough and fidgety and not at all what you might want after a hard day's lunch. And it's much the same story from anything else with a flamboyant badge. Astons, Ferraris, Lambos, Porsches. They're all built for Lewis Hamilton. Not someone called Hamilton, who just wants to get to Lewes. Even the people at BMW cock it up. They try ever so hard to make the 7-series big and soft and comfy. But like the naughty schoolboy who's doing his best to behave, they just can't help themselves. So, just as he sticks his hand in the sweetie jar, they stick their mitts into the 'sports' bin and fit even the squidgiest 7-series with grippy, low-profile tyres and a suspension system that firms itself up for the bends.

This is tremendous, of course, if you find yourself at the Nürburgring being chased by the Four Horsemen of the Apocalypse in helicopter gunships. But if you just want to get home − which is more likely in my experience − the inherent sportiness would drive you mad.

Big Audis are similarly afflicted and while Lexuses are not, they can be quite bland. I sometimes think that if you stole a Lexus, you'd be able to drive it around for a year or two before the owner remembered that he had one, and that it was missing.

So, you might not want a Mercedes. You may not like Germans. But if you want something big, well made and above all, comfortable, you have no choice.

Really? Aren't you forgetting something? I certainly was when I was driving that Maserati Quattroporte two weeks go. No really. I remember thinking: 'Well, this isn't good enough, so it'll have to be a Merc.' But what about the Jaguar XJR?

Like the Maserati, it has a 4.2 litre V8 engine. Like the Maserati, it has four seats and 400 bhp. Like the Maserati, many cows laid down their lives to create the interior, and like the Maserati, it is a handsome devil.

It was not always thus. When the new XJ series came along a few years ago, I was a bit shocked. It just looked like an old XJ that had got fat. But time, and a few styling modifications, have been kind and now, in black, with those aluminium gills on the flanks, a wire mesh grille and some big wheels, the supercharged R looks absolutely, head-turningly stunning. Not as good as the Mazzer, I'll grant you, but 2,454 times better than any Merc.

Better still, instead of a driver's door, the XJR is fitted with a time portal. Step through it and you are taken back to about 1956. I cannot tell you how old-fashioned it feels from behind the wheel. There's a big cat on the steering wheel boss but you think: 'No, this can't be. I'm in a Wolseley. Either that or somehow I've wound up in Queen Victoria's knicker drawer.'

So, a little bit cramped, a little bit claustrophobic and faced with a big slab of timber, you set off half expecting the wireless to provide you with Raymond Baxter and not much else. You're in a post office and the rest of the world is whizzing by in an e-mail.

Even the buttons and dials look and feel old-fashioned. But here's the weird thing, almost everything you can fit to a Mercedes is fitted to the Jag. Yes, the switch for the heated seats looks like it came from a Baird Telecaster but push it and you'll discover that it can not only warm your back but also, thanks to little air-con ducts in the fabric, cool you down as well.

Radar-guided cruise control. Yup, it has that as well and if you dive into the touchscreen command centre, you find it says Rear Multimedia. And never mind that it uses the same typeface as the *Doncaster Gazette* did in 1969.

What I'm saying is that with its television screens in the back, and its self-closing boot and its in-built telephone, the Jag has everything you ever use on your Merc.

Sure, Jag is owned by Ford, which has less money than most shelf stackers these days so one or two bits are missing. There's no infrared night vision, for example, but unless you are a doggist, why would you want that in the first place? Similarly, the seat bolsters don't punch you in the spleen every time you go round a bend – like they do on an M5 or in an Audi RS4 – but again, this is not something that's desirable. Or even pleasant.

The Jag, in short, is fully loaded with all the stuff you need, and everything you don't isn't there. Noise, for example. I'm not suggesting for a moment that a Mercedes E-class is the Grateful Dead with windscreen wipers but the Jag couldn't even make itself heard above a string quartet.

The XKR, it's two-door coupé sister, has the same engine but makes a hell of a racket. The XJR borders on sensory deprivation.

And despite those big wheels and fat tyres it's comfortable too. Really comfortable. Driving this is like floating on a lilo, on an oiled-up Thai teenager, in a warm bath, on a nice day, on a beach, in the tropics, while listening to Jean Michel Jarre. And that, come on, is what you want really.

You'd expect, of course, that a car this relaxing would be fairly hopeless if you were late for a plane. But no. It doesn't handle, steer or brake quite as well as a Merc, or more particularly, a BMW, but it's way, way better than the Maserati. And when it comes to oomph, Fritz had better be concentrating because Tommy Jag packs an almighty supercharged punch.

I suppose at this point you're all thinking: 'Yes. But I'm a busy man and Jags break down all the time.' Sure, that was the case when they were built by Red Robbo and his merry band of communists and lunatics. But you look at the customer satisfaction surveys now. Jag's a player. Right up with the Lexus you bought last February . . . and lost.

Best of all, though, is what the Jag says about you. A Merc says you're a chauffeur and that you have Lee Ryan from Blue in the back, talking about his new range of hair product. A BMW says you won't let anyone out of a side turning. An Audi says you're big in cement, a Lexus says you're a bit boring and a Maserati says you've gone nuts.

A Jag, though? Well, you could be a government minister, or you could be Arthur Daley. You could be Hannibal Lecter, or you could be the chairman of BP. You could be anyone. But whenever I see a Jag, don't ask me why, I always assume the driver has a gun in the boot. That makes you look a little bit cool.

Cool, and when you're stuck at the lights surrounded by a million Mercs, a little bit smug as well.

Sunday 21 October 2007

An avenger hitting dealers where it hurts

Volvo S80 SE Sport

As a general rule, you do not buy a Volvo because you want a sleek motorway cruiser or a machine that grips like a rabbit in flight. You buy one because you have many children, and because you occasionally need to transport wardrobes.

So why, you may be wondering, have they made an all-wheel-drive saloon car with a big V8 at the front and no space for even medium-sized furniture at the back. Have they gone mad?

No. Not really. But to understand why, you need to know a little bit about how the car industry works. It's very simple. The car maker makes cars that are then bought by a global network of dealers. Who then sell the cars on to you and me. This is known in financial circles as 'a licence to print money'.

I'm being serious. Because once you've decided that you'd like, say, a BMW, realistically the only place you can buy it is from the one dealer in your area. You can go to a dealer further away, of course, but don't expect your local chap to bend over backwards if something goes wrong.

All the dealer has to do then, is offer you a small discount to make you feel good. Then he takes this money straight back again by stitching you up with a load of extras you don't want or need. And a finance deal that is designed to ruin you, your children and your children's children. And then he offers to buy your old car for a pound. And you accept because selling it privately is such a godforsaken faff.

All those epsilons coming up the drive, kicking the tyres and trying to fob you off with a Nigerian bank draft that they assure you is as good as gold. Yeah right. Better to be rid of it for a pound . . . and try to forget it's going to get a polish and be sitting on the dealer's forecourt next week with a sticker price of £22,250.

Then it's time for a service. And that'll be £300. Unless some work needs to be done, in which case it will be £700. I know a chap who was charged the other day for someone to 'examine' the tyres on his car.

So, life as a car dealer is normally pretty rosy. Except for one tiny thing. It's okay if you have the franchise for BMW or Mercedes or Alfa Romeo because the car you use to go home at night will be fine and swanky. But what if your dealership sells Hyundais? Sure, you're making plenty of cash, but every night you have to go home in an Accent.

And it's the same story with Volvo. You bathe in the milk from a honey badger. You pour Cristal on your cornflakes and you gave your wife a diamond-studded vibrator for Christmas. You even have golf clubs made from an alloy of titanium, magnesium and mink. But you have to go to work every day in a ho-hum slab of Swedish ironmongery that has the pizzazz of a dead dog.

Oh sure, you've got the top of the range S80 with seats made from the bosom of a fin whale and an electric drinks dispenser. But it's still a Volvo. And you are still being laughed at by Nozzer and Ozzer at the nineteenth hole every Saturday afternoon.

Which is why, at the last Volvo dealer convention, you pleaded with the high-ups in Sweden to make a big V8. 'I could sell thousands,' you lied. And what's more, every other Volvo dealer in the world was saying the same thing.

So Volvo relented. And put a V8 in the front of the new S80

and now every Volvo dealer on the planet is happy. But what about you and me? The multitudes who must now buy this car if Volvo's investment is to pay off.

I suppose we should start with the engine. I assumed that since Jaguar and Volvo are both owned by Ford, it would be a Jag 4.2 under the bonnet. But it isn't. It's a jewel of a thing from Yamaha: 4.4 litres, silken power, no holes in the torque curve and a gorgeous V8 snuffle when you turn it on.

Twice in a day, chauffeurs waiting with Mercs outside expensive restaurants whipped round to see what had made the noise, and both times they looked amazed. Hearing this noise coming from a Volvo is like finding a baby that opens its mouth to scream, and then sounds like an antelope.

There isn't a bucketload of power on tap but because of the four-wheel-drive system, none goes to waste. You stamp on the throttle and no matter how greasy the road might be, the car just sits up and voom. Like it's been electrocuted.

This is a good thing because everything else on this car is a bit slow. The gearbox, for instance. You put your foot down and you have time to get through an Ian McEwan squash game before it kicks down.

Then there's the cruise control off switch. Of all the things in life that have to be instantaneous, this is number one. Even above a gun. But it isn't. Push it and the car sails on at seventy for what seems like two weeks before you get control back.

And then there's the sat nav. Not a Volvo strong point this since it steadfastly refuses to acknowledge that either the Oxford ring road or the M40 exist, but to make matters worse, it doesn't respond to your inputs properly.

'Mmmm,' it drawls, when you push the letter 'L'. Then 'Mmmm' again. And then: 'So, you want an L do you? Mmmm. Let me think about that.' After a while I began to think it might be on smack.

Worse than the slowness of the controls, though, is the suspension. Three settings are available: 'comfort', 'sport' and something labelled 'advanced'.

In the comfort setting, the car glides nicely from place to place, lulling you into a dreamy and creamy sense of security. And then, when you least expect it, you run over a manhole cover and all four wheels begin to pitter-patter like they've been connected to the San Andreas fault.

So you put it in sport and now there's no sense of security at all because the wheels pitter-patter permanently. Even when there's nothing for them to pitter-patter over. In desperation, you go for the advanced setting, which offers a combination of sports and comfort, so you end up with something that is neither. 'Advanced' over what, I wondered? An ox? A druid?

The problem is that Volvo is not intrinsically a maker of luxury cars. There is no culture, as there is at Jaguar, of making a car inherently sublime. And this can no more be achieved with trick electronics than you could make Ray Charles a cricketer by dressing him in white trousers and a box.

Some of the S80 is very nice. The interior, with its linen-look aluminium (I know, I didn't know what they were on about either, but it works) and that cascading centre console is a lovely place to sit. Spacious too.

Then there's the safety. Warning lights illuminate when someone is in your blind spot and then, on the dash, right in front of you is a huge red light that comes on from time to time. I have no idea why. But it doesn't half wake you up.

I also think it's a good looking car. And at £48,150 for the SE Sport model, fully loaded with options, you have to admit, it is exceptional value for money. Mind you, you'll lose your trousers with the depreciation.

And that's where you can be quite cunning. Because all of Volvo's 145 British dealers will have ordered a V8 S80 with all the bells and whistles, and in about six months they'll be flogging them. They know that to get them shifted they'll have to be much cheaper than rival offerings from Mercedes and BMW so you should be able to do a good deal.

And, for the first time, drive away from a car dealer's forecourt, knowing you ripped him off.

Sunday 28 October 2007

Living in the city and buying an off-roader is like permanently wearing a condom for the one day a month you might get lucky

BMW X5

I'm afraid that what I have under my bonnet this morning is not a snarling V8 or a sophisticated new type of smooth and mellow hybrid drive. It's a bee. You may have noticed in recent years that the motorway network is being stalked by a fleet of 'traffic officers'. They look like policemen with their high-visibility jackets and their moustaches and their blue and yellow four-wheel-drive patrol cars. But they are not.

They are employed by the Highways Agency to fill the gap left when the proper police abandoned the expensive business of patrolling the motorways and retreated to their desks.

The remit of the traffic officer is to get to the scene of a crash as fast as possible, ensure everyone is okay, clear the carriageway of debris and get the traffic moving again as quickly as possible. That sounds like a good idea, but unfortunately it's a government scheme. So it's all gone wrong.

The other day there was a small bump on the M40. There were a few broken indicators and I think one of the cars involved had lost its numberplate as well. No matter. Everything was on the hard shoulder. All of the drivers were well enough to exchange addresses. Everything was fine.

But no. The traffic officer in attendance had decided the crash was so severe that all three lanes of the northbound carriageway had to be shut. So, as you can imagine, the tailbacks were horrendous.

When I got to London, I made some calls and found that on that one day it was not only the M40 that had been shut, but the M25, the M26, the M5, the M4 and the M6 had also been closed at different times due to various minor crashes.

I therefore telephoned the Highways Agency, which began by denying the M40 had been shut at all. Then it said that yes, two lanes had been closed. And it stuck with this until I pointed out I had a photograph of the total closure. 'Oh well,' said a spokeschairperson, 'it might have been shut for fifteen or twenty minutes but we wouldn't know about that.'

What do they mean they wouldn't know about that? Do these people have any idea how much carnage is caused by shutting a motorway for twenty minutes? How can they think it's so trivial that it's not even worth reporting?

The Highways Agency actually says that congestion can have 'serious effects on our economy, our quality of life and [predictably] our environment'. Damn right it can. Missed planes. Ruined meetings. Spoilt suppers. Boiled engines. Frayed tempers. And all of that is even before you get to the effects on just-in-time production and 'best before' sandwiches.

Of course, it's easy to see what's happening. The traffic officers will have been told time and again that their safety is the number one priority. And that if they are dealing with the aftermath of a bump, they should do everything in their power to ensure they are not knocked down.

In some cases, this means they won't jump into a lake to save a drowning boy. On the motorway, it means they won't get out of their cars unless the road is shut.

Just listen to the traffic reports. Every day a major motorway is closed while some fat bloke with facial hair and a Napoleon complex picks up a lightly grazed door mirror from the central reservation.

The other day the M1 was shut nearly all day. The M4 in London has been closed on the past two Wednesdays. And the

A3 is hardly ever open. It's all getting completely out of hand.

In the past, a motorway was only ever shut because it was blocked by a truly massive pile-up. Now, though, I can't remember the last journey I made in which I wasn't wiggling through villages and suburbia to avoid closures. Closures that are only necessary for the safety of the traffic officers.

Here's an idea, then. Tell the motorway Wombles to stay in bed. This way they will remain safe and we can go back to the old days of having a bump and dealing with it ourselves without bringing the nation to its knees.

And before we finish with the subject. What are they doing in 4×4s? The only good news about this is that since they're government-owned vehicles, it is now obviously all right for us mere mortals to go out and buy ourselves a 4×4 as well.

And the choice we face is enormous. Porsche, Toyota, Land Rover, BMW, Mercedes, Audi, Volkswagen, BMW, Nissan, Subaru, Mitsubishi and the Americans. All can fit you up with something tall and thrusty and supposedly tough.

For the past week I have been mostly driving around in the new BMW X5. The old one was an ugly, American-made piece of nonsense that never really floated my boat at all. Sure, it was built to offer sports driving dynamics, but what's the point of that in a tall off-road car? It's like making vegetarian food that tastes of sausages.

You sense with the new one that some of that sportiness has been lost. For a kick-off, it's much, much bigger, and as a result, much, much heavier. And when you turn the key, the new 4.8 litre V8 engine doesn't so much zing as snuffle and grunt. I don't know what torque is but I bet it sounds like this: like a Mexican body-builder arm-wrestling a grandfather clock.

I have heard it said that the new version is nowhere near as nice to drive as the old one, but that rather depends. If you want to take it on a hillclimb or to Silverstone, then yes, I would agree. But for normal, everyday work, then no. The new one is better.

It floats and cruises where its predecessor would truffle and snout.

Annoyingly, however, the extra bulk makes it even more useless in town. I sometimes look at people in London squeezing up narrow streets in these massive cars and I think: 'Are you completely bonkers?' Yes, you might need something big and tall for your monthly trip to the cottage in Suffolk, but for crying out loud, why put up with the misery for the other 320 days of the year? That's like permanently wearing a condom for the one day a month you might get lucky.

City dwellers should have a Mini and rent something big when they need to go away. I'm really talking here to people in the countryside who'll be delighted to hear the new X5 – for the first time – is available as a seven-seater. Although I should point out the seats in the boot are small, cost an extra £1,300 and ruin the boot space. So I wouldn't bother. If you need seven seats, you're still much better off with a cheaper Volvo XC90.

The X5, then, should still be viewed as a five-seater, and a pretty good one at that. But one day while I had it, I found myself sitting in a jam – the A3 was closed again – next to a Mercedes ML 63, and I thought: Hmmm. Yet another American-made German five-seat off-road car. And given the choice, I'd take the Merc. It's better looking, smaller and that engine is just so joyously mad.

But of course, I wouldn't. What I'd actually do, without a moment's hesitation, is buy a Range Rover. You sit higher up in the big Brit, and because Land Rover does not make ordinary cars, there's no sense when you're on board that you're simply driving a taller version of a humdrum saloon. But you definitely get this impression in an X5, which feels like a 5-series, and that means it doesn't feel particularly robust.

Worse. At one point I was forced onto a kerb by a bus driver who set off without looking – surprise, surprise – and instead of just popping onto the pavement, the Beemer simply gouged huge chunks out of its front offside alloy wheel. I would like to make the bus driver pay for this. Actually, I'd like to see one done for attempted murder. But either way, BMW's big rugged off-roader was damaged by a kerbstone, and that really shouldn't happen.

It makes you wonder. Next time the road ahead is closed, could you escape up the embankment and across the fields in an X5? I think not. But in a Range Rover you could. I know, because I've done it.

Sunday 4 November 2007

All the luxury you need but no pizzazz

Volkswagen Phaeton

As I'm sure you know, the first recorded music you could buy came in the form of a wax cylinder. Such things must have amazed the people in their frock coats and their stovepipe hats, even though there were one or two problems. Like, for instance, they melted if you left them in the sunshine or in a warm room.

Oh, and they could not be duplicated. Yes, a performer could record his song onto a cylinder that he could then sell. But if someone else wanted to buy one, he'd have to perform his song all over again.

Also, because they turned at 120 rpm, the song could only last for two minutes. Which is why Pink Floyd could not be invented until the long-playing record came along fifteen years later.

Then we had to wait until the 1960s when William Lear, of Learjet fame, developed the eight track and convinced Ford the players should be fitted in Mustangs. And then it was another ten years before smaller cassette tapes took over. And you had to buy *Dark Side of the Moon* all over again.

Then after another ten years had dawdled by, someone worked out that music could be stored in a digital format, so we were given compact discs and everything went berserk.

Today, you have a video iPod and a wafer-thin television set. You have a portable satellite navigation system, Sky+, a digital camera, a widescreen laptop, a rampant rabbit, automatic sprinklers on your lawn and a mobile phone that plays 'Freebird' when anyone calls.

I even have a coffee machine that is programmed to deliver a hardcore XXX slug of caffeine in the morning, a more mellow blend in the afternoon and homo-no-caff after six in the evening. How cool is that?

This dramatic and frenzied burst of activity has created a new type of person. The gadget freak. And he is every bit as important to the world of consumerism as the last great marketing invention: the teenager.

Of course, to keep him happy, many new and useless things were invented. The home cinema. The La-z-boy electric re-cliner. The computerised barometer. Along with phones that take pictures, cameras that access the internet and even, I'm told, material that will be able to store and display information from the internet. This means that if, for some reason, you don't want to read *The Sunday Times* in newspaper form, or on the com-puter, or the television, or on your mobile phone, you can – and I'm not joking – read it on your own trousers.

See the problem? Everything that can be stored as a one and a zero is already stored. So now, in the absence of any new and exciting breakthrough, you're just being offered the same thing in a slightly different way. Usually Danish.

I recently bought a magazine called *Smart Life*. Billed as the international lifestyle technology bible, it is full of gadgets and gizmos that honestly and truthfully make me dribble. I want to own every single thing in it.

Did you know, for instance, that you can now buy a lavatory roll dispenser into which you plug your iPod so you can enjoy some four-four time while doing your number twos?

Or that you can buy a MediaBox? According to the blurb, it is an HDD media player with a 500GB capacity that can upscale the output from your PC to a full-on 1080p HD. I have absolutely no idea what any of this means but it's silver and black and I want one very badly.

The colouring and the style of the thing are everything. We are so consumed by the glowing LEDs and the flashing readouts and the smooth, clean look we don't really realise that everything in the whole magazine is stuff we've seen before, redesigned by Scandinavians in polo-neck jumpers and offered on the internet to idiots like me for £2,000.

No really. Having created the gadget freak with the concept that everything can be turned into ones and zeros, we are now being offered what we already have, only in brushed aluminium.

It's the Bang & Olufsen way. Put some simple Philips technology in a sleek black box and you can charge the earth. Which is why you are now being asked to pay £64 for a smoke alarm, just because it's Danish, and £534 for a chair just because it was designed by a man called Arne.

It's almost as though everyone in Denmark is employed to do nothing but think of a sleek new mounting system for an iPod. And that, of course, brings me on to the Volkswagen Phaeton.

I have written and raved about this car many times. And I see no reason why I should not write and rave about it again this morning.

Partly this is because I've spent the past few weeks trying to find the perfect large, comfortable car. And partly because I know the Phaeton is the answer but no one seems to agree. The only person I know who has one is the director-general of the BBC. And that's a miserable 3 litre diesel.

The one I have here is, in essence, a Bentley Continental GT minus the turbocharging and the chromed smooth-action ventilation knobs. It has the same 6 litre W12 engine, the same four-wheel-drive system and the same extraordinary attention to detail.

In a Phaeton, you could drive at 186 mph all day, when it's 122F outside, and the air-conditioning would maintain a constant temperature of 71.6F. This is guaranteed. Or rather it would be if the car wasn't limited to 155 mph.

It also has a dashboard that slides away to reveal the air vents and headlamp washers that do one headlamp at a time – so as not to reduce visibility too much.

There's more. It has the best seats fitted to any car, the interior is fitted with a dehumidifier so the windows will not steam up no matter what you are doing on them, and it has adjustable suspension that really does adjust. Turn a knob one way and it's like you're coming home on a cloud. Turn it the other and it feels like your hair's on fire.

As a luxury car – as a machine for going quickly and comfortably in sepulchral silence – the Phaeton is better than any of its rivals from Mercedes, Audi, BMW, Jaguar and Maserati.

Of course, you may think that £74,000 is a lot of money for a Volkswagen and you may be disinclined to spend that kind of money in a showroom full of men in donkey jackets buying Polo vans. But the main reason you stay away is because it looks so dreary.

This works well, of course, if you are the director-general of the BBC. You want people to think you slipped into a donkey jacket and bought a Passat. But most people, me included, need a bit more, I dunno, pizzazz and zestiness.

We know that when Volkswagen gave this car to a Belgian and asked him to fit a better looking body, the result was the Bentley Continental. So what I suggest is that VW now gives it to a Dane.

No really. If the Danes can make me want to refit my entire house with new radiators because they look nice, and install an iPod cum bog roll dispenser, I'm damn sure they could transform the excellent Phaeton basics into the absolute must-have accessory.

Let me put it this way. You all want an Aston Martin, don't you? You know it's made up of Jag and Ford bits but you don't care. You want one because it looks just so sleek and amazing. Right. And where was the designer of the V8 Vantage from? Well, let me put it this way. He's called Henrik Fisker.

Sunday 11 November 2007

Stay out of the real world, my little beauty

Mazda2

I do not like to be late. Actually, that's not strictly accurate. I don't know whether I'd like to be late because it's never happened. And it's never happened because I usually drive very powerful cars, which means I can always make up the time.

Last week, though, there was a disaster. I'd planned to leave at 11.45 a.m. for an appointment in Birmingham. But you know how things are. I couldn't find my phone charger. I'd lost my house keys. One of the dogs was missing. And did I turn my computer off? I'll just go and check and – Oh Christ, now it's 11.55.

This would mean averaging 60 mph and that's no bother in a Koenigsegg or a Caparo. But then I opened the front door to find that sitting there, all blue and useless, was a Mazda2. And for that little dollop of extra misery, it wasn't even the 1.5 version. It was the 1.3, and 1.3 litres, in liquid terms, is barely enough to quench the thirst of a dehydrated man. At a pinch, 1.3 litres might, just, be able to power an egg whisk but for making up time on a trip to Birmingham it's hopeless.

However, in the course of that journey, I had an epiphany. I was exposed to something cruel and unusual. Something I've not experienced for twenty years or more. I believe it's called the real world.

I've often wondered why there are so many people out there who hate cars, who find them noisy, dangerous, antisocial and unbecoming of a civilised state. Some of these people, for sure, have frizzy hair and eat only leaves, but others are, apparently, quite normal.

I can understand they might not find driving fun but I cannot understand why they won't accept that the car, at the very least, is a useful tool. Or rather, I could not understand until I tried that Mazda.

If you are looking for a small five-door hatchback, there are many reasons why you might be drawn to this car. Unlike anything else I can recall, it is actually smaller than its predecessor. And better still, it is lighter as well. It weighs less than a ton, in fact, which means you will get better fuel economy and more speed. I took a good long look around the cab – God knows there was time – to see if I could work out how this weight had been shed but other than the dash, which looks like it was made by John Noakes, it seems to be just as well equipped and just as robust as any other small car. And just as spacious as well.

What's more, being a Mazda, it's likely to be reliable. And when you add this to the low group 4 insurance bracket, the £9,999 price tag and the rather cheeky looks, it's easy to see why those who just want a tool might be tempted by such a thing. As small hatchbacks go, it's excellent.

But here's the problem. You see, while this may be the best of breed, it just isn't good enough for the real world. Coming out of Chipping Norton, on the road to Shipston-on-Stour, there's a long, slightly uphill straight on which you can overtake the dithering old fool who just spent twenty minutes in the town being confused by the double mini roundabout. And who is now in a such a state of shock, he's doing 3 mph.

Not in a 1.3 litre hatchback you can't. You drop a cog on the five-speed box, weld your foot to the floor and pull onto the other side of the road ... where ten minutes later you can still be found, sweating slightly, as you wonder whether you will get past before the long straight is over, or whether it would be prudent to brake and admit defeat.

Defeat seemed like a good idea. So I eased off, slipped back into the old man's slipstream and realised, with a heavy heart and sagging shoulders, that in a car such as this, overtaking is not on the menu. And as a result, you are forced to drive everywhere at the same speed as the slowest driver on the road. Often, this stretches the concept of 'movement'.

Eventually, and happily, the man in front died – I think he'd grown weary of spending so much time in his own company – and I could open the taps on the little Mazda.

It was horrible. Because it is built to a price, for people who don't like driving and simply want a tool, everything on it feels cheap and nasty. The electric power steering is too sudden. The suspension is too rubbery. The brakes are too sharp. So even at moderate(ish) speeds, it felt disconnected, unstable and twitchy.

Think of it as a motorway service station sandwich. It was not created to be the best sandwich in the world. The chef had nothing to prove. He simply wanted to offer some of the important food groups for the smallest possible price. There is no truffle oil. There is no homemade cheese. There is absolutely nothing to surprise and delight the enthusiastic motorist who wants something a little bit more than ham made from tyres, butter made from petroleum byproducts, and 129 carbon dioxides to the kilometre. Eventually, after what felt like several months, I reached the motorway and accelerated down the slip road. I had gravity on my side, and 85 bhp. This would have been great in 1957 but it sure as hell isn't enough in 2007 because by the time I reached the main carriageway, I was only doing fifty and that's too slow to join the inside lane without causing the onrushing lorry to have to brake.

So there I was, sandwiched between a truck full of Polish pies and Eddie Stobart, doing fifty-six . . . and there was simply no possibility of getting into the middle lane at all. I didn't have enough oomph to move out because, on the modern motorway, there is always something coming and with only 1.3 litres I couldn't match its speed before making the manoeuvre.

Small wonder people who buy cars such as this can't see

that driving is useful or fun. It isn't. It's either dull or terrifying.

And it gets worse because in Birmingham my car was valet parked in the hotel's 4 million-acre car park by a chap who was a) mildly surprised to see me step from such a thing and b) not on duty when I went to collect it four days later for the journey home again.

This meant I had to find it myself and that's pretty damn hard when you can't remember anything about it. Most of the hotel staff came to help, with one asking what it looked like. 'It's car shaped,' I explained, 'and possibly blue.'

Or red. I do believe the Mazda2 is a good small car but in the cut and thrust of modern driving, and especially on a motorway network full of BMW M3s and Romanian lorry drivers on speed, it is terrible. You would be better off on the bus or the train. Or walking on your hands and knees, while naked.

The fact is that, these days, you need power to survive and I really do think the government should stop fannying about with speed cameras and home zones and congestion charging. The cities are fine. It's the rest of the road network that needs to be addressed.

What I propose, then, is a ban, on any derestricted road, for any car that does not have at least 150 bhp under the bonnet. This way, you won't hate me for trying to get past in my Lamborghini and I won't hate you for being in my way. By keeping us apart, it will make Britain a kinder, more understanding place. And in addition, it will remove the single biggest danger on the roads today: big differences in speed.

We'll all be going quickly out there and that means we'll all have time to find our dogs and still arrive on time. The Mazda2, then, is excellent. But if I were running the Department for Transport, I'm afraid I'd have it banned.

Sunday 25 November 2007

Follow me, vicar, into the red zone

Mazda CX-7

Yesterday I jumped over a wall. It wasn't a very big wall, but even so I only just made it. And when I landed I was out of breath. And my hip hurt. This was all very disappointing. For forty-seven years I have jumped over small walls without a moment's thought, but from now on, I shall have to give the manoeuvre some serious thought and planning. One day soon, though I won't know it at the time, I will jump over a small wall for the last time.

It's the same story with sex. Everyone makes love at some point without knowing that they'll never do it again. I think, if they did, they'd put a bit more effort into the final performance. Maybe that's what John Entwistle was up to in that Las Vegas hotel room. Maybe he realised his ticker was on the blink and decided to go out in a blizzard of cocaine with a bright-orange hooker.

I sometimes wonder what I've done already for the last time. Skied? Flown a fighter jet? Seen the dawn at a party? It always fills me with great sadness and a resolve that I must never, ever, allow myself to be bored. Life is too short, and my time left too precious.

This is why I shall not be going to church any more. I've never been a fan of the baby Jesus, but now, as the summer of middle age begins to fade and small walls become too big, I can no longer tolerate the interminable hymns and the dreary psalms and the saccharine lectures on peace and imperialism and recycling from beardy in the pulpit.

In the past I could sit on my hands and bite my tongue and count the seconds, knowing that soon I'd be released into the fresh air. But today I just don't have the time to waste and I'm filled with a sometimes uncontrollable urge to throttle the vicar, goose the organist and make a break for freedom through the vestry.

I have a similar problem in the theatre. I'm told that Patrick Stewart's rendition of Macbeth, which finished yesterday, was extremely good. But it was Shakespeare, and he's second only to the Bible. He bores me. At no point will Portia crash a police car into a helicopter, and Shylock will not end up falling from the top floor of the Nakatomi Tower.

And, unlike with a film, or a TV show, or a dreary drinks party, you can't just leave when the boredom descends like an itchy blanket. You are imprisoned by the etiquette of theatre. You can't even commit suicide without attracting a chorus of shhes as you splash arterial blood all over the orchestra pit.

Then we have traffic jams. As I round a corner on the motorway to be confronted by a lava stream of red brake lights I don't just sigh – as a young person might – and relax, knowing that I'll get home eventually. I am overcome by a need to drive to the house of the person who caused the jam, be it the driver who crashed or the traffic Womble who shut the road or the boss of the construction company with no sense of urgency. And burn it down.

Being stuck in a traffic jam, watching your life ebb away in a relentless stream of inaudible flashes on the digital clock, is not annoying. It is terrifying.

And this brings me neatly on to the Renault Scénic. And the Citroën Picasso. And the Vauxhall Zafira. And the gone but not lamented Toyota Picnic. And all the other hateful mini-MPVs that sit in the showroom, reminding you that, like Lucy Jordan, you will never again ride through Paris in a sports car, with the warm wind in your hair.

I loathe mini-MPVs with a psychopathic passion. I loathe the way they are built, like zip-up slippers, purely for practicality. That they are so wilfully unstylish, so bereft of everything that makes a car interesting or fun. And that's why, in recent months, I've been delighted to see they're being overshadowed by a new range of off-road cars that can't really go off road.

I'm talking about the Nissan Kumquat, the Nissan Murano, the Land Rover Freelander, the Lexus RX and the soon-to-be-launched Ford Kuga. Yes, when all is said and done, they are mini-MPVs, but the inherent practicality is garnished with a bit of zest, some chunky tyres and a dollop of four-wheel drive. They are, if you like, Doc Martens zip-up slippers.

The new Mazda CX-7 is a classic case in point. They've gone a bit bonkers with the styling cursor at the front where it's all swoopy and mad, but, overall, this is an exceptionally good looking car. And no concessions are made to the terminally beige. It is not available with an automatic gearbox, and if you want a diesel, you'll have to look elsewhere.

The only engine on offer is a four-pot 2.3, which, thanks to the fitting of what feels a large and muscular turbocharger, develops a considerable 256 bhp. That means 0–62 is dealt with in an astonishing 8 seconds, and the top speed is electronically limited to 130.

This, then, is not a Doc Martens zip-up slipper. It's a full-on Nike Air slipper.

I especially liked how it felt in fourth gear, at 2700 rpm. At this point, the turbo has girded its loins, and you can feel it tensing, twitching, straining at the leash, eager to catapult you and your dicky hips out of the drudgery of middle age and into the red zone.

Yes, of course, there is a price to pay for all this oomph. And it comes at the pumps, where it will be revealed you're getting through the kids' inheritance at the rate of £5 every twenty miles or so in town. The good news is that the car itself isn't very expensive to buy. At £23,960, it costs less than anything that calls itself a rival.

The reason for this becomes clear when you step inside. It is like being stuck inside an IT consultant's left shoe. It's grey, with a splash of more grey. And there's nothing to play with. There is no satellite navigation, no trip computer, no curious buttons that don't appear to do anything and that you can study for years, trying to work out why they're fitted.

What you do get is a volume button on the steering wheel that, when you push it, makes a beeping noise. Why? As a general rule, I make the radio louder because I want to hear what's being said, not some stupid beep from the car. That annoyed me. I don't need a beep to tell me the radio is getting louder – I can hear it. I also don't need a beep to say the door is open, the key is in the ignition or I haven't put my seatbelt on. I am aware of all these things. The only beep I want is when I've left the lights on. And this goes for all cars. Should I ever come to power, I will make it law.

But, anyway, back to the CX-7 and some more problems. Because it is a high-riding, chunky-tyred 4×4, it doesn't ride as smoothly as a normal car. And it isn't quite as spacious in the back, or the boot, as you might have hoped. But the fact is this: you can't have the style and the high driving position without these drawbacks. It is like going out for a lot of drink and hoping all will be well in the morning. It won't be. There's a price to pay for looking good and having fun.

Of course, you can get round all of this with a sensible diesel-powered Renault Mégane. Plus, if you go down this road, it'll prepare you nicely for the day when you turn grey and a kindly nurse sticks a tube full of MRSA up your left nostril.

Me? Well, since I believe you should live life and not spend half of it in church, preparing for death, I'd take the Mazda, warts, beeps and all, every time.

Sunday 2 December 2007

For an axe murderer, it's a big softie

Subaru Impreza 2.5 WRX

Most people know the barebones history of rock'n'roll – some black men sang the blues but no one in white America would buy their music because it was the 1950s and, well, that sort of thing didn't happen.

Eventually, though, the music made it to England, where the misery of it struck a chord with working-class lads. Bands such as the Animals and the Rolling Stones copied it, and they did succeed in America, because, bluntly, Mick Jagger is white.

The thing is, though, I've never been able to see the link. I've listened to those crackly blues records from Memphis and I've listened to 'Jumpin' Jack Flash' and they appear to have nothing in common. Genetically, they seem as distant from each other as the sausage dog and the Magimix.

But the other night, while listening to a Radio 2 show, I heard a song from 1956 called 'Smokestack Lightning', and the DJs explained how you could hear the genesis of the Stones in there. They were right – you could. For me, this was a revelation.

And then they started talking about famous fathers and sons who have appeared in bands together. Which is exactly the sort of trivial nonsense I adore. And then they played 'Sylvia' by Focus and I began to think that I'd discovered a radio show designed exclusively for me. It was brilliant – so brilliant that I deliberately got lost so that I could hear more.

It's hosted by two chaps called Stuart Maconie and Mark Radcliffe, and because they have exactly the same Lancashire accent and exactly the same views on everything, you'll think – as

I did at first – that it's actually hosted by one man talking to himself.

No matter. Their knowledge of music is astonishing. I thought I was the only person alive who could name the guitarist with Focus but they actually know where he was born, where he went to school and, I shouldn't be surprised, what position his mother was in when he was conceived.

But these guys aren't anoraks – they are way beyond that. They are the people to whom people who make anoraks go to buy their anoraks. And they serve as a hugely useful introduction to this morning's sermon: the ongoing battle between the Subaru Impreza and the Mitsubishi Evo.

To normal people, who see cars as wheels, seats and expense, they are exactly the same, built in Japan as road-going versions of rally cars. To the untrained eye, they are indistinguishable one from the other. They are Ant and Dec, or, if you prefer, Maconie and Radcliffe.

They both have 2 litre turbocharged engines. They both have four-wheel drive and they are the same sort of size. Each is a family car with the heart and mind of an axe murderer. But to the trained eye they are not the same at all. To an anorak they really are chalk and cheese. They are Bad Company and Gareth Gates.

Last week, while plugging my new DVD on a morning TV show, I was approached by a young girl with earphones and a clipboard. Externally, she was much the same as any other behind-the-scenes girl in modern television. But she began, immediately, by telling me she had an Impreza . . . and I knew it wasn't going to stop there.

'It's the WRX STi RB5 two-door, PLS, SST . . .' she said for about half an hour.

After which she still wasn't finished: '994, PSP, Wii, LTD,' she continued. And on, and on . . . And that was before she even got to her boyfriend's Subaru, which led to another two hours of initials and numbers.

This is the thing with Subaru ownership: every last detail matters. Every tiny piece of the water-injection jigsaw is more important than your child's next breath. You don't own a car like this, you are assimilated by it. You become one.

With men I find this tiresome. But with girls I find it very sexy. So as this girl rabbited on with ever more initials and numbers, I was overwhelmed by a need to introduce her to a friend of mine who has a Mitsubishi Evo 9. This is the only girl in the world who put a topless photograph of herself on her Facebook page. I would love to see them argue about which is the better car. With a bit of luck, it might even end up in a fight.

I'm not going to say one is better than the other, because if I do, fans of the losing side will come to my house with crosses, petrol and much rage. But as an impartial observer I will say this: the Mitsubishi has always been the better to drive; the Subaru has always been the better to live with on a daily basis.

And that brings us on to the new Subaru Impreza WRX. In petrol-land this is one of the most important cars ever. Imagine a band comprising Mick Jagger, Jimmy Page, Eric Clapton, Phil Collins and bits of Radiohead. That's what this car is like to petrolheads. A pivotal, must-have moment of a car. Like its predecessor it has a turbocharged engine, 227 bhp on tap and four-wheel drive. But unlike its predecessor, it has a 2.5 litre engine and a hatchback body, and it's no longer bland to behold. Instead it's wilfully ugly.

I honestly began to imagine that it had been designed in a game of consequences: 'You do the back, then fold the paper over. I'll do the middle and we'll get that drunk bloke to do the front.' It's a hopeless mishmash that gets even worse when you step inside. This is a £20,000 car, and for that price you get a heater and . . . that's about it.

Honestly, I was amazed when I found it had dipping head-lamps. An Aga has more buttons than this. And as a result, anyone who just wants a 'nice hot hatch' will instead opt for a Golf GTI.

The Subaru enthusiast, however, will see the lack of equipment as a good thing. Equipment is weight. Weight blunts acceleration. Weight is bad.

Hmmm. This is undoubtedly true, but from the moment you set off you realise this is not set up to be a Lotus Elise with a hatchback. It is super-soft. Much softer than its predecessor. Much softer than a duck-down duvet. It glides like a Citroën.

Then there's the noise. Or rather there isn't. The flat-four engine just hums away quietly to itself and, if anything, sounds rather exasperated if you weld your foot to the floor and head for the rev-counter red zone.

And if you do head for the red zone, you will find that the natural tendency is for understeer. It was ever thus in an Impreza: it was one of the things that made it a more rewarding day-to-day companion than the furious and twitchy Evo. But in the new car the understeer arrives too early, and then you fall out of the seat. No, really. There are kitchen chairs with noticeably more side support.

This car is called Subaru Impreza, which makes you think it will be a bare-knuckle attack dog. But in fact you get a soft and rather elderly labrador.

Oh it's still pretty quick: 0–62 mph is dealt with in 6.5 seconds and the top speed is lots. But because of the understeer, the soft ride and the kitchen chairs, you never feel inclined to go for it. There's no sense at all that you're in a road-going rally car. It doesn't even have a six-speed box.

Of course, being a Subaru, it will be beautifully made, and it really is extremely comfortable, and quiet. But anyone drawn to these qualities will immediately be put off by the looks and the starter-handle-and-trafficator equipment levels. It is, in short, a car that appeals to no one.

My friend with the clipboard and headphones was talking

about it as though God himself had gone over to the dark side. 'What am I to do?' she wailed, as I imagined her naked with my friend Camilla in a big box of mud.

It's a good point. If you are a Subaru fan, what are you to do? Sure, there is a 300 bhp STi version of the WRX in the pipeline, and this will be harder and more focused. But it's no looker either, and the fact of the matter is this: the next Evo, the 10, is. The battle, then, between the Impreza and the Evo – it just got one-sided.

Sunday 9 December 2007

Just what you didn't want – a turbo toilet

Mini Cooper S Clubman

If you are a frizzy-headed, saggily breasted, left-threaded lunatic, Christmas is not a time for giving or receiving. It's not quality time for the family. Nor is it a time to worship the baby Jesus, because of course that's not multicultural or Winterval enough.

Christmas for these people is mostly a time of industrial-strength guilt. All year they feel guilty for being paid and comfortable but at Christmas they can really turn up the heat in the sauna of shame. They are guilty about the carbon vapour trail left by their cranberry sauce as it came over from America. They are guilty about the sheer volume of presents they bought for Tarquin. They are guilty about having central heating and a well-toned tummy, and teeth.

And so, to assuage the guilt, many have been buying charity Christmas presents for random families in Africa. All you do is make a donation to Oxfam and it will send a gift down the chimney of some mud hut in Mozambique.

You may think this is all jolly noble, and I'd have to agree if the presents were iPods or Manchester United football shirts or something the average African villager might actually want.

But unfortunately we are talking about a bunch of fair-trade lunatics so what they've actually been buying is goats. Hundreds of them. Oxfam says this is a brilliant idea, and ActionAid even posts a quote from Elias Nadeba Silva, a farmer, who was given one last year. 'I have great plans for my field,' he said, 'and my family is very grateful for ActionAid's help . . .

'But next year, no more goats. Okay? I'd prefer a copy of *Mothership* by Led Zeppelin.'

Other popular choices from well-meaning idealists in the media-fuelled parts of eastern London include cans of worms, piles of dung, catering packs of condoms and the materials for making toilets. Who wants that for Christmas? 'Daddy, Daddy. Santa's been!! He's been!!!! And he's brought me . . . an Armitage Shanks Accolade back-to-wall bog, which combines classical elegance with a contemporary style.'

I can only begin to imagine the look of desperation on the little lad's face. That crushing, all-enveloping sense of overwhelming disappointment. Someone in faraway England has gone to all the bother of buying him a Christmas present. It's probably the only one he'll get. And it's a bloody bog.

Think about it. We're told that we should never buy our wives or girlfriends anything with a plug, because this is bound to be something they need, rather than want. And exactly the same thing holds true the world over. No child anywhere *wants* a lavatory. You *need* a lavatory. You *want* teddies and footballs and BMX bicycles. And AK47s.

It is hard, honestly, to think of a more useless, patronising and stupid present than a toilet. Not even a gift-wrapped copy of the worst book ever written – *Versailles: The View from Sweden* – comes close. But after much sucking of my ballpoint, I have come up with something: a turbocharged Mini Cooper S Clubman.

I should make it plain from the outset that I like the normal Mini. I think that although it has a wheelbase longer than the Land Rover Defender, and therefore isn't mini at all, it has a lot of charm and so many natty design features, you really don't care that the back is suitable only for Anne Boleyn and that the boot couldn't handle even half a King Charles spaniel.

I was therefore expecting great things from the Clubman.

Because here is a car that offers all of the Mini's edge-thin, Conran-cute design stuff in a package that doesn't force you to amputate your passengers' extremities.

Or butcher your dog.

My expectations were lifted still further by an excellent review in this newspaper back in September, and then by the look of the thing when it arrived at my house. I loved the double doors at the back. I loved the huge speedo. And I loved the fact that this practical little car was fitted with a turbocharged 1.6 litre engine that pumped out 175 bhp. On paper, it's hard to think of any car that offers the modern motorist quite so much. And all for a shade more than £17,000.

Unfortunately, after a week, I have decided it's one of the worst cars in the world. About as desirable as a packet of dung or a can of worms. Truthfully? I'd rather have a goat.

The first problem is the single rear passenger door. It's on the right-hand side of the car, which is fine if you live in Germany or America, where everyone drives on the wrong side of the road – pull up at the kerb and your kids get out onto the pavement. But here in Britain, where we do things properly, your kids are forced to get out into the traffic.

Then there's the boot. Yes, access is good, and yes, you get 100 more litres of space than you do in the normal Mini. But it's still pretty small. As that September review pointed out, the boot in a Honda Jazz is 100 litres bigger.

Furthermore, you can see out of the back of a Honda Jazz. You can see out of the back of most cars, in fact. Seeing out of the back is jolly useful and is one of the reasons the Lamborghini Countach was not a big seller. But you can't see out of the back of a Mini Clubman. Glance in the rear-view mirror and all you can see is the pillar where the two doors meet.

It's a good job that speeding is now monitored by civil servants in vans, because there's no way you'd see a police car if it were on your tail. And it's a doubly good job because the natural cruising speed of the Clubman S is 110 mph.

The cruising speed of a car is a bit like the natural parting in your hair. It's just there, and you have to concentrate hard to make it go somewhere else. Weirdly, it has nothing to do with engine size. It's a combination of things – the resonance of the body, the suspension settings, the gearing. My Merc, if I'm not concentrating, sits at 85. It's its default setting. And that's fine. But fail to concentrate in the Mini, and it sails up past 100. You have to be alert to keep it down, and that's wearing.

But not as wearing as the torque steer. I do not know why the Clubman is so badly affected when the normal car, with exactly the same engine, is not. But I do know that there is no point paying extra for satellite navigation, because this is a car that goes where the camber of the road dictates. You, the man behind the wheel, have no say at all.

And woe betide the chap who decides to put his foot down hard coming off a greasy roundabout, because what happens next, in my experience, gets perilously close to dangerous. At best, it appears to be an extreme flaw.

And that's probably enough problems to be going on with, if I'm honest. Looking for good things in a car that torque-steers like a wayward horse and has no boot, no rear visibility, a silly door and a ridiculous cruising speed is a bit like looking for good things in a piece of fish that's dry, tasteless and bony. There's no point.

Anyone who grew up in the age of loon trousers knows that style can often win out over practicality. But with the Mini, the price is too high. There are just too many issues to make it work as a car. Think of it as loon trousers with no crotch.

And on that rather unusual concept it's time to move on to a seasonal close. Please have a wonderful Christmas. Drink too much. Eat too much. Don't feel guilty about the presents you give or those that you receive. Care not for your carbon footprint or the impact of your naked consumerism. Be happy. And remember, you are having a much better time than Gordon Brown because he has no friends and you've got lots.

Sunday 23 December 2007

Beemed back to the wild days of youth

BMW 135i

When I was growing up, and it wasn't that long ago, we had electricity for only three days a week, we drove cars that wouldn't start, we used rats to take away rubbish, and dead bodies, and a cup of tea was considered a luxury good.

And now we spool forward thirty years to find that round where I live there are women with crisp shirts and nice hair who make a living by decorating other people's Christmas trees.

Don't you find that amazing? That someone has persuaded a bank manager that there is a demand for such a thing, let alone such a volume of demand that it would overcome the extremely seasonal nature of the business? I can only presume that they charge £25,000 per tree.

Mind you, £25,000 these days is nothing. I know someone who paid that for a pair of binoculars. And £25,000 for a gun is considered good value. In just thirty years, then, Britain has been transformed from the Old Kent Road into Mayfair, the Community Chest and the entire bank.

And I was there when it all began. The year was 1982 and the place was Fulham. Specifically, Parsons Green, and, even more specifically, my local. The White Horse. When I started drinking there, it was a painter and decorator's pub and everyone drank stout. If you'd have strolled in and asked for a vodka, your head would have been kicked in before they'd got the rust off the optics. But then along came the privatisation of British Telecom and all of a sudden everyone had £200.

It was the start. The White Horse was given wooden blinds

and leather sofas, and friends of mine started dropping in after a day at work with enough money in their pockets to buy a house. One, a chap called Johnny who had an earring and a Ford Capri, suddenly remembered he was the Earl of Dumfries.

I think in my youth a City bonus was a chicken drumstick or some luxury crackers from Boots. But as Mrs Thatcher ran around privatising the water and the gas and the air, all of a sudden people starting getting enough each Christmas to buy an estate in Scotland. Or a small country in the Caribbean.

They were great times. Exciting times. Times when you felt anything was possible and that all you needed to become a billionaire was an idea. Any idea would do. I started writing about cars for local newspapers. Another mate came up with wheelie-bin cosies. Others bought and sold houses. And as all these businesses flew, it had a profound effect on the cars we all drove.

In the early days of the change, you couldn't really go to the White Horse unless you had a Golf GTI. Preferably in Lhasa green with a splash of Val d'Isère mud up the side. There is no modern-day equivalent to this phenomenon. You lived in Fulham back then. You had one. It was that simple.

But then, as the bonuses got bigger, people started upgrading to the BMW 323i. God, it was a good car. With its dainty pillars and uncomplicated styling, it was in many ways indistinguishable from a Ford Cortina. But unlike any Ford of the period, it started, it cost a bloody fortune and it went like stink.

And because it was rear-wheel drive, something with which the GTI brigade was unfamiliar, it was ever so easy to crash. This not only gave you something exciting to talk about in what had now become known as the Sloaney Pony, but it also gave you the opportunity to replace it with a 325i, which was even better.

This cost even more, but the amount of stuff it didn't come with was astonishing. No, really. There was no radio and you had to wind the windows down by hand. It was just a light body and a big engine. And we all loved it more than we loved our genitals.

Sadly, since then, the 3-series has grown into middle age. It's become fatter and bigger and slower. Deep down, a modern 3-series is still balanced and wondrous, but the excitement, the fizz, the thrill of those early cars is gone. Buried under a ton and a half of technology and kit.

Of course, because the 3-series became so enormous, BMW was able to launch the 1-series beneath it in the line-up. And that would have been fine but unfortunately it was styled by the same chap who did Corporal Jones's butcher's van in *Dad's Army*. Even Queen Victoria would call it old-fashioned, with its sit-up-and-beg stance, its almost vertical windscreen and those idiotic swoops on the flanks.

All of this would have been only mildly annoying if it was thrilling to drive and more spacious inside than an art gallery. But it isn't. The boot is microscopic, the rear legroom is suitable only for people who haven't been born yet and the big-selling diesel is about as much fun as herpes. If this car were a person, it would be Piers Morgan.

Now, though, BMW has given its baby hatchback a boot to create what it calls the coupé, and frankly that looks like a recipe for even more calamity and disaster. Booted hatchbacks never work. You need only look at what happened when VW turned the Golf into the Jetta to know I'm right.

And then you have only to look at the 1-series coupé to know I'm wrong. It is by no stretch of the imagination a pretty car. But neither is it offensive. Which means it has exactly the same non-styling-driven appeal of the early 1980s 323i.

What's more, the version I tested came with a big 3 litre twin-turbo six under the bonnet. That's 306 bhp, and that's good too.

Step inside and it gets better.

You get the bare minimum of kit. Just a big, fat, chunky wheel, a snickety-snick six-speed manual box and, er, a rear-view mirror. I had hope in my heart as I set off; hope that, after twenty-five years, BMW was back in business making small, fast, simple sports saloons.

It is. Initially the brakes feel too sharp, but after a mile or so you adapt your driving style to suit and then you can sit back and revel in the joy of it all. The ride is perfectly judged; firm but not so taut that it pops your eyes out on every cat's-eye. And on a motorway it settles down to be nicely on the right side of comfortable. The seats are bang-on, as is the driving position.

But it's the engine that impresses most of all. It has one small turbo to spin up the instant you apply the power, and then a bigger one that trundles into life later to keep the power coming . . . in bigger and bigger lumps. This, and there's no other way of saying it, is a great engine. A masterpiece. It doesn't zing like the BMW straight-sixes of old but there's so much muscle you don't notice.

Then you leave the motorway and the road gets twisty and it's like settling into your favourite armchair. The steering, the feel, the way you can adjust your line through the bend with the throttle. There is no other car made today in this sector of the market that gets even close. If you love driving, this is up there in a class of one.

Of course, a Mitsubishi Evo or a Subaru Impreza will grip more and slingshot you from bend to bend with more urgency, but if you prefer a more flowing style – less grip and more handling – then you would be better off with the little Beemer.

Faults. Well, the rear legroom is a squeeze, and it's not what you'd call cheap. With no extras at all it squeaks in at under £30,000, but add one or two bits and it'll shoot up to £34,000. That's a lot.

Except, of course, it isn't – not these days when people are spending that, and more, on family holidays and kitchens.

The fact of the matter is this. The 135 coupé is the best car BMW makes. I have no hesitation at all, then, in giving this long-awaited return to form the rare accolade of five stars.

Sunday 30 December 2007

Part II

The straight's story

I had wanted to go to Norway for an offshore powerboat race. They'd fly us out there, put us up in a hotel full of hot and cold running Vikings, even let us drive the boats at 150 mph down a fjord. But it was all too butch for Adrienne. 'We're going to Mykonos,' she said. For several reasons this was A Bad Idea. First, the Greeks will arrest you for anything: looking at their planes, insulting their flag, being Turkish. I was once arrested on Crete for being beaten up. Second: the food. Most civilised countries use the fruit from a vine to make wine. The Greeks eat the leaves, throw the grapes away and make their wine from creosote.

In fact, the only good thing about this part of the world is that in 3 million years it won't be there, and the loaf that is Greece, and all the crumbs that have fallen off it, will be dragged to the bottom of the sea. But Adrienne was insistent. We were going to Mykonos. The former home of Homer and home now to half the world's homos.

'If it has to be Greece, wouldn't Lesbos be more fun?' I asked, but it was no good. I was sent off to get air tickets. But all flights to Mykonos were full. I ended up talking to Marquis Jets, who offered us exclusive use of a Falcon 2000. This was my last hope. 'Adrienne,' I said, 'we have a private jet. We can go anywhere you want. Where's it to be? Oslo? Trondheim?'

'Mykonos,' she said defiantly, and went back to cutting the sleeves off her T-shirts.

Adrienne is best described as a Stanislavsky hack. She likes to get into the part. She was all Pringle-ised in Cheshire and arrived in Iceland looking like a dead fox. Fine, but in the land of the fairies, I didn't think method journalism was a good idea. 'Can I suggest you don't take those see-through white trousers?' I said. She gave me a look. 'Well, can I suggest you wear something under them that's a bit more substantial than that thong?'

I should explain that I'm not homophobic. It's just that, with the possible exception of Adrienne, none of my best friends is gay. I was born in the socialist republic of South Yorkshire, where it was possible to be homosexual but unwise to own up. And today I live in Chipping Norton, which doesn't have a big gay scene. Adrienne was dismissive. 'Yes, but you work in the media, which is very gay.' Sure it is, but I have lunch with Richard Littlejohn and work on *Top Gear*, which is about as homosexual as a Brunellian rivet.

Initially, there was no evidence that I'd flown into the Med's khaki buttonhole. It was the same as all the other Greek islands. None of the houses was finished, and neither was the sewage plant. There were signs outside all the restaurants saying, 'Breakfast. Lunch. Dinner. Greek food' – as if the local stuff could not be considered a meal – and the beer had about as much potency as a choirboy.

But you can't escape the fact that you're in the Med, which makes it all better. It's something about the cicadas and bougainvillea. It doesn't matter if it's Capri, Corsica, Minorca or Malta, they're all either fine or the best places on Earth. Even the Greeks can't completely mess this up.

We found ourselves on the medieval edge of the town in a bar watching the sunset. An English couple strolled by and noted us, me in my George Clooney outfit, Adrienne in her sailor-boy suit and obvious thong. 'Ooh, there's Jeremy Clarkson,' said the girl. 'I never knew he was gay.'

This was a big moment. She'd go home and tell her friends she'd seen me with some ladyboy in Mykonos and that I was homosexual. Then her friends would tell their friends, until a couple of hundred people in some suburb of Leicester would know that the mop-haired bloke from *Top Gear* is queer. So how did that make me feel? Let me put it this way: the next day a barmaid thought I was German, and that was a damn sight worse.

At midnight we went to Pierro's, the oldest of Mykonos's gay night spots, which was all muscles and drugs. Adrienne posed a lot, but one of the dancers told me she'd got it all wrong. 'He looks like a straight guy dressed for a gay club in Miami.'

I never realised this: there are a lot of different ways to be gay. And something else: we used to choose holidays on the strength of the weather. Now, it seems, people are choosing on the basis of what sort of sex they'll get. Ibiza for quantity. Bangkok for quality. And if you want it rough with Schwarzenegger, on PCP, up an alleyway, never mind the food, Mykonos is right up your street.

When I bumped into two American girls – knowing that many straight girls go to gay clubs because they can dance without being bothered – I began cautiously. Within fifteen minutes we were getting on well enough for Adrienne to go all pouty. They were all touchy-feely; one said I had lovely skin and looked twenty-eight. Then I found out they were married. To each other. Apparently, this is legal in Vermont, and when they got back to the States they were going to a sperm bank so they could both get pregnant at the same time. 'Won't that be cool?' said the pretty one with the pierced tongue. Well, not for the children, no.

The next day we hit the all-nude Super Paradise Beach and I decided to spend the day cruising the sand in search of the perfect bosom. But all I found was a perfect tit. 'Adrienne,' I said, 'have you noticed how the design of the basic breast can be so different? I've seen dog's noses, melons, fried eggs, wobbly ones, pointy ones, spaniel's ears, Ulrikas ...' 'No,' she said, 'but have you noticed all the different penises? Look at that one. It's huge.' This was a worry. When two chaps are together, it just isn't done for one of them to point at another man's penis and say: 'My, what a whopper.' Just in case it's actually sort of average.

Then it happened. In a bar on top of the cliff I was approached. There were three of them: muscle-bound Americans called Steve, Doug and Doug. 'I'm not German,' I whimpered as they pulled up chairs at my table. 'Yeah, we can tell,' one of them drawled. 'And I'm not gay either,' I added.

They wanted to talk about the choreography they'd organised for the closing ceremony of the Commonwealth Games. I wanted to talk about darts and speedboats and why there is no such thing as the perfect breast. In the end, we talked about Mykonos, which, they said, is tranquil. But Mykonos is not tranquil. And it's especially untranquil when you've been joined by Adrienne. She'd strutted in the club, pouted on the beach, minced in the town, and hadn't had so much as a sniff. Whereas without even trying, Mr Hetero had got himself a couple of Dougs.

We finished off with a visit to the beach where *Shirley Valentine* was filmed. And guess what? This shrine to heterosexual love was deserted. Adrienne made a good point: 'In real life, Tom Conti would've been f★★★ing Shirley's husband.' Nice to have you back, mate. Let's do Norway sometime.

Sunday 22 December 2002

Simpsons – Table Talk

Last time I tried to eat in Birmingham, it was 1997. At the time, *Top Gear* was based in the city and I regularly had to stay the night. This meant starving, because then – and this was only eight years ago – there were no restaurants. Not one. Well, not if you'd had chicken madras for breakfast and an onion bhaji for lunch, and you fancied something less ratty for supper.

Imagine that. Imagine the second city of any other country having no restaurants.

Imagine asking the concierge at a hotel in Los Angeles if he could recommend somewhere to eat, and being told: 'Ooh, you've got me there.' Or Lyons. Or Turin.

I loathed Birmingham. I loathed the fat girls who tottered down Broad Street on their silly shoes. I loathed the Bullring, the haircuts and the way that accent made everyone sound sub-normal. If Einstein had been from Birmingham, nobody would have taken the theory of relativity seriously.

Birmingham, until very recently, was like a rugby player's bath after all the water has drained out: empty in the middle, with a ring of scum round the outside.

But now, as you no doubt know, there's a spotty department store and some fountains. And to complete the metamorphosis, it has two restaurants – both of which, worryingly, have been given one Michelin star.

In my experience, a single Michelin star means the owner has been concentrating on the food to the exclusion of everything else. And the food, for me at any rate, is only 10 per cent of the dining experience. Give me a white tablecloth, good company, elegant glasses, no draughts, perfect service from waiters who never interrupt anecdotes, lots of ashtrays, clever lighting, and, frankly, I'd be happy with a cluster of skunk's dingleberries served on a bed of wallpaper paste.

Of course, neither of the new Michelin-starred restaurants in Birmingham allows smoking in the dining room, so we used a pin to select Simpsons in Edgbaston, asked if we could come at 8.30 p.m., and were told no, because there were some people coming then. In other words, you come when we say, you don't smoke and you will be allowed to genuflect at the altar of our chef's magnificence. Well, we all thought as we headed up the M40, this is a bit like going to church.

Of course, AA Gill would have taken Elle Macpherson and the Pope, but, this being me, I took my wife, who's a brunette, and a couple you've never heard of. There was Kate, who thought that going to Birmingham was 'terribly exciting', and Will, who says his favourite food is jelly.

Simpsons has a car park with marked-out spaces for a dozen or so cars. Quite what cars they had in mind when they were painting the lines, I can't imagine. Not our 4WD Volvo, that's for sure. And there's a similar lack of room in the bar. When the man on the next table decided that what he'd really like for a starter was his girlfriend and set about eating her face, I was so close, I could hear every slurp. Mind you, she was a lot more appetising than most of the stuff on the menu.

The real puzzler was the way the puddings and the main courses seemed to have been mixed together. So the roast coquelet came with hazelnuts and sherry-vinegar sauce, the pigeon came with pear, and the venison with fig marmalade and juniper-berry sauce. I know it's a personal thing, but I don't like sweet and savoury in my mouth at the same time. It's why I wouldn't ever choose trout-flavoured ice cream. Or Eton mess garnished with cocktail sausages.

Still, I thought I'd give this mix'n'match cuisine a bash and started with seared duck foie gras with – wait for it, a roast banana and some banana puree.

Strangely, the combination tasted like a Zip fire lighter. But then my wife's seared scallop in Indian spices, with a caramelised cauliflower puree, was like Vim. Of course, your usual correspondent, who understands the history and science of food, would know why our dinner tasted of various household products. 'Fig marmalade in February?' he'd scoff, knowledgeably. 'Well, of course it'll taste like Fairy Liquid.' But all I can do is tell you it was horrid.

Kate's main course was the big disaster, though, because it seemed to have the same flavour and nutritional value as one of the napkins. Me? I ate an entire pig. Its blood, its belly, its feet, the lot.

That was good(ish), as was my wife's mushroom risotto – although her green salad didn't turn up for ages and then, when it did, was actually made up mainly of tomatoes. Will didn't know what he was eating because he'd burnt his tongue that morning on some railway tea.

All in all, then, a fairly disastrous culinary experience, which is of no consequence to me because I don't care about the food particularly. What I did care about, however, was the overbright lighting and the Herculean obsequiousness of the staff. The head waiter was a clever and decent cove, but the others were way, way too effusive.

They need to relax, dim the lights and provide some bloody ashtrays.

But here's the thing. As I retired to the bar afterwards, I had a chat with some of my fellow diners, all of whom were BMW M3-driving, golf-playing local businessmen – and they absolutely loved the place. They loved the notion of telling their colleagues the next day that they had eaten in a Michelin-starred restaurant and that it had cost £60 a head.

And this is my problem. I am used to eating out in the capital and was using metropolitan standards to judge a restaurant that's in Birmingham. That's unfair.

Yes, Simpsons would last about five minutes in London. But how long do you think The Ivy would last in Birmingham? They'd be horrified at the tattiness of the customers' clothes and disgusted to find shepherd's pie and fish and chips on the menu.

Eating out in Birmingham, or any big provincial city, is not something you do because you can't be bothered to cook. It's something you get dressed up for. So you want it to be formal. You want to be treated like a king and lit like a film star while they bring you mountains of incomprehensible food that you couldn't make at home, even if you wanted to.

Pigeon and pear? Banana and duck liver? That's far too pompous for me. But when you've lived in a city that has had no restaurants at all, it's the bee's knees – served on a bed of black-olive gnocchi and flying-fish wasabi.

Sunday 20 February 2005

I was a superyacht pirate

By any standards it was an ambitious question. 'Dad,' I said plaintively, 'I know I'm only twenty-two and everything but do you think there's any chance that I could borrow the boat in the south of France for a couple of weeks this summer?'

Of course the answer would be 'no'. This was not like asking to borrow a fiver, or the car. This was a six-berth gin palace with two turbocharged Volvo engines. And I had the responsibility and maturity of a praying mantis. 'Yes,' he said. 'Sure.'

Before being allowed to take it out of La Napoule, the marina where it lived just outside Cannes, I had to take a national motor cruising certificate of competence.

Which involved driving around the Solent for a week.

I learnt how to park and which buoys meant what and how not to decapitate too many swimmers. And then, on the last night, we were made to sit a mock exam, so we'd have some idea of what to expect when we sat the real thing.

The next day our teacher handed out the real exam with something of a glint in his eye. Not surprising, really, since the papers were exactly the same as the mocks we'd sat the night before. Even I couldn't fail this one. And I didn't. Brilliant.

He can boast about a 100 per cent pass rate. And I got my ticket for a life on the ocean wave.

The holiday that followed, with four friends, is still the most enjoyable I've ever been on. Some say that oysters are the best aphrodisiac, but trust me on this, boats in the south of France are better. Honestly, next time you're out with a girl, offer her some snot in a shell and see how far you get. Then offer her a night on your gin palace in Cannes and I can guarantee you'll be making the two-headed beast within the hour. Even if you are twenty-two with a concave chest and legs like pipe cleaners.

And no money. This was the only blot on our untroubled horizon. Even then, in 1982, filling the boat's tank cost £200 and this was something we had to do every other day. Hard when you earn £22 a week and spend £44 of that on beer.

But not impossible. Not when you convince the girl at Barclays in Antibes that your grandmother has just died and you desperately need cash for the trip home.

She fell for this story six times.

Oh, and it also helped that we never actually paid for anything we ate. We just sort of got the bill and ran. And that meant we had just enough fuel to crash into pretty well everything between Le Lavandou and Monte Carlo.

One day, after a long and completely free lunch, we decided to go to the Ile de Port Cros. We'd been told it was a nature reserve and, being young, thought this meant there'd be lots of ladies' areas to look at. So that they'd look at us, I devised a plan. 'Listen up, chaps,' I said. 'We're not going to do any of that namby-pamby backing up to the jetty malarkey.

'No,' I said. 'I shall drive straight at the pier at thirty knots and then at the last moment spin the boat and drop it dramatically alongside the pontoon. I have a motor cruising certificate of competence. Trust me.'

All went well until I slammed the engines into reverse and the boat came off the plane. Because only then did I realise the stern drives were on power tilt and the propellers had shot clean out of the water. I therefore had no braking at all, which meant we didn't stop alongside the jetty. We just went straight through it.

With a 9 ft hole in the pier, I have no idea how all the day trippers got back on the ferry to Toulon that night. Because we were gone, on our way from the scene of the accident as fast as possible. And straight into the jaws of another.

I'm forty-five now and I know that when the air goes clear in the south of France you can be assured a mistral is coming. But I didn't then, not until the wind hit.

It was a big one. So big that lots of windsurfers were in real trouble. After we'd rescued four and told the coastguard helicopter to go away, because it was hovering overhead and making our cigarettes hard to light, one of the boat's engines overheated. And then a rope we'd thrown to some poor chap with a bad gash on his head was blown back and round the only functioning prop.

We tried cutting it off, but in 70 mph winds the sea was just too rough. So we had some beers and decided to make port on the overheating diesel. This was fine until I made it into the harbour, a small one on the eastern side of Cannes, full of wooden sardine boats and Disque Bleu men in berets mending nets. Have you ever tried to stop a nine-ton boat propelled by a gale when all you have in the braking department is one poorly engine? Much to the annoyance of a local fisherman whose boat we smashed to splinters, it can't be done.

Happily, while the argument raged between the fisherman and the windsurfers we'd rescued, one of our party was able to get the rope off the good prop and we were able to run away. Again.

Man, we celebrated that night, which meant we finished up the next morning with a girl on the boat. Nothing unusual in that but this one wouldn't get off. We had a rule. No falling in love. No, 'Oh but she's really fit, can she stay?'. Girls had to be gone in the morning.

We offered her money. We offered her a cab. But she just sat there refusing to move. So we put her to work, asking her to lean over the back and pull in the fender as we nosed out of the port. Sadly, from her point of view, just as she did this the boat suddenly accelerated and I'm afraid she fell in.

Her rage was huge, but not as huge as that of the owner of a nightclub in Juan-les-Pins who charged us £140 for five small bottles of beer. In 1982, for crying out loud. As punishment we attached our boat to his jetty and yanked it, along with all his sunloungers, off into the Med.

This really was one amazing holiday. Uninterrupted blue days and wild endless nights. A blend of wanton destruction, unbelievable expense and lazy afternoons on that flying bridge listening to the wavelets lapping on the hull.

You pull up off a beach in your boat and there's no wandering around for quarter of an hour trying to find a big enough spot to sit down. There's no sand in your sandwiches and every time you wake up you aren't confronted by the unedifying spectacle of a German penis.

You have your own fridge, your own air-conditioned shelter from the sun, you have a bed with sheets for a lie down, and when the sun sets you don't have to walk back to a superheated car for the 4 mph trudge back into town. You go for an evening cruise. Then, that night, you casually mention to the prettiest girl in the Whiskey a Go-Go that you have a boat in the harbour and whehey . . .

Top five happiest moments of my life? Well, one was off the Pampalone beach near St Tropez when the Radio Monte Carlo DJ interrupted Steve Winwood's 'While You See A Chance Take It' to say the Falklands war was over. And that we'd won.

So last year I decided that what I wanted most of all was a boat of my own. A Fairline Targa 48 to be precise. Until someone told me that the access to the engine was much better on the Targa 52. And then my boy, who's nine, said he much preferred the Princess V50.

I became obsessed, studying the classified ads in the boat magazines, and just not listening when people trotted out the same old clichés. The only two good days you have with a boat are the day you buy it and the day you sell it. And if it floats, flies or fornicates you're better off renting.

I wanted to re-create those heady days of 1982 and I wanted my family to come, too. So to convince them I was right, last year I chartered a jet-powered 50 ft Riva in Corsica.

We had a brilliant holiday. Each morning we'd go to the market in Bonifacio to buy cheese and sardines and rough Corsican rosé. Then we'd go to a quiet cove or maybe Sardinia, which was just an hour's blast away. One of our favourite spots was among some piercing, jagged rocks that jutted out of the sea like Neptune's teeth.

The water here was eerily green, so that snorkelling in it was like drifting silently through a Lara Croft movie. The kids loved it. I loved it. And my wife loved it.

Sort of. I think she loved it most of all because we had a skipper to drive the boat and then, at night, we went back to a house she'd rented as a back-up.

Wisely, as it turned out, because on one night we did sleep on the boat and it was horrid.

It's fine when you're twenty-two and so off your face you don't mind that some plumpton from Nancy is sitting on yours. But when you're old it's too hot, too cramped, and too like being in a caravan.

I came home thinking that for a boat to make sense it has to be at least 65 ft long with proper lavatories and proper bedrooms, not bunks wedged into empty spaces behind the microwave. The trouble is that sixty-five-footers are really very expensive. A million quid. And to park them anywhere you need a mooring that is just as much again.

So instead we've bought a lighthouse. It's on the coast of the Isle of Man. And it has its own harbour. This hasn't cured my longing for a boat. It's made it even worse.

Sunday 11 December 2005

Behind Jeremy lines

There's nothing gentle about the descent into Baghdad airport. To confuse the insurgents who lie in wait with rocket-propelled grenades and anti-aircraft missiles, the pilot of the Hercules transport plane doesn't select a glide path until he's pretty much over the runway. By which time it's more of a plummet path.

Twenty thousand feet below, four Apache gunships patrol the desert, their Hellfire missiles and chain guns ready to atomise any-one who fancies taking a pot shot at us. Meanwhile, at the airport itself, ice-white barrage balloons full of spy-in-the-sky cameras float in the dust-streaked, windless sky, monitoring the perimeter for signs of activity.

Up on the Herc's flight deck, two crew chiefs – big, hard special-forces men – stand behind the pilot scanning the skies for the telltale smoke trails left by incoming ordnance. They are fidgety and nervous. In January, an RAF Hercules was brought down by an anti-tank shell; and now we're two days into Ramadan, a good time for the Muslim fighter to die. Although on our approach the threat came from an even more dangerous quarter. 'There,' said one of the big guys urgently, and sure enough, bearing down on us, fast, from the west, was an American fighter plane.

To avoid the impending collision, the pilot set the flight controls to 'tactical', ducked under the fighter, banked hard and, with a rush of negative G-force that lifted the crew chiefs clean off their feet and into a state of weightlessness, we started our free-fall, engine-screaming, super-fast descent into Baghdad. It's important at times like this to get the soundtrack right. Vietnam had Hendrix and the Doors. I needed something more up to date. So before setting off, I'd made a special playlist on my war-Pod. The Five Best Songs for a Combat Landing into Iraq. And so, with the Hercules hurtling towards Baghdad, in the manner of a wardrobe falling from the top of a tower block, I was listening to U2 belting out 'Vertigo'.

Oh man, what a rush. Especially when the coalition pilot, an Italian, hauled back on the stick, sending a shudder of face-bending G through the airframe. As we weaved through the screen of helicopter gunships on our final approach, I turned to Adrian, smiling the smile of a very happy man, and couldn't believe what I saw. He was fast asleep.

And he stayed that way until we'd floated over a badly repaired pothole in the middle of the runway and, with an almighty bang, landed. The worst two war correspondents in the world had arrived in Baghdad.

Over the years we have become used to journalists being on the scene of the battle within hours of the kickoff. And I bet you've never wondered how on earth they get there. Only the RAF flies direct from Britain to Iraq and the only planes they can use, the only ones that are fitted with missile counter-measures, are three thirty-five-year-old Tristars. These things predate video recorders.

Nevertheless, Adrian and I were due to board one of them on a Sunday at oh-my-God o'clock. 'Why,' I wailed, 'does it have to be so early? Why don't you forces people ever set off anywhere at tea time?' A silly question, as it turns out. They have to leave in the dark in Britain so disaffected youths from Bradford can't pass the departure time to their mates in Iraq; and they have to land in the dark as well.

It didn't matter, though, because it turned out all the Tristars were broken and the trip was in grave danger of being called off. This was horrible. When I'd first been asked to go to Iraq, my response was: 'Ooh yes.' Mr Bush had made it plain that the war was over and that the whole country was returning to normality. Mr Blair always makes it sound like Bourton-on-the-Water over there. But do you know what? He's lying. At present, 350 roadside bombs and twenty car bombs go off every week in Iraq. And in Baghdad alone, there are twenty-five attacks of one sort or another every day. So far, around 2,000 Americans have been killed in action, and that's rising at the rate of one every eight hours. Once every four hours, one of them has a limb blown off.

My insurance company reckoned I had a one-in-a-hundred chance of being killed, and charged a premium exactly twice what I'd been offered to write the story. These figures caused some concern on the home front. Adrian's girlfriend made him write a will. My wife, having discovered the insurance would only pay up if I were killed, not if I died of a heart attack, called Adrian with some very specific instructions. 'If he starts to go a bit blue, shoot him,' she said. And me? I was worried about the very real possibility of being beheaded, live on the internet. I didn't think I'd be able to go with much of my dignity intact, frankly.

So as the trip was endlessly postponed, I vacillated between relief and disappointment. I wanted the thrill but I didn't want my head cut off. And then the phone rang. The trip was back on. The RAF had chartered a Monarch Airlines Airbus, which, because it had no anti-missile gubbins, would take us to Qatar.

Then it was off again. The Turks had refused permission for any military plane to overfly their country and that was that. In the end, we went to war with BA, landing in Kuwait, and then hitching a ride to Iraq on the Hercules. Cool, eh?

There were many things we could have done in Baghdad if we'd been journalistically inclined: we could have sought out the Iraqi Islamic party and those from the Conference of the People of Iraq, to find out why they're at odds with the Committee of Muslim Scholars. But instead we went tank-racing.

They were not puny little armoured personnel carriers, either. They were the real deal. Two Abrams M1A1 main battle tanks. These turbine-powered gas-hogs look complicated but, in fact, are designed so that even the most idiotic knuckle-dragging one-eyed swamp-man from Buttsville, Iowa, can get to grips with the motorcycle-style controls. Sadly, they were beyond the ken of Adrian, who, looking bewildered and frightened, set off backwards, slowly at first, then very quickly, straight towards one of Saddam's ceremonial lakes. Annoyingly, with a jolt that reared the front of the tank a full 3 ft in the air, he stopped just before he hit the water, and then with a tremendous roar surged forwards as though perhaps he had suddenly caught epilepsy, or was on ketamine.

At one point, he tore past the crowd of onlookers at full speed, which might have been hugely impressive had we not seen his face. He didn't look bewildered or frightened any more. He looked like a man who was steaming at 45 mph in a 68-tonne tank and couldn't find the brake pedal. He looked terrified.

The big problem in my tank was the heat. It was like sitting in the top right oven of an Aga. Certainly, it was hot enough to make the bottle of what looked like Coca-Cola I'd found on the floor seem tempting. 'Can I drink this?' I asked my commander.

'Well, you can,' he said, 'but I wouldn't because it's the driver's piss bottle.' Jesus H Christ. How much sweat do you have to produce for your urine to turn the colour of Coke? Whatever, I drove the tank around for a while, feeling rather chuffed when I heard one grunt saying over the radio: 'Anyone wanna guess which is the car critic and which writes about recipes?' Afterwards, Adrian was like a small boy. 'I won, I won,' he chanted. Nobody had been aware of a race, least of all his white-faced commander who, as we left, was seen hunched over Saddam's ornamental lake, vomiting.

After twenty-four hours in the fortified Green Zone, sipping tea, meeting generals and trying to sleep in the same room as A A Gill, the All England Snoring Champion, I finally stumbled onto a Big Story, only for the life of me I can't remember what it was. What I can remember is going for lunch in Uday's palace, the one where he used to feed women to his lions.

Now it's an American army canteen, so, as you can imagine, security is tight. As tight as it was when they'd checked our car in Kuwait. God, they were useless. I could have hidden an elephant in there and they wouldn't have found it. All that stood between me and my lunch in Baghdad was an adenoidal teenager who, in an irritating nasal whine, said I didn't have a pass. And then failed to do anything about it.

Over lunch – a burger, surprisingly, followed by two buckets of ice cream – someone dropped a metal tray. I heard the crash and thought: 'Oh, someone's dropped a tray.' But the 400 soldiers in there whipped round like Saddam himself had just burst into the room with an atomic bomb. They were a nervy bunch, and I can't say I blame them. Not when the only thing that stands between them and half a million very angry locals is Kevin the Teenager.

So what's it like to be shot at? Well, the first time, on our helicopter flight back to Baghdad airport, it was only a rocket-propelled grenade and, frankly, using one of these to bring down a fast-moving helicopter is like using a dart to bring down a hummingbird. So it was no big deal. But the second time was different. This time we were in a Lynx, sitting sideways by an open door over the ruined city of Basra, when someone fired a surface-to-air heat-seeking missile at us. The pilot, known to his men as Lord Flasheart, was chatting away when sensors on the helicopter detected a missile launch and jettisoned a fanned array of flares to provide an even hotter target than the engine's exhaust. It didn't work. The missile was still coming . . .

Before going to Iraq, Adrian had read a 1925 book, with no pictures in it, called *Mesopotamia: The Babylonian and Assyrian*

Civilisation, and another, by Wilfred Thesiger, called *The Marsh Arabs*. Neither had really given him much insight into how a Lynx might fare in a Sam attack. So he was the colour of porridge. Me? Rather more wisely, I'd read all of Tom Clancy's work, so I knew we weren't being chased by a fearsome Sam-18. People without shoes would struggle to afford such a thing. More likely we had a 1960s Sam-7 on our tail, and those things are confused by just about everything. So, while a Lynx helicopter may be as old as a Morris Traveller, it is fast and chuckable. I therefore knew we'd get away.

I also knew that afterwards, it'd be good fun going back to the launch site to find the little shit who'd pulled the trigger. And giving him a face full of hot lead. I even selected a suitable tune on the war-Pod. 'Bad to the Bone', by George Thorogood. Unfortunately, the rules of engagement for British troops serving in Iraq seem to have been written by Alastair Campbell. And are hammered home in a hard-hitting video presented, coinciden-tally, by the former *Top Gear* front man Chris Goffey. They say, in essence, that unless the enemy has already shot at you, and you're certain he's preparing to shoot at you again, you cannot shoot back. So we had to leave Sam-7 man alone, meaning he was free to come and have another go at another helicopter the next day.

Adrian thinks this is fair enough. He reckons you can't win by fighting like with like. Damn right. You win by fighting like with hate. The British have tried a soft-beret, hearts-and-minds approach in Basra, and on the day we were there we were fired at in the helicopter, mortared twice, then raked with fire from a fearsome DShK 12.7 machinegun. The Americans are criticised for their gung-ho policy, but are they inflaming the situation? Well, so far they've lost around 2,000 from a total force of 155,000. And we've lost nearly 100 from a force of around 7,800. Do the maths, and you'll find there's not much difference in the ratio, roughly one death for every seventy-eight men.

Strangely, our chaps are remarkably cheerful, referring to difficult patrols as 'sporty' and using Monopoly-board names for all the streets at their base. They don't seem to mind the threat of death, or the lack of power or the thirty-second ship shower they're allowed once a day. They do, however, mind the pay. The Hercules crews get an extra £5 a day for being out there, but lose the £10-a-day fuel allowance they're paid at home. This pisses them off. It pisses them off nearly as much as the twenty-minute phonecard they're given every week for calls home. Murderers in jail get thirty minutes. Then you have the squaddie who, on his two-week leave in England, was forced to take a job as a bouncer at the U2 gigs to make ends meet.

To make matters worse, those trained in close protection could leave tomorrow and get up to £250,000 a year in the private sector, guarding journalists, oil-company execs and Iraqi officials. Sure, there'd be no army medevac chopper waiting in the wings, but £250,000 a year? Tax-free?

Occasionally you see a white-faced soldier in the canteen, his hair matted with sweat, taking half an hour to eat a carrot. You think: 'Christ. What have you just been doing?' I suppose if I was a proper reporter I'd have asked, but more often than not someone was in the middle of a funny story, so I never did.

Life for the troops is pretty hard. Most work sixteen hours and then crash in their twelve-man tent for eight. The helicopter-maintenance boys regularly pull twenty-four-hour shifts, desperately trying to keep the mostly ancient fleet flying. Rest days are rare, and fairly useless, because there's sod-all to do. They can't leave the base for fear of being beheaded. They can't sunbathe because if they get burnt, they're put on a charge. They can't get drunk because the ration is two tins of beer a day. And they can't have sex because, they claim, 70 per cent of the girls at the base are lesbians.

The good thing is that because they aren't allowed to do any fighting, they have plenty of time for cleaning, which means the camp is spotless. It's not well equipped, though, which was a problem for Adrian, who had brought so many changes of clothes, there hadn't been room in his bag for stuff like a towel, or a sleeping bag or a pillow. Or indeed anything you might actually need in a desert army camp. I went to buy cigarettes. The base shop only sells Marlboro reds. Why bother with low tar on a battlefield?

Interestingly, the only clothing on sale were Arctic padded jackets. Can't you just tell this is a government operation? Yes, if you then toddle off to the stores. The troops call it the Window of No, because no matter what you want, they haven't got it. Or they have got it but they won't give it to you. Tommy, our guide, had been wearing a pair of trousers two sizes too big since he arrived and can't get replacements. They didn't have a towel for Adrian. And while he was trying on some hats, which he thought would go well with his Roger Moore safari suit, there was another mortar attack. Possibly. It's hard to say for sure because the Tannoy system had obviously been salvaged from one of the railway stations Beeching closed down in 1963. It was completely incomprehensible, but we did think at one point the chap might have said 'You're damned,' so we donned our flak jackets and our hard hats, put the kettle on, and settled down to watch Northern Ireland vs Wales on Sky Sports. Actually, Adrian put his hard hat on. Sadly, as a joke, he'd bought one for me which was the size of an egg cup, so it wouldn't fit. But since we were indoors, on a base with a twenty-five-mile perimeter fence, the chances of being hit seemed remote.

It seemed a bit weird, if I'm honest, being mortared while five hours away Ryan Giggs was doing football.

I felt Iraq was more interesting, if only I could find the right story. And that's hard when you're sitting in a storeroom on an army base, watching Adrian try on hats, and the only information you have is from a Tannoy system that doesn't work. You have to rely for hard news on the military, who only talk in abbreviations, so they're even less comprehensible than the public-address system.

We therefore went to the ranges to try out an AK–47. Adrian was very good, pumping round after round into the bull's-eye. I, on the other hand, was struggling to hit Iraq, so I wandered off into a nearby tent, where I found upwards of fifty Iraqis waiting for Adrian to give them their gun back.

At last. A chance to be a proper journalist. A chance to ask about their hopes and fears, and what on earth they were doing on a British base, being taught how to shoot. It turned out they had a question for me. There was much chatter, much nodding, then an expectant silence as the interpreter translated. 'Who,' they all wanted to know, 'is the Stig?'

It seems the Shi'ites love *Top Gear*, so I was asked to pose for photographs. None of them was rude enough to ask why on earth another bloke wandered in and lay down at their feet so he could be in the picture too.

Finally, night fell. It's not a proper night, of course, thanks to the eerie flickering light from the burning oilfields, and the odd forty-watt bulb, which is all Iraq's feeble national grid can provide. Or, more likely, all that Gordon Brown's pathetic war budget can afford. But at least there's enough juice for the beer coolers.

Two tins. And I figured I'd be drowsy enough to get a decent night's kip in the superheated tent with old Sinus Face. The base's sniffer dogs get air conditioning. The soldiers don't. But it was not to be. At 11 o'clock, with yet another mortar attack in full swing, one of the Tristars thundered onto the runway and an army bod said we had to be on it.

I like to think the authorities were genuinely concerned for our safety. That it had been the busiest day in the whole two-year conflict and there'd been some political pressure to get the civilians out. But no. The Tristar had brought in teams from Fleet Street, along with all the big TV networks. And I'm afraid they wanted our beds for the proper journalists.

Sunday 6 November 2005

Things can only get redder

The flights to Moscow are full of ox-pecker businessmen. They're all bright-eyed and bouncy with anticipation, keen to ride the rhino of Russia's oil and gas boom by drip-feeding it with a selection of boutiquey Euro luxuries: shotguns, power-boats and fusion-restaurant concepts.

On the way back, however, they don't look quite so good. Bankrupted financially by Russian business practices, and morally by a Klondike-esque nightlife, they are nursing empty wallets. But every single one will whisper, in a conspiratorial, blokes-only sort of way: 'You can forget Amsterdam and Reykjavik. For a really good night out, you have to get yourself to Moscow.'

So that's what Adrian and I did.

Actually, that's not strictly true. I wanted a good night out. I wanted to eat my supper from the toned belly of a Ukrainian hooker while snorting pink cocaine from the back of a golden swan. Adrian, on the other hand, wanted to queue for bread, and beat himself with twigs while sampling the workers' struggle for control of the factories.

Before leaving, therefore, he fixed a translator who was an artist and would show him some of the struggle, while I called the people from Russia's *Top Gear* magazine, who knew some people who might be able to help with the swan and the naked Ukrainian.

So, at the airport Adrian was met by his rather dreamy trans-lator in a smashed-up taxi, and I was met by a Maybach. Also, there was a Cadillac Escalade full of policemen in paramilitary uniforms, sub-machineguns and a selection of potato-faced meat machines who talked into their cuffs a lot.

Adrian looked at the taxi and the dreamy translator. And he had a struggle for, oooh, about one second, deciding whether to go with them or get in the creamy Maybach with me.

It, and the sub-machineguns, all belonged to a businessman we shall call Matthew, and at first I thought it might be a bit of an ego trip. I mean, he publishes magazines and makes fountain pens.

But this meat-'n'-metal protection was not for show. Three years ago, Matthew was kidnapped by Chechen terrorists. He was beaten, handcuffed to a former special-forces soldier, blindfolded and taken to a flat somewhere in the uniformly grey, monolithic, high-rise outskirts of Moscow.

The Chechens called his father, who lives in Spain, saying that unless they received $50 million within five days, the boy would be killed. His father roared back: '$50 million? F*** off!' And with that he turned off his mobile. For two days.

Matthew waited five days for his kidnappers to drop their guard and then leapt out of a fifth-floor window. It's hard to say what shattered his legs, the impact, or the bullets fired by the guards as he fell. But whatever, he crawled to a nearby road, flagged down a passing motorist, and over the next seven months watched the entire gang being sent to prison, where, he says quietly, all of them met with accidents and died.

I liked Matthew enormously. And here's something truly amazing. Adrian, who dislikes people until he gets to know them and then dislikes them even more, liked him enormously too. Partly, I suspect, because Matthew could get us into restaurants.

He suggested Pushkin, where Clinton and Kofi Annan eat when they're in town. It served borscht but other dishes too. I wanted to savour it all, since everything cost a billion, but Adrian was in a hurry. He'd wangled an invite to a special party and had a surprise for me.

So did Matthew. To get us to the party, we had the Maybach, of course, and the Cadillac meat-wagon, but now we had a Lamborghini as well.

Our convoy sent the security at the party into a complete tizzy. Their meat and our meat rushed about speaking into their cuffs and tapping their ears, and pretty soon we were inside a room of pulsating sweat and testosterone. We were ushered through the outer zone, past girls of such ravishing beauty that I barely noticed most were pretty much naked, into the VIP enclosure, which was full to bursting with photographers. All were crowded round a large wooden crate where, plainly, something big was happening. Adrian assured me that this was my surprise, and after he'd pushed me to the front he almost said: 'Da daaaa!'

It was Gwyneth Paltrow, sitting in the crate on a roped-off bar stool, all on her own. Quite what she was doing there I have no idea, because as I drew breath to ask, the photographers turned their attention on me. Not even my meat was big enough to deal with the onslaught, so we put our heads down and, leaving Gwyneth in her big box, barged our way back to the cars.

On our way to the next party, the opening of a restaurant, I think, for girls at least 7 ft tall, we saw the first of many car crashes. Crashing, it turns out, is something the Muscovites do a lot.

In Soviet days, you could have a flashing light on your car if you were connected in some way to government. And this is still the case. Tax inspectors. Lollipop ladies. Men from the ministry of fish. They all have what they call 'blinker cars'. But now, for $500, anyone can buy a licence to have a blinker car. This means that at every road junction, almost everyone has the right of way, and Moscow echoes almost permanently to the sound of tinkling glass and tortured metal.

We steered through it all and made it to the party, where I assumed, from the massed ranks of tanned and elongated flesh, that my Ukrainian hookers had turned up. Sadly not. They were just girls out on the town, trying to hook up with an oligarch. This counted Adrian out. In fact, he claimed he was starting to feel like Madge, so soon we were back in the Lambo-bach-illac convoy for a sprint over to a lap-dancing bar. So there you are. The Russian night out. Expensive girls. Expensive food. And a dirty great Lamborghini. The only difference with London is that your wife's at home.

If I'm honest, Adrian spent most of the night looking like something heavy had landed on his foot, and I spent most of the night talking to a girl in our party whose grandfather, Vladimir Chelomei, had been made a hero of the Soviet Union for inventing what became known as 'Satan': the SS–18 intercontinental ballistic missile. For more than twenty years, this was the launch vehicle for Russia's nukes. For a generation, it brought sleeplessness and terror to 500 million people in the West. Me included. Yet here I was, sitting in a bar full of naked Ukrainian ironing boards, chatting to its inventor's agreeable granddaughter. Tell me the world is not a weird place. I dare you. I double dare you.

So where was Madge going to find his struggle? 'In an art gallery,' he said with the grin of a maniac.

Apart from seeing what would happen if I relieved myself on Lenin's tomb, I couldn't think of anything I wanted to do less. So we did a deal. 'If you can name a single Russian artist, we'll go.' He couldn't. So we didn't.

I'm not saying Moscow can't stun you, though. I've seen two views in my life that have genuinely taken my breath away: Cape Wrath and Hong Kong at dusk. And now a third. Red Square.

We came at it from the south, through the new arch by the Museum of Something Not Interesting. And even though a portion of the cobbled centre was taken up by a makeshift ice rink, the rest was so beautiful and so evocative I actually gasped: St Basil's, the silly onion-shaped church whose designers were blinded after they'd finished it to make sure they never did any such thing again; the blue fir trees that are replaced quietly, and overnight, when they grow taller than the placenta-red Kremlin walls they shield; and the big department store lit up like Harrods.

You find yourself whizzing round and round like an eight-year-old in a shop full of train sets, not quite believing that an image you've seen a million times in pictures could be so much more eye-wateringly spectacular in real life. Best square in the world? Oh yes, and by quite a margin.

Later, in a market where you could buy cheese made from a Bolshevik's armpit sweat, there was a kerfuffle. A man had stepped forward with a pen and paper to ask for my autograph, but long before he could utter a sound, my meat had pulled his arm off. The pen and paper were examined, and when both were discovered to be harmless, the man was allowed to proceed with his request. Which he did without a trace of indignation.

For the most part the centre of Moscow looks like London. You really can see that the two cities were joined at the hip before everything went tits-up in 1917: the same architecture, the same sense of history, the same retail experiences, and the same silly six-figure restaurants. I've never been so far and felt quite so at home.

What's more, just as though we'd been in London, Madge failed to find much struggle and I never got to dip a quail's egg into a Ukrainian teenager. We had a nice time in what appears on the surface to be a nice place.

There's nothing to indicate that you're in a twenty-first-century Wild West. Even the guard at Lenin's tomb was smoking a fag like he wouldn't have cared if I'd wee-ed on it. Or him. And yet the autograph-hunter seemed to demonstrate that there is an inbuilt fear of muscle and authority. You don't question any-one with more money or biceps or contacts than you. The price of asking for an autograph is a severed arm. The cost of a speeding ticket is a quiet bribe. You get the best table in the house with a small glare.

We saw this, too, on our run back to the airport, when we

were given a police escort. Blue lights flashing, we tore down those special lanes reserved in England for buses, but in Moscow for the rich and powerful. After Plod had barged slower traffic out of our path on the motorway, we swept straight up to the VIP lounge, breathless with a mix of cheek-reddening embarrassment and butterfly-tummy excitement.

Then, after we'd thanked our meat for murdering the autograph-hunters, and waved a tearful goodbye to the Maybach, we found ourselves on the plane, back in the clutches of a real democracy. In economy class.

I prefer theirs.

Sunday 28 January 2007

I'm a space nut

Thirty years ago, the Voyager spacecraft were launched. Their mission was to head straight out from Earth into deep space, where they would broadcast songs by whales, messages from Jimmy Carter and directions to Earth, in the hope that an alien culture would drop by for tea and biscuits.

The little ships are doing well. Voyager 1 is around 9.6 billion miles from the sun, doing just over 38,000 mph through the termination shock region between the edge of our solar system and interstellar space. Voyager 2 is way beyond Pluto, forging a path through the myriad tiny ice planets that cling precariously to the sun's gravity. It's all just too excellent for words, the notion that we've sent a message in a bottle out there and now it's just a question of waiting for Mr Spock to land in Hyde Park.

But, unfortunately, the Voyager craft do quite a lot to undermine the whole business of space travel. You see, by the time they get to the next solar system, the next place where life might be found, Jimmy Carter will be dead, whales will be extinct, the sun will have burnt up, Earth will have been sucked into a black hole the size of a grapefruit, and anyone dropping by for some cucumber sandwiches is going to be pretty cross they made the journey for nothing.

What's more, the Voyagers demonstrate clearly that we're never ever going to be whizzing around space seeking out new life and new civilisations, because it's all just too far away. Think about it. If we'd put a twenty-year-old man on Voyager, he'd now be fifty and he'd still be in our own solar system. By the time he reached our next-door neighbours, he'd be about 6 thousand million billion. Or, to put it another way, dead.

What's to be done, then? Do we just give up? Do we just say: 'Oh well, the world's big enough for our purposes and, all things considered, it's fairly cosy. So let's build a shopping mall at Cape Canaveral, turn Baikonur into a museum and I'll see you at the pub on Saturday'?

No. Don't you want to go to the termination shock region? It sounds like a ride at Alton Towers but it's better than that. It's where the sun's influence ends, where the solar winds drop from 1.5 million miles an hour to nothing, and the bow of our solar system forges a path through the interstellar gases. Don't you want to know what that looks like? What it sounds like? What it feels like to be standing on the prow of a solar system as it smashes through space at tens of thousands of miles an hour? I do. And I don't think we should give up on the dream because of something trivial like the laws of physics. In the same way that sixteenth-century man built ships to see what was on the other side of the ocean, we must build technology to get round the problem of being too slow. We cannot pack in the idea of exploration because we can only do 38,000 mph. We have to find a way of proving Einstein wrong. We have to peel away our Gatso mindset, our obsession with avoiding risk, and build a machine that will take us up to and beyond the speed of light.

We've explored our own world. We've been to the top of it (well, I have) and the bottom. We've climbed the highest mountains, explored the harshest deserts and plumbed the deepest oceans. And now it's time to quench our thirst for knowledge by moving on. By which I mean up.

I should explain at this point that I'm a space nut. When I see photographs of gas clouds taken by the Hubble telescope, they are, to me, like pictures of faraway beaches in travel brochures. They are an invitation to come and see for myself. When I lie on a tropical beach on a clear night, the hairs on the back of my neck rise as I grapple with the concept of infinity, the idea that somewhere out there is another Jeremy Clarkson lying on a tropical beach on a planet exactly like Earth, thinking exactly the same thing at exactly the same time.

And that it's a mathematical certainty that there's another Earth, exactly like ours except that Wales is the shape of a sperm. And another that is exactly the same except that their Fiona Bruce has yellow hair. Every possible permutation of our world must be out there, and that's before you get to every possible permutation of every other imaginable world.

Are we alone in the universe? Of course not. Not if it's infinite. And we're not going to find out whether it is by going to the pub and getting all excited because our mobile phone has a new ring tone. Sadly, that is precisely what we are doing. You may think, as you look at the satellites whizzing hither and thither in the night sky, that much is being done behind our backs. Well, sorry to disappoint you but while there are hundreds of thousands of pieces of space junk in orbit round the world, there are only 800 active satellites, and most are boring. Sixty-six per cent were put there so you can speak to your kids during their gap-year in Belize. Seven per cent sit there helping you find a street in Reading. Six per cent are used for military espionage, 5 per cent for predicting weather, and a similar number waste their time looking at polar bears and melting ice. In total, 760 are pointed at Earth. Just forty are for looking outwards. At the rest of the universe.

So what of the International Space Station? Well, so far as I can tell, it's nothing more than a ramshackle garage where astronauts spend their days fixing bits of equipment that have gone wrong. What's it for? I'm afraid I haven't a clue. Hubble? Brilliant pictures. Glad it's there, but when all is said and done it's just a big Nikon.

All we ever hear about space now are a few hopefuls claiming that they'll soon be running tourist flights to the cosmos. Richard

Branson said in 2004 he'd be taking paying customers for a God's-eye view of the planet in their jeans and T-shirts by 2007. But he isn't, yet. The first attempt to put a cheap and reusable spacecraft into orbit was aborted after the pilot heard a long bang. The second nearly came to grief when the plane that is used to take the craft up to 47,000 ft went into a dangerous spin after separation.

Space has stalled. And to get it going again, I'm afraid we need a war. War has always been good for humankind. Obviously, it's not so great when you're on the battlefield with a big leak in your torso and an arrow in your eye, but, truth be told, battlefields have very little to do with the eventual outcome of the conflict. That's rarely decided by the soldiers and the generals. It's decided by the tools they're given. Charging a machinegun nest advances you and your men 3 ft while, back at home, scientists are advancing the whole world by 300 years.

The world's first electronic computer was built at Bletchley Park not so some spotty youth could spend his afternoon shooting his mates in the face but to crack German codes. Jet planes were built not so you could go to Tenerife but because Germany needed a faster fighter. Radar was developed not so you could land more safely at Heathrow but because we needed to find U-boat periscopes in the middle of the Atlantic. Almost everything we take for granted today came from war. And the war that gave us more than anything else was the fifty year standoff between Russia and America.

When Russia launched Sputnik fifty years ago, it was nothing more than a small radio, but the beeps it transmitted, when translated, told the listening world: 'This is Russia and we'd like you all to know that our German scientists are a hell of a lot better than America's German scientists.' Or, in English: 'You're going home in a f***ing ambulance.'

Duly insulted, America set up Nasa, found billions to finance it, and embarked on a programme that would prove the Russians, er, right. Having been the first to orbit the world, they became the first to put a dog up there, and then a man. They were also the first to the moon (no, really) and the first to Venus.

The space race became what really ought to have been known as 'the ego war'. And it was brilliant. Because unlike in other wars, casualties were restricted to just twenty-two astronauts and seventy ground personnel, and the benefits to the rest of us were immense. As America's German boffins struggled to outdo Russia's German boffins, we got golf clubs made from metal that can remember what sort of shape it's supposed to be. And people with heart defects got a small vascular pump based on the fuel pumps used in the shuttle. We got the ability to track hurricanes, we got satellite navigation, we got live football matches played on the other side of the world, we got scratch-resistant lenses in our sunglasses, we got solar panels and flat-screen televisions. When a doctor takes your blood pressure, he uses a system devised by Nasa for monitoring the heart rate of its first man in space, Alan Shepard.

The cold war and the space race that resulted were fantastic. It was the greatest lurch forward since Victorian England decided that it could use coal to get itself an empire.

And then the Russians decided to give up, so now it's all gone wrong. Nasa's astronauts have stopped pushing the outside of the envelope and keep busy instead by getting drunk and trying to murder one another. Space is run by the infernal health-and-safety industry, which won't let a brave young test pilot go up there if there's even the slightest concern that he might not come back again. Space exploration is for the benefit only of share-holders, and programmes are run and operated by the lowest bidders.

As a result, the magic of space exploration has gone. Instead of getting up at 3 a.m. to watch a fuzzy man bouncing around a sound stage in Nevada, we turn over and go back to sleep. We look today at the space shuttle and think of it as an ugly and

outdated lorry that blows up when it takes off and disintegrates
when it comes back again. I don't. I see a machine that generates
37 million horsepower but produces nothing from its exhausts
except water. I see a fabulous creation that lights up the night sky
with its power and is doing 120 mph by the time its tail has
cleared the launch tower and 17,500 mph by the time it's cleared
the atmosphere. I see a machine that could get from Florida to
Spain via space in twenty minutes, and can deal with the furnace
of re-entry. A furnace that burns three times hotter than the
surface of the sun. And best of all, I see a machine that glides back
to Earth with no power, somehow kissing the runway at exactly
211 mph.

And I always think to myself: that's brilliant. But where would
we be if Russia and America were still at one another's throats?
The termination shock region, probably, where, who knows,
they might have come back with a cure for the common cold, an
easy-to-wire plug and iPod earpieces that don't get all tangled up.

I listened three years ago to George Bush's vision for our future
in space, and I have to say that it made a deal more sense than his
vision for our future down here on Earth. He talked of building
a new long-distance space exploration vehicle to replace the
shuttle, which will be retired in 2010. He spoke of establishing a
permanent manned base on the moon from where all deep space
missions could be launched. And it wasn't like he'd been watching *Star Trek* the night before either, because he reasoned that
moon launches would not have to overcome as much gravity as
they do on Earth. He even revealed that the moon's 'soil', as he
put it, contained elements that could power rockets and even
be used to manufacture breathable air. 'We do not know where
this journey will end,' he said, 'yet we know this: human beings
are headed into the cosmos.'

There was much cheering and whooping from the audience
when he made these remarks, but none from me. Watching an
idiotic president promising a bunch of space geeks that they'd

have a moon base and ray guns and warp speed to the Andromeda system was all very well, but without impetus it was never going to happen. That's why I'm delighted to see Russian bombers back in Nato airspace and radioactive poison all over the restaurant tables in London. And it's why I'm delighted to note that Russia, buoyed by its new wealth and power, has announced plans to build a moon base for missions to Mars.

It means we can go back to the good old days. It means we can go to the stars.

Sunday 7 October 2007